Routledge Revivals

Authorship in the Days of Johnson

Originally published in 1928, this book discusses the complex relationships between authors, patrons and publishers in the 18th Century and the ideals and struggles for copyright. It examines the power of booksellers over authors and the effect on authors of copyright security and the lapse of patronage.

Authorship in the Days of Johnson

Being a Study of the Relation Between Author, Patron, Publisher and Public, 1726-1780

A.S. Collins

First published in 1928 by George Routledge & Sons Ltd.

This edition first published in 2024 by Routledge
4 Park Square, Milton Park, Abingdon, Oxon, OX14 4RN

and by Routledge
605 Third Avenue, New York, NY 10158.

Routledge is an imprint of the Taylor & Francis Group, an informa business

© 1928 A.S. Collins.

The right of A.S. Collins to be identified as the author of this work has been asserted by him in accordance with sections 77 and 78 of the Copyright, Designs and Patents Act 1988.

All rights reserved. No part of this book may be reprinted or reproduced or utilised in any form or by any electronic, mechanical, or other means, now known or hereafter invented, including photocopying and recording, or in any information storage or retrieval system, without permission in writing from the publishers.

ISBN 13: 978-1-032-90845-8 (hbk)
ISBN 13: 978-1-003-56009-8 (ebk)
ISBN 13: 978-1-032-90853-3 (pbk)
Book DOI 10.4324/9781003560098

AUTHORSHIP IN THE DAYS OF JOHNSON

BEING A STUDY OF THE RELATION
BETWEEN AUTHOR, PATRON,
PUBLISHER AND PUBLIC, 1726–1780

BY
A. S. COLLINS

LONDON
GEORGE ROUTLEDGE & SONS, LTD.
BROADWAY HOUSE: 68–74 CARTER LANE, E.C.
1928

*Made and Printed in Great Britain
by Hazell, Watson & Viney Ld.
London and
Aylesbury*

CONTENTS

CHAPTER I

AUTHOR AND BOOKSELLER

		PAGE
(i)	Effect on authors of copyright security and of the lapse of patronage	7
(ii)	Power of booksellers over authors and of 'the trade' over other booksellers	15
(iii)	Grub Street	23
(iv)	Prospects of authors. Their bargaining power. Prospects improve. Liberality of booksellers and their general attitude	28
(v)	Personal relations between author and bookseller .	45
(vi)	Review of advance from 1726 to 1780 . . .	51

CHAPTER II

THE COPYRIGHT STRUGGLE

(i)	The Act of 1710	53
(ii)	The survival of piracy intermittent in England. Importation from abroad and from Ireland. Its treatment	56
(iii)	Lapse of copyrights under Act of 1710. Booksellers petition Parliament. Their claims and failure .	68
(iv)	Question of perpetual ownership raised. Indirect attempts to secure it. Typical arguments. Bullying tactics	82
(v)	Donaldson begins his attack. Perpetuity won in England, lost in Scotland, finally lost in England. Counter-replies to the pleas of 'the trade' . .	92
(vi)	Effect of loss of claim to perpetuity. Attitude of booksellers and of authors. No drop in prices . .	105
(vii)	The ideal of copyright. The position in 1780 . .	111

CHAPTER III

AUTHOR AND PATRON

(i)	Patronage in the days of Charles II and Queen Anne. Its highest point	114
(ii)	Decline under Walpole and George I . . .	118
(iii)	Pope—his rise to independence. He rejects pensions and has no use for patrons	123
(iv)	Young, Savage, Gay, Swift, and Thomson. Their lives and the light they throw on patronage . . .	137

CONTENTS

		PAGE
(v)	Political patronage under Walpole	163
(vi)	Social patronage. Queen Caroline. Peterborough, Oxford, Chandos, and others	171
(vii)	Writers themselves patrons—Pope, Warburton, Johnson	177
(viii)	Dedications. They become scandalous	180
(ix)	Value of the last years of patronage. Its help to Thomson, Fielding, and others	184
(x)	Decay of patronage. Writers self-supporting. Literature passes to middle classes	189
(xi)	Vulgar patrons: attacks by Johnson, Foote, Churchill, and Goldsmith	193
(xii)	Revival of patronage by George III and Lord Bute	199
(xiii)	Patronage after 1760. Sterne. Comparison of 1730 and 1770. Chatterton and Crabbe	206
(xiv)	Conclusion: Conditions in 1780	210

CHAPTER IV

THE GROWTH OF THE PUBLIC

(i)	From dependence to independence	213
(ii)	Survey of patronage and its relation to authorship	214
(iii)	Author and bookseller. Copyright up to 1774. Effect of 1774 on public and authors. Position in 1780.	221
(iv)	The reading public. Increased by periodical essay, newspapers, magazines, reviews, romances, novels, circulating libraries, education, number-books, and children's books. Women readers and writers. Improvement in morality and taste. Growth after 1750. Lackington. Popular reprints	232
(v)	The play-going public. Prospects of dramatic authorship. Revival of Shakespeare. Position about 1770	259
(vi)	Conclusion	269

AUTHORSHIP IN THE DAYS OF JOHNSON

CHAPTER I

AUTHOR AND BOOKSELLER[1]

(i) Effect on authors of copyright security and of the lapse of patronage. (ii) Power of booksellers over authors and of 'the trade'[2] over other booksellers. (iii) Grub Street. (iv) Prospects of authors. Their bargaining power. Prospects improve. Liberality of booksellers and their general attitude. (v) Personal relations between author and bookseller. (vi) Review of advance from 1726 to 1780.

(i)

AT the beginning of the eighteenth century the profession of letters was in a precarious position. Till 1695 the press had been under the control of a Licensing Act which required that no book should be printed without the consent of a Licenser. The primary object of that Act had been the suppression of all writings which, in the opinion of the authorities, might be undesirable in the interests of Church or State; but it also resulted in the protection from pirates of the authors or proprietors of books, since a Licenser would not give permission for one to print what another had already undertaken. In 1695, however, the gagging of the press by this method, open to all the abuses of placing petty officials in positions of absolute authority, was given up. The Act required renewal for a fresh term, but, influenced by the desire for the free expression of opinion within the bounds of ordinary law, Parliament allowed it to lapse, and with it lapsed the check upon

[1] The word 'bookseller' is used throughout in its eighteenth-century meaning, which roughly corresponds to our modern 'publisher.'
[2] The term 'the trade' is also used throughout in its eighteenth-century meaning of the inner circle of 'monopolizing' booksellers.

such printers as had no respect for the literary property of others. That necessary control over the less orderly of their calling had in former times been exercised by the Stationers' Company under the powers of their statutes, but in course of time their control had become inefficient. By-laws, especially enacted in 1683 during an earlier lapse of the Licensing Act, had proved ineffectual, and from 1695 there seemed no sure means of stopping any printer from printing the next day what another had printed the day before, and those who were ready to do so were not wanting. Another by-law of 1694, imposing a fine of one shilling on each copy of a pirated work, proved useless.[1]

IN such circumstances the relation of author to publisher existed on a very insecure basis. How could a bookseller pay highly for the rights to a work whose profits another might steal from him by a cheaper edition ? Such a state of things was impossible, for, while it continued, there could be no advance, no security, no incentive. The booksellers themselves, being the most concerned, were the active party in petitioning for relief. They approached Parliament on the question of obtaining an Act which should acknowledge their rights and maintain them by adequate penalties, first in 1703, again in 1706, and finally with success in 1709. The House of Commons did not seem conscious of any great importance in the matter, and it was only after an additional plea on the part of the printers and papermakers of London in 1709 that the third petition of the booksellers began actually

[1] See A. W. Pollard, *Copyright in the Eighteenth Century* (*Biblio. Soc. Transactions*, 1922).

to have effect. Even then the action of Parliament did not fulfil the expectations of the petitioners, whose Bill appears to have gone into Committee as one to secure the owners of copy in their property for ever, and to have emerged drastically revised as one that did not secure but "vested" the property in its possessors for a limited period. That period was, in the case of books published prior to April 1st, 1710 (on which date the Act came into force), the space of twenty-one years, and in that of books published after that date of fourteen years, to be renewed for another fourteen if the author were still alive at the expiration of the first. That all might know what books enjoyed copyright, the condition of registration in the Hall book of the Stationers' Company was made, and all actions were to be brought within three months of the offence. The penalties of invasion of copyright were forfeiture and destruction by damasking of the remaining copies of the unauthorised edition, and a fine of one penny per sheet, half of which was to go to the Crown and half to the bringer of the action.

FROM April 1710, therefore, an author had a definite property with which he could bargain with a bookseller; and it was certainly none too soon that this property was given him. *The Tatler* was moved to speak very seriously " of a set of wretches we authors call pirates, who print any book, poem or sermon, as soon as it appears in the world, in a smaller volume and sell it, as all other thieves do stolen goods, at a cheaper rate." Of such was Mr. Henry Hills, junr., who made a business of reprinting in duodecimo all the best-selling poems and sermons; and, as the day of reckoning drew near, there was a corresponding scramble of pirates to make the most of their remaining days. To all this the Act for the Encouragement of Learning put an effectual stop; piracy was henceforth only occasional, and an author had a real bargaining power which a bookseller might estimate in terms of cash, knowing that the value to be placed upon a given work depended for the future on the public taste and could not be prejudiced or depreciated by the dishonesty of others. The existence of such a bargaining power was an essential condition of any stability whatever in the relationship of author and bookseller, but that bargaining power was itself liable to considerable fluctuation under the influence of external forces, political and social, affecting the craft of authorship.

THE Hanoverian Succession had altered the whole face of affairs in England. The fact that the King could speak no English, that his son, also, could speak but little, and that for years no minister except Lord Carteret could talk German, removed the possibility of any considerable influence of the Throne on the government of the country, and so from 1714 England entered on a period of more complete Parliamentary rule than had so far been the case. Parliament, therefore, and the Lower House in particular, became the source of ministerial power, and henceforth ministers must either control the Commons or the Commons would control them. The course of things where the prevailing atmosphere of political life was corruption, took the inevitable turn. Party warfare was for the time dead, killed by the failure of the Tory intrigues with the Pretender to come to a successful head before the death of Queen Anne; the Tories were for a generation or so powerless, and a House of Commons consisting of only one party could not stand before the systematic corruption practised by Walpole, who from 1721 was in fact, if not in word, the first minister of the Crown.

LUCRATIVE offices and ready money were the essentials for securing the obedience of members and for buying boroughs, and it followed that, even if ministers had been so inclined, there were no longer available for the reward of writers those official positions and pensions which writers had begun to regard as the prizes of literary men in the later years of the Queen, and especially in the time of Harley's administration. But had there been ample means to hand for the patronage of literary merit, we may doubt if Walpole would have continued the growing custom of the political patronage of writers. "He loved neither writing nor reading, and if he had a taste for art, his real love was for the table, the bottle and the chase."[1] As to encouraging men of letters to aspire to administrative offices, he had seen too much of the poor practical abilities of such men, who were too frequently bad at business, weak and ineffective politicians, and feeble debaters. When he made Congreve a Commissioner of Taxes, he said, "You will find he has no head for business." At such times as he had occasion to employ political writers, he was content with the poorest, never read their work, and paid them highly. The result was that authors, unless they

[1] J. R. Green, *Short History of the English People*, chap. ix, sec. x.

were politicians first and authors second, were driven to seek a living elsewhere; they turned, of necessity, to the booksellers.

ANOTHER tendency of the age which led authors to rely more upon the booksellers was the decay of patronage on the part of the wealthy. That kind of patronage only flourishes when learning is confined to comparatively few, and those few are able to find in the people of wealth and rank, themselves a small circle, some to support and appreciate that learning. As the number of potential patrons grows, the tradition of patronage of the learned dies among them, unless there is some prominent example to follow; each looks to another to see if his neighbour is a patron of men of letters, and between their doubt and hesitation men of letters remain without the patronage of any. Again, as authors multiply, it becomes all the more difficult for the would-be patron to single out the deserving few from the undeserving many, and the scattered patrons whom taste, not example, impels to help the needy authors are unable to extend their assistance to all.

IN the thirties of the eighteenth century the number of patrons was slowly decreasing and the gaps were not filled. The Court, which might have set the example, was notoriously contemptuous of writers, and the attitude of Walpole was equally plain. In addition, the leading author of the time, Pope, may have contributed something, if indeed anything was possible, to the failure of men of rank to appreciate the claims and needs of men of letters. Pope was so proud an exponent of the independence of the literary character that the thoughtless might well begin to wonder whether patronage were really advisable; and the *Dunciad* might strengthen any opinion that there could be no honour in patronizing the race of literary aspirants. But however that may be (and the argument is probably fallacious), the decline of patronage was unmistakable, and one who adopted authorship was more and more led to the booksellers. Patronage might shelter a few, but they must be suppliant. The many and the resolutely independent, like Johnson, were beyond its bounds. The booksellers were becoming the only resource of a writer.

BOTH the political situation and the decline of patronage had added to the power of ' the trade ' (by which name the booksellers were known) by making them more necessary, and their power was still further increased by the growing swarm of writers who resorted to them for a livelihood. Johnson, writing in 1751, said that " the authors of London were formerly computed by Swift at several thousands, and there is not any reason for suspecting that their number has decreased."[1] Indeed there can be little doubt that they had not only not decreased but rather multiplied, and in the early years it would almost seem as though they had threatened to outnumber their readers. In 1756 we find Johnson humorously suggesting that the best profession for the great surplus to choose was soldiering, since they were inured to the greatest hardships and privation. The effect on the bargaining power which the legal gift of copyright had given an author was seriously damaging. It only remained high if an author had powerful

[1] *The Rambler*, No. 145.

patrons and great talent; talent, even genius unsupported at the outstart by patronage, must struggle for some years to rise clear of the crowd and might very likely go under before recognition could come; on the position of the author with just average ability the effect was deplorable, the hopeless overcrowding of the profession destroying that modicum of comfort which would have been spread among fewer.

THE evil was that writing was not a profession in the sense in which we could speak of the law as a profession; the craft of letters was a last resource of the shifty, needy and incompetent. We may believe that the creative spirit of Fielding was bound to express itself in literature sooner or later, but he gives us an example of that attitude to authorship as a calling which treats it, as teaching was also long treated, as a refuge for those who can do nothing else. He " had no choice," he told Lady Mary Wortley Montagu, " but to be a hackney writer or a hackney coachman." It was the same with Savage, who, says Johnson, " having no profession, became by necessity an author."[1] Collins, we are told, in 1774 " came to London a literary adventurer, with many projects in his head, and very little money in his pocket."[2] Francklin (1721-84) " for the greater part of his life was compelled by want of lucrative preferment to write for the press and the stage."[3] Edward Moore, after being unsuccessful as a linen-draper, " turned to literature as a last resource "; and in 1754 Shebbeare, a chemist, tried political writing as possibly more

[1] Johnson, *Lives of the Poets*, ed. G. B. Hill (Savage).
[2] Johnson, *Lives of the Poets*, ed. G. B. Hill (Collins), iii. 335.
[3] *Dict. Nat. Biog.*

profitable. Such are but a few examples, and if there were men like these who in some degree succeeded, how many more must there have been with less talent, injuring the prospects of each other and of men more gifted than themselves, by clogging a calling to which they were only drawn by necessity and vain hope unsustained by ability.

(ii)

THE only condition of things which could have absorbed in any degree of comfort the greater part of these good, bad and indifferent scribblers would have been a flourishing trade of bookselling,[1] itself the outcome of a wide reading public, and this condition was in the first quarter of the century very far from being actual; in the second quarter it had begun to develop, in the third it was steadily advancing, and in the last it may be said to have been fairly established. The power of the booksellers was great by reason of the decline of political and social patronage of writers, and because of the growing number of the writers themselves; it was greater still because of the absence of a public; and it became crushing by virtue of the absolute monopoly by 'the trade' of the means of publishing. There were few booksellers, and between them little or no rivalry. The eighteenth century was the age of co-operation in 'the trade,' as the nineteenth was one of keen competition; and the small group of co-operating booksellers, consisting of the more important members, was able to pursue a policy of exclusion which was

---

[1] For the history of bookselling, see F. A. Mumby, *The Romance of Bookselling*; C. Knight, *Shadows of the Old Booksellers*; H. Curwen, *A History of Booksellers*.

only broken through in 1774 after persistent efforts of the Scotch booksellers, who, together with those in the English counties, had multiplied considerably since the middle of the century. PRINTERS had long been subsidiary and had ceased to be the dominant factor in publishing which they had been in the time of Shakespeare; they were now merely agents hired by the booksellers and shut out from any participation in the higher walks of the trade. Johnson wrote in 1739 in *The Gentleman's Magazine*: " We can produce some who threatened printers with their highest displeasure, for having dared to print books for those who wrote them." In 1762 Baskerville, the pioneer of improvement in printing, told the same tale in a letter to Horace Walpole: " The Booksellers," he complained, " do not chuse to encourage me, though I have offered them as low terms as I could possibly live by; nor dare I attempt an old Copy till a Law-suit relating to that affair is terminated."[1] It was an attitude very galling to the printers, and one which excited disapproval among the public generally. Dr. Clarke, a friend of Bowyer the printer, affirmed in 1765 that " the thoughts of *governing the Booksellers*, either for gain or glory, would give me a greater pleasure, than any other object in trade,"[2] and he felt sure that, in saying so, he had his friend's hearty concurrence. And, again, there is noticeable among the arguments opposing the grant of a relief Bill to the London booksellers in 1774 this one of a monopoly detrimental to printers. " A few persons," it was said, " who call themselves

---

[1] Nichols, *Literary Anecdotes*, iii. 453.   [2] *Ibid.*, ii. 461.

booksellers, about the number of twenty-five, have kept the monopoly of books and copies in their own hands, to the entire exclusion of all others but more especially the printers, whom they have always held it a rule never to let become purchasers of copy."

By co-operation the printers were subdued and in the same way intrusion of particular booksellers or others into the 'clique' was prevented or punished. One rare example of successful intrusion was that of Cave [1] and his *Gentleman's Magazine*, which also opened up a new and prosperous channel for those who would live by their pens. Cave had first offered a share in this undertaking to some half of the London booksellers without their having the courage to venture on so original an enterprise, but when 'the trade' saw this remarkable success within their sacred preserve, they at once opposed it with *The London Magazine* the next year (1732), although without being able to overtake Cave. But, as a rule, their opposition soon stifled such attempts. Dodsley's *Public Register* (1741) was first crippled by the threat, engineered by rival booksellers, to tax it as a newspaper, and its failure ensured by the same men exerting their influence on the newspapers to refuse its advertisements; as a result it died after twenty-four weeks.[2] Similar was the fate of *The Universal Museum*, started in 1762 by Arthur Young, the political economist. He was warned beforehand by Johnson that such an effort would never succeed unless the booksellers had the property, and true enough, Young was in five months obliged

[1] See Memoir of Cave, Nichols, *Literary Anecdotes*, v. 1–58.
[2] R. Straus, *Robert Dodsley*. pp. 70–1.

to hand it over to them. Likewise the booksellers had interests in standard histories which the work of a real historian like Hume was bound seriously to affect; there was, therefore, the usual attempt to maintain their monopoly, and in 1757 the outcome of a scheme to thwart Hume's success was the enlistment of Smollett on the booksellers' side. They could not eclipse Hume, but at any rate their scheme had " a very discouraging effect " upon his sales. It was in order to appease any of these booksellers that Dodsley when issuing his series of *Old Plays* in 1743 decided that the trade must " have a handsome allowance."

To make all sure, they kept up the limited circle of their monopoly by strictly regulating the sale of copyrights. When the charge of keeping all the rights in a few hands was preferred against them, the booksellers' always replied that they were sold at public sales to which any member of the trade was entitled to admittance. But in actual practice catalogues were only sent to a chosen few, and others were rigorously excluded. When the rights of Thomson's *Seasons* were offered for sale in 1769, Donaldson, the intruding Scotsman, was sent a private notice that his presence was not desired.

THE only good of this system of co-operation was in the power it gave to a group of booksellers to combine in the publication of expensive works, by which means the risk was shared and the expense more easily faced. The first combination was established about the year 1719; it consisted of seven booksellers and was known under the name of the Printing Conger. The term

'Conger,' says Nichols,[1] may be derived from Congeries or Conger eel, and the latter etymology is certainly very applicable when we consider the above-mentioned power of these booksellers to swallow up all the lesser brethren. But the Printing Conger, and the New Conger which was formed by another group in 1736, and the Chapter which replaced both (taking its name from the Chapter Coffee-house, where its members met for the transaction of business) were all justified by good works. There were many publications which no single bookseller could undertake, either because of the expense of printing, or of preparing, or from the uncertainty of the demand for them, or because their appeal was only to a narrow class. By combining the booksellers insured themselves against any great loss, were generally enabled to make a profit, and were also of great benefit to literature, to the learned world and to authors. Most prominent in this way are Johnson's *Dictionary*, undertaken by seven booksellers; his *English Poets* and their *Lives*, in which thirty-six were associated; and Gibbon's *Decline and Fall*. The system was also rendered necessary by the way in which the property of certain books was divided into many shares, ranging from two to fifty or more, so that all were interested in the reprinting of the particular work in which they had a share.

BY the end of the century co-operation in this way was becoming less usual; the breakdown of the monopoly, with the consequent entry of competition, was one reason, and the growing wealth of individual publishing firms another.

[1] Nichols, *Literary Anecdotes*, i. 340.

It continued for some years among the London publishers in one form, because those who still claimed " an equitable title by usage " to the rights of old books found it the best way of clinging to what remained of their former property. They seemed to aim at leaving no bookseller of any importance unpossessed of a share in unprotected copyright, and in 1805 there was sold a one hundred and sixtieth share in Johnson's *Dictionary* for £23. On the whole, the only benefit to authors of this system of co-operation lay in the possibility it gave of big literary undertakings, exhaustive histories, dictionaries, and works edited with copious commentaries.

SUCH was the formidable body of men with whom an author had to deal. Their supremacy was only challenged by the presses of the two universities, whose rights and privileges continued unaffected by the Act of Queen Anne, by any private presses which might be set up, and at one time by a Society for the Encouragement of Learning.

THIS latter society [1] was set up in 1736, under the presidency of the Duke of Richmond, and with a managing committee which included among its hundred odd members James Thomson, the poet. Its avowed object was to enable authors to publish their work without having to resort to the booksellers. To accomplish this the society was to bear the expense of printing, and was to be reimbursed out of the profits, the author keeping the copyright. In other words, however excellent its intention was towards authors, it was an open attack on booksellers, and as such it was doomed

---

[1] See Nichols, *Literary Anecdotes*, ii. 90–7.

to failure. The promoters gave a sample of their quality at the beginning; nothing could suit them but to launch forth with some publication of great eminence, and they tried to secure Bentley's *Manilius*; Bentley, however, abruptly refused, and published it through the usual channel of 'the trade.' The secretary, again showing the spirit of the Society, wrote to a friend of " this discouraging and ungenerous act which will be recorded to the learned world, perhaps, when he is dead and rotten. Such men," said he, " deserve fleecing from booksellers." At last the Society did bring out a few books, useless works of obscure scholars, and even then not without contracting with some of those same " fleecing booksellers." Cave recommended to them in 1741 Johnson's *Irene*, but they declined it. Finally by 1748 so much expense had been incurred with so little benefit to authors or learning that the project was abandoned. The whole was ably summed up by Ralph: " Their Plan was too narrow,—They also forgot, that the Booksellers were Masters of all Avenues to every Market, and, by the Practice of one Night's Postage, could make any Work resemble *Jonah's Gourd* after the Worm had *smote* it."[1]

THE University Presses were equally insignificant rivals to 'the trade' and not interested in the works of ordinary writers. Certain books such as the *Prayer Book* they possessed the sole rights of printing by royal privilege, and in others, such as Lord Clarendon's *History of the Rebellion*, their rights were based on original gifts, secured by Act of Parliament. The booksellers were

[1] J. Ralph, *The Case of Authors by Profession or Trade* (1758), p. 60.

ready to sell their books, provided they were given the usual discount, but as the University authorities seemed unable to grasp the necessity of allowing discounts, and were, moreover, of very poor business ability as a whole, the booksellers generally left them to prosper as well as they could, unless they were called in by contract, as sometimes they were to redeem situations of particular chaos. Their general attitude is explained thus by Johnson: " The booksellers, who, like all other men, have strong prejudices in their own favour, are enough inclined to think the practice of printing and selling books by any but themselves, an encroachment on the rights of their fraternity; and have need of stronger inducements to circulate academical publications than those of another; for, of that mutual co-operation by which the general trade is carried on, the University can bear no part." [1] Nichols, writing to Bowyer in 1765, said that for the last seven years the Cambridge Press had cleared £1,500 annually, which was probably an unusually high average. If we may judge from a letter of Baskerville in 1762, they did not seem anxious to encourage others to lease their privileges: " The University of Cambridge," he wrote, " have given me a grant to print their 8vo and 12mo Common Prayer Books; but under such shackles as greatly hurt me." [2]

OF private presses the only one of note was that set up in 1757 by Horace Walpole as a hobby, which could be used for charitable purposes. Staffed by a man and boy, none too reliable, it went, of necessity, but slowly, and from the

[1] Boswell. *Life*, ii. 425. [2] Nichols, *Literary Anecdotes*, iii. 453.

narrowness of its extent was quite negligible as far as the booksellers were concerned; yet its struggles give us interesting sidelights on the attitude of 'the trade.' "The London booksellers," Walpole wrote in a moment of depression, " play me all manner of tricks. If I do not allow them ridiculous profits, they will do nothing to promote the sale; and when I do, they buy up the impression, and sell it at an advanced price before my face. This is the case of my two first volumes of *Anecdotes* for which people have been made to pay half a guinea, and a guinea more than the advertised price."[1] " Literature," he wrote at another time, " must struggle with many difficulties. They who print for profit, print only for profit; we who print to entertain or instruct others, are the bubbles of our designs. Defrauded, abused, pirated. . . ."[2] If he had taken it up for amusement, he found very little in the long run, and wondered whether the " booksellers cheat me the more because I am a gentleman." Possibly they did, but in any case 'the trade' never seem to have had any scruples about harassing those who plied their trade, but were not of their number. However, being rich enough to survive cheating, Walpole was able to help some deserving people by his Strawberry Hill productions.

(iii)

THE natural result of such power being concentrated in the hands of a few booksellers and of the number of writers being so great was the penury and squalor of Grub Street.

[1] *Letters*, ed. Toynbee, vi. 19.   [2] *Ibid*, v. 154.

Every writer whom a bookseller was unable to discern at once as one whose talent was likely to be commercially successful must take his place in the crowd and gain a living by the hackwork for which the booksellers could find a market in the, as yet, small public. The struggle to rise from the ranks of the hacks was arduous, but Johnson, Smollett and Goldsmith, among others, won through, and, as the century advanced, it became rapidly easier and quicker to do so. The conditions in the early days were beyond doubt most wretched, but they were not so bad as they were made out to be by Macaulay and Thackeray. Thackeray, indeed, not content with accepting the Grub Street myth in all its horror, went so far as to say that Pope by the *Dunciad* helped to spread and perpetuate the wretchedness of the hacks, and that he "contributed, more than any man who ever lived, to depreciate the literary calling."[1] The conditions, however deplorable, were inevitable, and if they had stopped the flow of those who could not write, they would have been of good service to the profession of letters.

IT appears that the booksellers did what they could to find writers employment and to treat them as well as possible, but, not being philanthropists, they did not try to reform that state of affairs, born of the times and made worse not by them but by the insistence of men who would turn to literature as a last resource; and we must remember in addition that such figures of the Grub Street myth as Savage and Boyse were people whom nobody could help. The dis-

[1] Thackeray, *English Humorists*, 1853, p. 215, and see pp. 214-17.

gruntled Ralph might assert in 1757 that "there is no difference between the Writer in his Garret, and the Slave in the Mines,"[1] but it was not so and had not been so; a writer of any ability could escape from his garret as Johnson did, and as Goldsmith did; it was only Goldsmith's incurable extravagance that kept him from comfortable circumstances. Indeed by 1760 Grub Street was altogether better than it had been in 1730, about which time Pope wrote: "I believe, if anyone, early in his life, should contemplate the dangerous fate of authors, he would scarce be of their number on any consideration. The life of a wit is a warfare on earth"; and in 1730, things were really not so bad as they would seem to Pope with his abhorrence of poverty, and as they must appear to those who brood too closely on the sombre hues of the *Dunciad*, and give undue prominence to Hogarth's sketch of the Distressed Poet, "in a garret writing for bread, and expecting to be dunned for a milkscore." If the remuneration of a bookseller's hack was low, the cost of living was also low, and was estimated by Johnson to have been at about 1730, some £30 a year.[2]

THE state of Grub Street in Little Britain in the time of Pope is described thus by Roger North, who died in 1743: "It is wretched to consider what pickpocket work with the help of the press these demi-booksellers make; they crack their brains to find out selling subjects, and keep hirelings in garrets, on hard meat, to write and correct by the great; so puff up an octavo to a sufficient thickness, and there is six shillings current for an

[1] *Case*, p. 22. [2] *Life*, i. 105.

hour and a half's reading and perhaps never to be read or looked upon after." Savage said of himself as one of Curll's hired writers : " Sometimes I was Mr. John Gay, at other Burnet or Addison ; I abridged histories and travels, translated from the French what they never wrote, and was expert in finding new titles for old books. I was the Plutarch of the notorious thief." Johnson was another of these compilers of lives and miscellaneous articles, prefaces and similar work, but also one of the few who " can be said to produce or endeavour to produce new ideas." The majority were mere " drudges of the pen, manufacturers of literature who set up as authors," and indeed hardly worthy of being esteemed authors at all. The bookseller West defined such a man in his *Recollections* of the latter half of the century as a garretteer, whose " business is to abridge, compile, write notes, and make a liberal use of the scissors, paste and brush, for the publishers of weekly or monthly numbers of Bibles, Voyages and Travels, Dictionaries of Arts and Sciences, Histories of the War and of the World, etc., for which all the names of the greatest divines, historians and travellers are sometimes adopted with the alteration of a letter or two, or a different Christian name." [1]

It was the interest of the bookseller to allow as little for writing, and of the hack to write as much as possible. Taking Johnson as an example, and judging from his letters, where we find him sign himself " Yours impransus," and apologises for not replying the evening before because he had no light by which to write, the average writer was

[1] W. West, *Fifty Years' Recollections of an Old Bookseller* (1837), p. 71.

certainly very poorly paid. According to Washington Irving, who was, however, biassed, Newbery, the bookseller of children's books fame, " coined the brains of authors in the time of their exigency, and made them pay dear for the plank put out to save them from drowning." But it was surely something to the credit of booksellers that they rescued at all these men who threw themselves recklessly in the sea without any particular aptitude for swimming, and who, when they were rescued, were none too profitable and were only kept at work by the fear of starvation. Those who would work well at their drudgery had the chance of doing well, as the quack Doctor, " Sir " John Hill, did in the fifties of the century, compiling weekly issues of voluminous works on Botany, Husbandry and other necessary subjects, by which he sometimes gained as much as £1,500 a year. Grub Street never passed away, but as there grew up a larger public, there was a greater demand for this miscellaneous work, and it was better paid ; but Grub Street is a division of the poor we shall always have with us, and its general condition seems to have been the same in the twenties of the next century when Borrow was compiling his lives of Newgate prisoners and writing the apocryphal history of Joseph Sell.

GRUB STREET is a side of the literary profession which we cannot pass by, as standing outside the main relation of author to bookseller, for it did not consist only of the dregs of the profession, but it dragged down the better men, lengthened their struggle, and increased their hardships in the rise to fame ; nor was Grub Street only the province of the inferior booksellers, but even the best had their drudges while they gained their reputation by contracts with first-rate authors. Horace Walpole was speaking not of a section, but of all, when he said, " Our booksellers here at London disgrace literature by trash they bespeak to be written, and at the same time prevent everything else from being sold."[1] Of course, they did not hinder the sale of those good works of which they had acquired the property, but by encouraging the trash they naturally checked the good. The writer, said Goldsmith, " despairs of applause and turns to profit which invites him."

(iv)

THE chances of an able writer were almost to the end of the century very dubious, unless special circumstances favoured him. Prospects were good or bad according as an author had or had not independent means, powerful patronage, or a fair social standing. To those who had not these things, necessity or a craving for literary expression could be the only inducements to turn writer. Johnson, after a year or so spent in writing for Cave, made strenuous efforts to escape to teaching in 1738. The degree of M.A. being necessary, Pope, who had heard of Johnson's case, asked his friend Earl Gower to petition Swift to secure a Dublin degree, and Lord Gower wrote describing Johnson as " choosing rather to die upon the road [i.e. to Dublin], *than be starved to death in translating for booksellers*; which has been his only subsist-

[1] *Letters*, v. 448.

ence for some time past."[1] That, probably, was exaggerating Johnson's feelings, but the strength of his desire to gain some better livelihood is shown by his trying to take up the legal profession when the teaching project had fallen through. Goldsmith, similarly, after a short trial of literature, returned to the Peckham school and did his best to obtain a medical appointment abroad; the *Enquiry into the Present State of Polite Learning* was written with the intention of providing funds for his journey to Coromandel, where the post in question was. But by that time all did not agree that literature was so bad a profession, for we are told that in 1763 Robert Lloyd, the friend of Wilkes and Churchill, drudging in the Fleet Prison on any miserable work on which the booksellers chose to employ him, found it "not so bad as being usher at Westminster"; although obviously it was bad enough.

THE booksellers had so powerful a grip on an unknown writer whose merit the public did not know, that such a writer had to take whatever was offered him. Johnson, we are told, would have taken even less than 10 guineas for *London* in 1738 but for the fact that Paul Whitehead, whom he despised, had just received a similar sum for a worse poem. Cleland was said to have been tempted by the offer of 20 guineas from Griffiths, the bookseller, to write a book "too infamous to be particularized," *The Memoirs of a Woman of Pleasure*, on which Griffiths made a profit of some £10,000.[2] But where a man had a small income, like Hume, he could drive a fair bargain.

[1] Boswell, *Life*, i. 133.   [2] Nichols, *Literary Anecdotes*, ii. 458, note.

Indeed, Hume's bargain with Norne in 1737 for the rights to the first edition of the *Treatise of Human Nature* was distinctly in the author's favour. Hume received £50 and twelve copies, while Norne had a complete loss, the impression falling " dead-born from the press." Anstey's social position gained him £200 for his *New Bath Guide* after two editions had already been published; while Goldsmith, because he had no social position, received for his *Traveller* only 20 guineas. Johnson, having made a name, had £125 for *Rasselas* in 1749 [1]; in 1762 Goldsmith received only 60 guineas for *The Vicar of Wakefield*, because " then [his] fame had not been elevated." [2] Harvard, a small writer, whose *Charles I* had in 1736 had a great success on the stage, was refused the usual fee of £100 for the copyright, because his general reputation was so low. Such was the influence of social position or literary reputation on the bargaining power of a writer.

ON the whole it was only the household stuff of literature that was really well rewarded; popular histories, natural histories, dictionaries, biographies, travels and scientific works were in constant demand, and booksellers paid well in order to get good work. Goldsmith's agreement for his *History of Animated Nature* was for 800 guineas; for a *Grecian History* he had £250 after a debt had been deducted, and 250 guineas also for a *History of Rome*; for his best work he received far less, *The Good-natured Man* going for £150, *The Traveller* for £21, and the copyright of the Chinese letters for a mere 5 guineas. " The

---

[1] Boswell, *Life*, i. 341.   [2] *Ibid.*, i. 415.

writings by which one can live are not the writings which themselves live."[1]

THE more limited scale of remuneration in the higher walks of literature was to an extent justifiable. It is difficult to decide quickly on the merits of original work, and more difficult still to estimate the appeal of any given work to the public. " You have only your own opinion," said Johnson, " and the public may think very differently. Both Goldsmith's comedies were once refused " ; and at another time, " My judgment I have found is no certain rule as to the sale of a work." Then if a critic of Johnson's standing felt the need for caution, it was clearly unreasonable to expect booksellers to undertake anything new without some assurance, and it was, moreover, an age when ' the trade ' was most in need of advancing along sure and careful lines, until it should be firmly established. Booksellers were, as a rule, inclined to estimate a work by quantity rather than quality, but they often made a point of calling in wiser heads than their own. Dodsley, when Akenside asked £120 for the copyright of his *Pleasures of the Imagination*, " carried the work to Pope, who, having looked into it, advised him not to make a niggardly offer ; for ' *this was no everyday writer.*' "[2] Johnson acted as Cave's oracle in literary matters. " Millar," wrote Boswell, " though himself no great judge of literature, had good sense enough to have for his friends very able men to give him their opinion and advice in purchase of copyright."[3] Further, a bookseller had no security that the work even of a writer of great reputation might not result in a

[1] For Goldsmith's prices, see J. Forster, *Life and Times of Goldsmith*.
[2] Johnson, *Lives* (Akenside), iii. 412.   [3] *Life*. i. 287.

loss. Millar offered Mallet £3,000 for the copyright of Bolingbroke's works, and Mallet, having refused because he thought the offer inadequate, found to his dismay that no one would now read Bolingbroke.

LITERARY property was indeed, as Nichols said, " a field which required some degree of speculative sagacity to cultivate." If a bookseller found that he had underestimated the value of a work, he could always, and did sometimes, make an increase on the price he had paid for the copyright. Millar had given Fielding £600 for *Tom Jones*, but, finding the sale above his expectations, he added another £100; Goldsmith for a similar reason received an addition of £50 to the £100 paid for his *Good-natured Man*; Johnson was given an additional hundred guineas on the price agreed upon for the *Lives of the Poets*; in 1776 the £100 Blair had for his sermons was doubled by Strahan because " the sale was so rapid and extensive, and the approbation of the publick so high."[1] It was more usual, in fact, for a bookseller to find that he had made greater profit than he anticipated, than to find that he had made a loss. *The Vicar of Wakefield* was almost a unique loss. Newbery seems to have doubted its value when he had bought it, and refrained from publishing it for three years, and there was still a loss on it of £2 16s. 6d. after three editions had been sold. Collins, the bookseller of Salisbury, is said to have sold his third share in 1784 at a loss of fifteen guineas.

SUCH a loss, however, was very exceptional. The chief booksellers were rapidly growing

[1] Boswell, *Life*, iii. 98.

wealthy and important men, magistrates and members of Parliament. Millar made more thousands by Fielding's works than he paid hundreds; Smollett's history " alone proved a little fortune to the printer and bookseller "; by Johnson's *Lives* the booksellers in twenty-five years, said Malone, probably got £5,000; Cadell told Robertson that he and Millar made £6,000 out of Robertson's *History of Scotland*, for which they had given £600; Dodsley made so much in ten years out of Anstey's *New Bath Guide* that he gave the author back the copyright, and out of Gray's *Elegy*, for which he gave nothing, he made £1,000 in a few years. Murray, setting up as a bookseller himself in 1768, wrote: "Many Blockheads in the Trade are making fortunes; and did we not succeed as well as they, I think it must be imputed only to ourselves."[1] " Young man," Osborne was used to say to apprentices, " I have been in business more than forty years, and am now worth more than £40,000." That was the case with all the prominent members of the trade, and it was undoubtedly due to the steady growth of the public.

BOOKSELLERS, when they had a public on which to rely, could afford to be generous; and we begin to find bigger and bigger prices being paid for copyright as we pass the middle of the century. In 1726 Swift had only received £200 for *Gulliver's Travels*, and in 1742 *Joseph Andrews* only brought Fielding £183 10s., but *Tom Jones* and *Amelia* were rewarded with £700 and £1,000 respectively. Hume between 1754 and 1760 received the sum of £3,400 for his history, which,

[1] Smiles, *A Publisher and his Friends* (1891), i, 5.

said the author, "much exceeded anything previously known"; Robertson in 1769 was paid £4,500 for his *Charles V*; where Dodsley gave 220 guineas for Young's *Night Thoughts* in 1742, he gave Percy in 1765 300 guineas for his *Reliques*, and Churchill for *The Duellist* in 1763 had £450. Lyttelton's *History of Henry II* was in 1767 considered worth £3,000; in the same year Strahan gave £500 for Steuart's *Principles of Political Economy*, and in 1776 he gave the same sum for the first edition only of Adam Smith's *Wealth of Nations*. The usual price for an exceptionally successful play, which had been £50 in the time of Queen Anne, had become £100 by 1730, and by 1780 had risen further to £150, as we see by such examples as Hannah More's *Percy* (1778) and Cumberland's *West Indian*. Indeed, there is ample testimony to the great improvement in prospects which had taken place in the profession of letters by the last quarter of the eighteenth century. To take but two examples, we find eloquent witness to the fact in Henry's *History of England* (1771-80) which brought the author £3,300, although of no more than average merit, and in the £30,000 which Hannah More is said to have made by her pen. The sum of 300 guineas which was all Johnson gained by his *Lives of the Poets* (1777) is in this light misleading. It was no higher because, as Boswell said, "[Johnson] had less attention to profit from his labours than any man to whom literature has been a profession."[1] According to Malone, "had he asked a thousand or even fifteen hundred guineas, the booksellers who knew the

---

[1] Boswell, *Life*, iii. 110

value of his name would doubtless have readily given it."

WARBURTON in 1762 gave the opinion in a pamphlet on literary property[1] that the real effects of the Act of 1710 had been for the worse, and contrasted eighteenth-century literature with that of the days of patronage, especially in Greece and Rome, to the disadvantage of his own day. Considered abstractly, there was much to say for his view, but considered practically there could be no point whatever in the discussion. There were no longer many patrons, and if resort were not had to the booksellers (for which purpose the 1710 Act was essential), then literature would have been reduced to the ranks of the independent; there could have been no Smollett, no Johnson and no Goldsmith. The complaint which gave rise to this abstract discussion was that this complete dependence on booksellers, this constant necessity of writing whether one would or no, for a living, was most detrimental to true literature and resulted in a flood of trash for whose absence the world would be all the better. It was certainly true, as Johnson said of Collins, that "a man, doubtful of his dinner, or trembling at a creditor, is not much disposed to abstracted meditation or remote enquiries"[2]; he is more or less driven to write fluently and badly. Added to which, there was the lowering influence of the public demand, which booksellers made little or no attempt to direct. They fed the prevailing public taste, requiring of their writers only such stuff as the common reader was greedy for, until the public appetite was glutted, the late style became a

[1] *Letter from an Author to a M.P.* (1747), B.M. 518, k. 4 (9).
[2] *Lives of the Poets*, iii. 335.

"drug," and another kind of trash appealed in its stead. But, on the other hand, this writing for booksellers to keep body and soul together did give much good. Johnson tells of Collins that as soon as he inherited a legacy, he gave up working [1]; further, we have the word of Grainger that Johnson himself never thought of working if he had a couple of guineas, and the Doctor avowed that he never wrote but for " want of money, which is the only motive of writing I know of."

THE dependence on booksellers, then, cut both ways; if it made Goldsmith write nearly endless volumes of history to pay off the debts from which he was never free, it also made Johnson, at Dodsley's suggestion, set to work on the *Dictionary*. In fact all this talk, for Warburton was not alone, arose purely from the desire to find arguments against booksellers and their claim to perpetual copyright, since security in their writings was fully as essential to authors of independent means as it was to those who had to bargain with their pens for subsistence.

BUT it is noticeable how much of the best work came from those who were independent. It may be that to those particular men, irrespective of their position, were the peculiar mental gifts given, or more probably it fell out so because of the condition of authorship; there may have been potential philosophers and historians who were denied expression by the public demand for lighter matter, and literature can no more be exempt from the working of the law of supply

[1] Cf. Churchill, of whom Cowper wrote:
"Lifted at length, by dignity of thought,
And dint of genius to an affluent lot,
He laid his head in luxury's soft lap,
And took too often there his easy nap."

and demand than any other profession; to live on the public, a writer must please the many, not the few. Hume, having resolved to maintain independence by frugal living on his slender patrimony, was able to prepare his early writings in country retirement either in England or France, and in 1747, before he became opulent through his history, he had a reserve of a thousand pounds. Robertson was supported during the composition of his *History of Scotland* by the comfortable income of a living near Edinburgh, and was by 1764 in possession of a " revenue exceeding what had ever been enjoyed before by any Presbyterian clergyman in Scotland." [1] Gibbon, too, was always in comfortable circumstances, even when not enjoying a salary of £750 as a Lord Commissioner of Trade with nominal duties. Gray, again, was able to produce his poetry at leisure, disdaining to take any money for his copyrights, with the single exception of the £40 given by Dodsley for the *Odes* in 1757. Of such men it can hardly be said that they followed the profession of letters; they were primarily clergymen or politicians for the greater part of their time, and learning and writing were to them recreation; they wrote not to get a living, but because they could not live without writing, because to them " vita sine literis mors est," as Robertson prefixed to his note-books.

THE relation between these authors of independent means and their booksellers was very different from that of their poorer fellows, who wrote to live and had to take the best offer a bookseller would make them, lest they should cease to live

[1] D. Stewart, *Life of Robertson* (1801), p, 50.

at all. It was Robertson who said that " an author should sell his first work for what the booksellers will give, till it shall appear whether he is an author of merit, or what is something as to purchase money, an author who pleases the public " ; and his saying was perfectly true. But if we can conceive a struggling author with no one to back him having succeeded in writing a *History of Scotland* at all, we may be sure he would not have got from a bookseller the £600 which Robertson did, who had made a small name by his defence of Home's *Douglas*, and had considerable friends to recommend him. It was to the Robertsons and not to the Goldsmiths that the copyright gave a fair bargaining power ; the latter might often be denied the opportunity even of testing that " something as to purchase money," the opinion of the public. Laurence Sterne, prebendary of York, had not sufficient recommendation to induce Dodsley to give even £50 for the first two volumes of *Tristram Shandy* in 1759, and *Tristram* might have slumbered another ten years like Johnson's *Irene*, and had no further adventures, had not Sterne been enabled by a friendly loan of £100 to print a small edition at York. Then indeed, praised by Warburton as the English Rabelais, " a fashionable thing," " nothing else talked of, nothing admired " but *Tristram Shandy*, Dodsley offered £650 for the second edition and two more volumes. It was a typical example of the unadventurous nature of booksellers at that time, afraid to run the risk of publishing unless the author could bear the expense, or reliable opinion testified to the probability of success.

In the second half of the century, however, the prospects of authorship were distinctly improving, because the public was so quickly expanding. To the many literary aspirants who sought his advice in those days when he was the recognized Great Cham of letters, Johnson summed up his attitude thus : " If the authors who apply to me have money, I bid them boldly print without a name ; if they have written in order to get money, I tell them to go to the booksellers, and make the best bargain they can."[1] There was now a public which could support a good work, and a writer confident of his merits was quite justified in printing for himself if he could. Churchill in 1760 could find no bookseller willing to give more than five guineas for his *Rosciad*, and so he undertook the publishing himself with great success ; although it must be admitted that his circumstances were particularly favourable, since nothing sells like good topical satire. But if we take the other extreme, we find there, too, an example of successful appeal to the public by the learned Mrs. Carter, whose *Epictetus* in 1758 brought her £1,000.

WHERE a writer had to bargain with booksellers, he likewise was on surer ground ; a publisher might reject a work through bad judgment, but where he paid, he paid better. Goldsmith was *déterré* in a much shorter period than Johnson ; and where Johnson, after some nine years, received only 15 guineas for his *Life of Savage* and a year later was glad to revise Madden's poem, *Boulter's Monument*, for 10 guineas, " which was to me at that time a great sum,"[2] Goldsmith, after two

[1] Boswell, *Life*, ii. 195.   [2] *Ibid.*, i. 318.

years, was getting £20 for a catchpenny life of Voltaire and next year (1760) was employed by Newbery to contribute two papers a week to *The Public Ledger*, roughly at the rate of £100 a year. By 1766, in fact, the payment of booksellers was sufficiently good for Goldsmith to say, in reply to the temptations of an emissary of Lord Sandwich, " I can earn as much as will supply my wants without writing for any party."[1] It was his love of gambling and his extravagance in living in society beyond his means that always crippled him. The booksellers paid him well; but however much they had given, it is most likely that poor Goldy would have succeeded in spending more. Johnson " always said the booksellers were a generous set of men," and Anderson tells us of Smollett that " the booksellers for many years were his principal resource for employment and subsistence. For them he held the pen of a ready writer, in the walk of general literature, comprehending compilations, translations, criticism and miscellaneous essays, and towards him they were as liberal as the public enabled them to be. They were almost his only patrons; and indeed a more generous set of men can hardly be pointed out in the trading world. By their liberality, wit and learning have perhaps received more ample, more substantial encouragement than from all their princely or noble patrons. Accusations indeed of injustice, selfishness and meanness, have been long reiterated against them, by disappointed authors; and, in some instances, they may be well founded; but the large sums which have been paid for manuscripts by the booksellers

[1] J. Forster, *Life of Goldsmith*, ii. 71.

of London, in the course of the eighteenth century, are sufficient to rescue the venders of literature from the reproach of suffering the dispensers of knowledge to consume themselves in the operation."[1] For example, Smollett's popular *History of England* in 1758 brought him some £2,000.

THE support of the public was, of course, the determining factor, and on the whole the payments of the booksellers maintained a very fair correspondence with it; " the measure of their liberality," said Gibbon, " is the least ambiguous test of our success." To this liberality Nichols, the antiquarian printer, also bears witness, allowing as one must for the bias favourable to the trade which permeates what he flattered himself he might call his *Typographical Annals of the Bowyer Press.* He wrote of Robinson the bookseller (1730–1801): "As his success in business proceeded, he extended his liberality to Authors in no common degree; and it will be difficult to find an instance where he did not amply gratify the wish of the party if at all compatible with prudence or even the distant probability of return. It was his opinion that liberality to Authors was the true spirit of bookselling enterprize, and, perhaps, little can be done if occasional failures are allowed to break in upon this system."[2] Nichols, in fact, feared " he gave rather too much than too little," with that typical bias which we have to discount in his judgments; but Lackington, the secondhand bookseller of the last quarter of the century, was if anything biassed the other way, and a man whose disapproval spoke with

---

[1] Anderson, *Life of Smollett* (1806), p. 37. [2] Nichols, *Literary Anecdotes*, iii. 446.

no small voice, and his testimony is the same as that of Nichols. " Publishers," he thought, " at least many of them, would be allowed to possess more liberality than any other set of tradesmen, I mean so far as relates to the purchase of manuscripts and copy-right."[1] Further, there is no doubt that Robinson was quite right in his opinion that liberality was a sound business principle; it was the one on which the chief booksellers in the days of Johnson's fame acted; it was the principle of such men as Dilly, Millar, Strahan and Cadell.

BUT if the spirit of booksellers was admittedly liberal in regard to purchasing copyright, it was very illiberal towards an author who wished to use them merely as publishers of his work, while keeping the copyright himself; they would not be content with the rôle of a bookseller in the present-day sense of the word. They did not always buy the copyright for its whole period, but would buy it for, perhaps, the first edition with a division of profits on future editions, as Strahan did in the case of the *Wealth of Nations*, or they might be content with a division of profits from the beginning, as in Strahan's agreement to give Gibbon two-thirds of the profits on the first volume of *The Decline and Fall*. These and variations of these methods were favoured by booksellers; but where they had no further interest in the sale of a work than in the discount on each book sold, their attitude was different. In 1728 we find Lindsay, translator of a certain Mason's Latin *Vindication of the Church of England*, writing to Dr. Zachary Grey : " Your

[1] Lackington, *Memoirs* (1803), p. 225.

promoting its sale will be a great obligation to me; for you know the booksellers will not promote any thing which is not their own property."[1] In 1742 a certain Rev. Francis Wise, writing in a similar connexion, declared: "It is incredible what mischief the booksellers are capable of doing to an author, by discountenancing the sale of his book."[2] We have seen, too, how Horace Walpole in 1764 wrote of a Strawberry Hill impression, that the booksellers, "if I do not allow them ridiculous profits, will do nothing to promote its sale."[3] Lackington, moreover, at the end of the century was most emphatic on this trade tendency. "In general," he affirmed, "where authors keep their own copyright they do not succeed, and many books have been consigned to oblivion through the inattention and mismanagement of publishers, as most of them are envious of the success of such works as they do not turn to their own account. [Authors] should sell their copyright, or be previously well acquainted with the characters of their publishers."[4] That some works having a poor sale while the author had the copyright, had a rapid one when it was sold, was asserted by Lackington to be indisputable; they were purposely kept back, he said, that the booksellers might obtain the copyright for a trifle from the disappointed author. "I am sorry that such should be found, but I am sure to the fact. It is inconceivable what mischief booksellers *can* and often *will* do to authors, as thousands of books are yearly written for to

[1] Nichols, *Literary Anecdotes*, i. 373, note 2.
[3] *Letters*, ed. Toynbee, vi. 19.
[2] Nichols, *Illustrations*, iv. 441
[4] Lackington, *Memoirs*, p. 229.

London that are never sent."[1] And though Lackington was very fond of scandal, more especially against Wesleyans, there is no reason to doubt here the validity of his statement on the whole. Perhaps the most eminent work subjected to this booksellers' boycott was the first volume of Hume's *History*, which was first published in Edinburgh. There it had a very considerable sale, 450 copies being sold in five weeks, but in London only 45 copies were disposed of in a year, which Burton attributes to trade influence. Its success when Millar agreed to push it and to undertake the subsequent volumes was certainly very remarkable, if it were due solely to Millar's exertions, and it is a matter of surprise that the public, which had of late years been buying Hume's philosophical essays so that they were a common topic of conversation in educated circles, should have so held aloof from his *History* unless it was checked from buying it by the booksellers. BUT if the latter could and often did hinder the sale of a book, they were equally skilled in promoting it. Millar in 1749, fearing on second thoughts that he would not be repaid for the £1,000 which he had given Fielding for *Amelia*, had resort to two tricks. He advertised that " to satisfy the earnest Demand of the Publick, this Work has been printed at four Presses ; but the Proprietor notwithstanding finds it impossible to get them bound in Time, without spoiling the Beauty of the Impression, and therefore will sell them sew'd at Half-a-Guinea " ; in addition he told the other members of ' the trade ' at a sale held just before the publication of *Amelia*, that

[1] *Memoirs*, p. 229.

he must withhold from them this latest work of Fielding's because there would be such a demand that he could not afford to allow them the usual discount. The ruse succeeded to perfection, and the impression was quickly bought up.[1] Somewhat less creditable was the strategy of Smollett in 1751, when he incorporated into *Peregrine Pickle* the scandalous memoirs of Lady Vane, which largely contributed to its good reception; and another trick of the trade is evidenced by Newbery's device for ushering into the world Goldsmith's *History of England* in 1763, by which it appeared as a series of letters from a nobleman to his son, was variously attributed by the public to Lords Chesterfield, Orrery and Lyttelton, and in consequence sold remarkably well.[2] In such ways did the booksellers tempt the public to buy books, of whose copyright they were the owners.

(v)

THE intimate personal relations between authors and booksellers were, on the whole, friendly, sympathetic and helpful. One might perhaps have expected to find more friction between two sets of men so much contrasted, but their close and constant connexion with each other seems to have given a mutual insight into and appreciation of the best qualities on both sides. Millar must have seen that Thomson's habit of not rising till midday was not merely the result of indolence; Dodsley did not respect Johnson the less because he lived " in poverty, idleness and the pride of literature "; Newbery must have

[1] Dobson, *Fielding* (1883), p. 152.   [2] Forster, *Life*, i. 301.

felt that Goldsmith's follies were compensated by his talents, and were, perhaps, their necessary complement. The authors, on their side, saw that booksellers must be men of business, and could not be philanthropists, and were, therefore, not so galled by the chains of commerce by which literature was bound. There were, naturally, lesser men who would say " booksellers are persons whom I would not willingly have dealings with,"[1] and that " booksellers, since the days of old Ben, have been a shuffling set of selfish knaves," but the more important writers, possibly with the exception of Pope, esteemed booksellers more highly. Nor is Pope an exception whose word can go for much ; his own keenness for money was responsible for his attitude to publishers, for his attack on their commercial spirit in the *Dunciad*, and for his quarrel with Lintot. Dodsley, he wrote in 1735, had just set up as a bookseller, and " I doubt not, as he has more common sense, so will have more honesty, than most of [that] profession "[2] ; to the poet, booksellers were mostly fools and knaves, because he was too easily irritated and too anxious for his own profits. Johnson, on the other hand, " uniformly expressed his regard "[3] for the booksellers in his later days, although earlier he had occasionally denounced " the avarice by which booksellers are frequently misled to oppress that genius by which they are supported."[4] But in the years when Boswell knew him, he always said, " the booksellers are generous, liberal-minded men,"[5] and affirmed that " the mer-

[1] Nichols, *Illustrations*, iv. 436.
[2] Pope, *Works*, Elwin and Courthope, x. 126.
[3] Boswell, *Life*, i. 438.
[4] *Ibid.*, i. 305, note 1.
[5] *Ibid.*, i. 304.

cantile ruggedness of that race "[1] was then a thing of the past. The following passage from a letter shows that he appreciated their position: " I suppose with all our scholastick ignorance of mankind, we are still too knowing to expect that the booksellers will erect themselves into patrons, and sell under the influence of a disinterested zeal for the promotion of learning."[2] Gibbon called Cadell " that honest and liberal bookseller "; and Boswell said that " Mr. Strahan's liberality, judgement, and success, are well known "[3]; while Goldsmith added his tribute when he said, " I look to the booksellers for support; they are my best friends, and I am not inclined to forsake them for others."[4] Indeed, there is a pretty story of Goldsmith which, if not true, is at least in spirit indicative of this pleasant sympathy. Carnan, the tale goes, gave for one of Goldsmith's works " so large a sum that the Doctor said he thought it would be ruinous to the poor man," and sent him back his purchase money, which the bookseller, however, declined to accept. Of Carnan's predecessor, Newbery, we know that he and Goldsmith got on very well together. Newbery cared for the poet's lodgings, saw that Mrs. Fleming, his landlady, was paid her £50 a year, and helped him with loans to such an extent, that when he died in 1767, Goldsmith was about £200 in his debt. Cowper, again, was very happy with his publisher, Johnson, but in a different way; the poet found him " a very judicious man," and his letters tell how they " jog on together comfortably enough," Johnson suggesting helpful

---

[1] Boswell, *Life*, i. 305, note 1.   [2] *Ibid.*, ii. 425.
[3] *Ibid.*, i. 288.   [4] Forster, *Life*, i. 380

alterations which Cowper thankfully accepted. And, again, the relation between Hume and Strahan is well illustrated by their long, detailed and intimate correspondence, only marred by occasional lapses on the part of the historian, as when he accused Strahan of deception or, by his plaintive suspicions, irritated him into writing, " Do learn to put a little confidence in me."[1] But such incidents are by the way, and the earnestness of Hume's apology for the charge of deception shows the value he placed on their friendship. " There is no man," he wrote, " of whom I entertain a better [opinion], nor whose Friendship I desire more to preserve, nor indeed any one to whom I have owd more essential Obligations."[2] SUCH is the strain common to most authors in speaking of their booksellers, such the general, happy tenor of their connexion in the early years of George III. The Dillys, we are told, " in their dealings with authors were very liberal, and Charles in particular was known for his kindness to young aspirants." Robert Dodsley was spoken of by Boswell as the " worthy, modest and ingenious Mr. Robert Dodsley." Beattie, Hume and Robertson lent their names in support of the petition of the London booksellers for relief in 1774. Looking further back we find that Thomson was relieved from much monetary anxiety because " Millar was always at hand, to answer or even to prevent, his demands,"[3] and in return, when he had money, the poet undertook to recompense Millar for his losses on the unpopular poem of *Liberty*. Cave, though hardly " the universal encourager of merit " that Nichols

[1] Hume, *Letters*, ed. G. B. Hill, p. 269.   [2] *Ibid.*, p. 271.
[3] L. Morel, *James Thomson*, p. 122, note 1.

called him, took considerable interest in his writers; it was through his influence that Johnson's *London* was accepted by Dodsley, and he also tried to get *Irene* taken up by the Society for the Encouragement of Learning. Fielding, too, owed many an occasional loan to Millar in the days of his play-writing, when his best clothes were as often as not in the pawnshop; and Johnson once owed release from prison to Richardson's payment of a debt.

SUCH incidents show a spirit of sympathy and helpfulness on the part of the booksellers, although their actions were also largely in their own interest, for an author indebted to them was bound to supply copy, and an author in prison was of diminished value. But it was more their sympathy than their interest which prompted them. Richardson, for example, had " a reputation for being kind to clever men "—a fact which drew Goldsmith to solicit, with success, the office of press corrector from him. Collins, when confined to his lodgings by a prowling bailiff, was advanced by a bookseller, on the promise of future work, " as much money as enabled him to escape into the country."

FURTHER, there was a tendency among booksellers to respect their authors. Steevens, in his preface to *Shakespeare* (1778), wrote of Tonson: " He had enlarged his mind beyond solicitude about petty losses, and refined it from the desire of unreasonable profit. He was willing to admit those with whom he contracted, to the just advantage of their own labours, and had never learned to consider the author as under-agent to the bookseller. The wealth which he inherited or acquired, he enjoyed like a man conscious of the dignity of a profession subservient to letters." What Steevens said about Tonson might about 1780 have been said of several of the leading booksellers. They had an esteem for men of letters which contrasts pleasantly with the words of such of their contemporaries as Adam Smith, who authoritatively and contemptuously pronounced that the "unprosperous race of men, called men of letters, must necessarily occupy their present forlorn state in society much as formerly, when a scholar and a beggar seem to have been terms very nearly synonymous."

FAR from holding any such view, the leading booksellers cultivated an intimacy with authors which must have been of great value to both. Such a practice could not but result in greater harmony, a greater readiness to meet each other's wishes, and a more complete understanding. If the authors gained in one way, the booksellers in another had the benefit of securing good advice on works of whose acceptance they were in doubt. For example, Strahan had in 1777 rejected Blair's sermons,[1] and only agreed to take them on Johnson's recommendation, to be rewarded by a most remarkable sale.

SUCH interchange of opinion could take place freely in a convivial atmosphere, and this personal relation we speak of was undoubtedly seen at its best in such a setting as the dining-room of Messieurs Dilly in the Poultry, who were, says Boswell, "my worthy booksellers and friends

---

[1] Strahan was, however, on the whole the best judge of literature in the trade. Gibbon's first volume had been stinted to five hundred copies "till the number was doubled by the prophetic taste of Mr. Strahan." Hume wrote to him: "I thank you for your corrections, which are very judicious."

... at whose hospitable and well-covered table I have seen a greater number of literary men, than at any other, except that of Sir Joshua Reynolds."[1] It was an age of convivial hospitality, and the festive board brought together not only bookseller and author, but bookseller and bookseller. For many years it was the custom to initiate trade sales by a dinner in whose genial atmosphere differences might be smoothed away and profitable schemes auspiciously inaugurated.

(vi)

IN review, we may say that the profession of letters shows rapid progress in nearly all respects during the half-century 1726 to 1780, and that at the end of that period its prospects were distinctly good. The determining factor had been the rise of the public; that had resulted in booksellers having more demand for writers, thus relaxing the pressure of their monopoly; the increase in trade led naturally to a rise in the payment of authors, Millar, for example, gaining the praise of Johnson for having "raised the price of literature."[2] Years of toil in Grub Street were no longer the depressing approach for a poor aspirant, whose period of probation was become less arduous and far shorter. The trade itself was in 1780 prosperous and generous; and in generosity, at least, it was probably higher than in the period that follows. Knight, in his *Shadows of the Old Booksellers*, estimates that Gibbon's profits in 1777 were some 59 per cent. higher than they would have been in 1840.[3]

[1] *Life*, iii. 65.   [2] *Ibid.*, i. 288.   [3] New Universal Library, p. 199.

AUTHORSHIP IN THE DAYS OF JOHNSON

THERE are only two writers whose records do not afford credit to the booksellers of 1770 to 1780, but neither do they shed discredit. Chatterton had alienated many by his poetic forgeries and his satirical epistles; he proudly refused all help, and it does not appear that he approached any of the more eminent booksellers. Crabbe, on the other hand, would deal with none but the first publishers, and refused to adapt himself to circumstances in any way; instead of being willing, as Johnson and Goldsmith were, to write what was wanted, Crabbe would write nothing but what pleased himself.[1] Neither the tragedy of Chatterton nor the first ill-success of Crabbe can, therefore, with justice be cited as exceptions to the liberality of booksellers or the good prospects of authors.

[1] Compare with Crabbe's attitude: "As one of the little occasional advantages which he [Johnson] did not disdain to take by his pen, as a man whose profession was literature, he this year (1756) accepted of a guinea from Mr. Robert Dodsley, for writing the introduction to *The London Chronicle*, an evening newspaper." (Boswell, i. 317.)

CHAPTER II

THE COPYRIGHT STRUGGLE

(i) The Act of 1710. (ii) The survival of piracy intermittent in England. Importation from abroad and from Ireland. Its treatment. (iii) Lapse of copyrights under Act of 1710. Booksellers petition Parliament. Their claims and failure. (iv) Question of perpetual ownership raised. Indirect attempts to secure it. Typical arguments. Bullying tactics. (v) Donaldson begins his attack. Perpetuity won in England, lost in Scotland, finally lost in England. Counter-replies to the pleas of 'the trade.' (vi) Effect of loss of claim to perpetuity. Attitude of booksellers and of authors. No drop in prices. (vii) The ideal of copyright. The position in 1780.

(i)

WE have noted before the state of insecurity into which authors and booksellers were thrown in 1695 by the lapse of the Licensing Act. It was in vain for the members of the Stationers' Company to pass a by-law in May 1694 " to prevent the rights of books entered in their registers from being invaded by evil-minded men" under penalty of a fine of twopence on each offending copy. The power of the Company over printers and booksellers was no longer strong enough to be a deterrent to unscrupulous men, anxious to earn a living, and, if the members could not enforce order among themselves, there was no relief to be had at law. The best a bookseller could do was to threaten legal action against would-be pirates, in hopes that the mere bluff would prove effective. But whether they had legal support in their copyright property or not, the booksellers continued to assume and to act on the assumption that the acquisition of a copyright gave exclusive and perpetual property in a work. The practice continued in the early years of the eighteenth century of purchasing from authors the perpetual

53

copyright of their books. It was to "secure" this that Parliament was petitioned, with the result that the Act of 1710 was obtained with a limited protection, but with no mention of any perpetuity.

FROM the reports handed down of the passing of this Act,[1] it appears that it was drastically revised in committee, and there can be little doubt that the opinions of lawyers and others on the vast claims of the booksellers were unfavourable, and that they were communicated to the booksellers. It seems hardly credible that 'the trade' in 1710 can have believed that this perpetuity was any longer theirs at law, or that the legal authorities (and Lord Somers was in 1710 still a prominent member of the Ministry, actively interested in Parliamentary affairs) can have doubted that the new Act excluded any such interpretation. But for twenty-one years, in most cases, 'the trade,' whatever they thought, could have no immediate interest in the continued validity of their claim. All books published before April 1st, 1710, were legally protected until April 1731, and new books, if the writer died shortly after publication, would be safe enough till the late months of 1724. There was time enough to reflect upon the position.

MEANWHILE, the desired security was achieved. Piracy did not cease entirely, but it was henceforth within bounds. Pamphlets written around 1709 in support of the petitioning booksellers all spoke glibly of the Common Law rights, but pleaded that its remedies were insufficient. It only gave damages, they said, to the extent of the

---

[1] An account of the stages of the Bill is given in a pamphlet written for Donaldson, B.M. 518, k. 4 (16).

losses suffered, and those losses it was never possible adequately to estimate. " The subject of our request is," said one of these sheets, " that you would be pleased to strengthen the Common Law in our case."[1] Interpreting the Act as the House of Lords in 1774 interpreted it, we cannot say that the booksellers got what they wanted, but they did get this one request of theirs for penalties, independent of these unascertainable damages. A bookseller could now procure the destruction of all pirated copies and a fine of one penny on each pirated sheet, of which fine, however, the bookseller had only half, the Crown having the rest. We should expect therefore to find that, when pirates were prosecuted, the booksellers sought to inflict these penalties on them; but such was not the case. Having secured penalties, they declined to exact them, and chose rather to obtain in a Court of Equity injunctions to restrain piratical publications, as a more expedient method. Against the penalties it was urged that they were too small and would never be fully paid, as the number of books actually printed could not be ascertained. All they required was the suppression of the rival, and, as an injunction did that, and was, moreover, easily and quickly obtainable, to file one became the usual procedure. It was only necessary to present a prima-facie case of right to the work in question, and the injunction, readily granted, was always acquiesced in by the pirate.

[1] *More Reasons humbly offered to the Honourable House of Commons for the Bill for Encouraging Learning*, B.M. 1887, b. 58 (6).

(ii)

IT could hardly be expected that any Act of Parliament, however stringent, would stamp out piracy. There would always be one or two booksellers ready to run the risk, seeing that, with reasonable secrecy and precaution, an impression might be well circulated and sold before the owners could be sufficiently sure of their mark to set the law in motion. Thus we find injunctions being filed every now and then in respect of works clearly within the terms of the Queen Anne Statute. In 1722 Knaplock obtained an injunction against Curll for printing Prideaux's *Directions to Churchwardens*, and Tonson one against Clifton for Steele's *Conscious Lovers*; in 1729 Gilliver employed the same means against Watson's pirated edition of the *Dunciad*; in 1737 this same Watson came under an injunction, filed by Ballax, for pirating Gay's *Polly*[1]; in 1761 Dodsley had to try to put an end to the growing practice of pirating in magazines, by filing an injunction against Kinnersley for abstracting part of *Rasselas* and printing it in a periodical; in 1771 an injunction was obtained against the printers of *The Journal of Sidney Parkinson*, the rights of which were included among those of the other papers concerning the South Sea voyages which Hawkesworth was to edit for Strahan; and in 1774, while the great copyright battle was only just subsiding, some Edinburgh booksellers invaded Dodsley's rights to *Chesterfield's Letters*, on the specious argument

---

[1] For much of the copyright question, see Sir J. Burrow, *Question of Literary Property* (1774).

that Dodsley was not the original assignee, and were restrained by an injunction.

SUCH examples of occasional piracy throughout our period are nothing more than was to be expected, and confirm the fact that in the suppression of piracy the Act was quite successful, even though its penalties were laid aside. But there were, of course, many more piracies than there were injunctions against them. Thus in 1735 there seems to have been a pirated edition of Pope's works by Curll, of which the poet wrote to Fortescue, " We cannot find who is the pirater of my works, therefore cannot move for an injunction, though they are sold over all the town."[1] In 1735, too, Dodsley's popular play, *The Toy-shop*, was widely pirated. In 1729 Bowyer had to insert the following advertisement in *The Evening Post*: " Yesterday two illegal, false, and spurious editions of *Polly, an Opera ; being the second part of the Beggar's Opera*, were published ; the one in octavo without the Musick, printed for Jeffrey Walker in the Strand, the other in octavo with the Musick at the end, printed by J. Thomson. This is to advertise all booksellers, printers, publishers, hawkers, etc., not to sell, or cause to be sold, any of the said editions, the sole property of the said book being according to Act of Parliament vested in the Author, for whom the book is printed with the Musick on copper-plates in quarto. Prosecutions with the utmost severity will be put in execution against any one who shall presume to sell any of the aforesaid illegal spurious editions."[2] Such adver-

[1] Pope, *Works*, ed. Elwin and Courthope, ix. 130.
[2] Nichols, *Literary Anecdotes*, i. 404 and note.

tisements doubtless proved effective, for they were frequently made by publishers, but generally more concisely. It is possible that the threats of prosecution " with the utmost severity " led to private settlements without recourse to the Court of Chancery, and in any case they gave warning to all well-wishers of the author or of his publisher to avoid the false edition.

PIRACY was at times quite a minor trouble. Mr. Straus, Dodsley's biographer, says of the years round 1738 that " about this time [Dodsley] was forced to take measures to secure himself against the piracies which were then so prevalent."[1] In 1739 Brooke issued this notice concerning his *Gustavus Vasa*, which was selling well because of its prohibition by the Lord Chamberlain for political reasons : " Whereas a pyrate Edition of my Play is publish'd, I humbly hope none of my Friends who did me the honour to subscribe will think me in the wrong in taking this Method to secure my Property. And I hereby give Notice to all Booksellers and Pamphleteers that whoever can be prov'd to sell any other Edition than this shall certainly be prosecuted with the utmost Severity."[2] Thus for years piracy remained a real danger which it was foolish to ignore, and which made authors and publishers cautious. Dr. Birch, the antiquarian scholar, wrote in July 1752 to his friend Bishop Hayter : " The lateness of the season having determined the Proprietors of Archbishop Tillotson's *Life* to suspend the publication of it till October, their apprehensions from their piratical brethren will restrain me for some months from distributing the presents

---

[1] R. Straus, *Robert Dodsley*, p. 47.   [2] *Ibid.*, p. 320.

which I intended."[1] It is manifest that the temptation to forestall the work would have proved unconquerable, if a chance copy had come the way of a none too honest bookseller.

BUT where piracy was most irritating and irrepressible was in those miscellanies of accumulated thieving, the magazines. They claimed the right to abridge and to précis without infringing copyright, and it was often difficult to draw the line between so-called abridgment and downright piracy. Of Johnson's *Idler* papers, which appeared in *The Universal Chronicle* in 1759, Boswell wrote that " this paper was in such high estimation before it was collected into volumes, that it was seized on with avidity by various publishers of newspapers and magazines, to enrich their publications."[2] As a result there appeared in *The Universal Chronicle* a most high-sounding and threatening notice from Johnson's pen against this " little regard to justice or decency," and " shameless rapacity." The proprietors, it said, would in retaliation take the best works owned by the pirates, print them in small copies at an humble price, and give the profits " for the support of penitent prostitutes," who were more deserving than such men as their injurers, " prostitutes in whom there yet appears neither penitence nor shame." The piracy of *Rasselas* by Kinnersley in 1761 was sufficient to obtain an injunction, but the whole system was too profitable to die out until there was a clearer legal ruling and higher public spirit in the trade. The same tale had to be told of Goldsmith's essays when they were collected and published in 1764. The author

[1] Nichols, *Illustrations*, i. 824.   [2] *Life*, i. 345, note.

in his preface said : " Most of these essays have been regularly reprinted, twice or thrice a year, and conveyed to the public through the kennel of some engaging compilation. If there be a pride in multiplied editions, I have seen some of my labours sixteen times reprinted, and claimed by different parents as their own. I have seen them flourished at the beginning with praise, and signed at the end with the names of Philautos, Philalethes, Philalutheros, and Philanthropos."[1] Such was the form piracy tended to take, when the reprinting of single works became too dangerous. But we have seen that there was by no means an absence of pirates of the latter too. And it is not difficult to imagine the state of chaos in which authorship would have struggled without the safeguards of the Act of Queen Anne. THE gravest flaw in the Act of 1710 was that the grant of copyright was confined to Great Britain, leaving an author's works as unprotected in Ireland as they would have been in France. Where a demand for an English work was expected in France, as there was for Richardson's novels and Robertson's histories, the author's interest was confined to securing a good translator who should take the field before the others set to work, and, in the same way, an author or publisher was only concerned in respect to Ireland in securing that a Dublin bookseller who was likely to produce a good edition should have the copy before the others. It was too early to expect any international copyright, but one might have expected an extension to Ireland. The flaw was, however, due not to the English Parliament but to the nature

[1] Forster, *Life*, i. 376.

THE COPYRIGHT STRUGGLE

of the Constitution. The Irish Parliament was a separate body, and till the Revolution it had claimed that no law enacted by the English Parliament was valid in Ireland, even if especially extended to that country, unless reaffirmed by the Irish legislature. After the Revolution several important laws had been passed affecting Ireland, and these were acquiesced in without express opposition. " Molyneux, however, in his celebrated *Case of Ireland's being bound by Acts of Parliament in England stated*, published in 1697, set up the claim of his country for absolute legislative independency."[1] The claim was not allowed to go unchallenged, but no unnecessary steps were taken to force a decision, and, at the time this Act was passed, it was customary for the English Parliament not to extend ordinary laws to Ireland. The Irish, on the other hand, had little to gain and much to lose by any extension of copyright to their own country, as their booksellers relied chiefly on material stolen from English writers; piracy was the source of their income, and the Irish Parliament patriotically upheld them. One attempt was made by the English booksellers to gain the extension to Ireland, but a Bill drawn up in 1737 proposing to prohibit the reprint of English copyrights in Ireland after June 1st of that year did not pass the English Parliament, and the position remained unremedied till the Act of Union in 1801.

ONE typical and notable example of Irish piracy is shown in Swift's letter to Pope from Dublin in 1729, saying: "As for your octavo edition

[1] Hallam, *Constitutional History of England* (1854), iii. 401.

[of the *Dunciad*], we know nothing of it, for we have an octavo of our own, which has sold wonderfully, considering our poverty, and dulness the consequence of it."[1] Such was the gap between England and Ireland in the middle of the eighteenth century that there is a story of a certain Rolt having gone to Dublin in 1745, and there reprinted as his own work Akenside's *Pleasures of the Imagination* which had been recently published anonymously in London ; and though the story is probably untrue, it is not impossible. But the state of things is best described by a pamphlet issued in 1753 by Richardson in respect of his *Sir Charles Grandison*.[2] It had been his intention to publish the novel first in Dublin through Faulkner, the leading bookseller and friend of Chesterfield, before he himself issued a London edition. The arrangements, however, were upset by the dishonesty of two of Richardson's printers who conveyed the sheets to three other Irish booksellers. Faulkner said that, in order to protect his own interests, he was compelled to join them, and so three pirated editions of nearly half the work appeared in Dublin before a single volume was ready in London. Of these treacherous workmen Richardson's pamphlet stated : " He is further assured, that these worthy Men are in Treaty with Booksellers in *Scotland*, for their printing his Work, in that part of the United Kingdom, from copies that they are to furnish ; and also, that they purpose to send a Copy to *France*, to be translated there, before Publication : No doubt for pecuniary Considerations." Then the pamphlet continued : " It has

---

[1] Pope, *Works*, vii. 163.
[2] *The Case of S. Richardson, of London, printer* (1753), B.M. 816, m. 12 (53).

been customary for the *Irish* Booksellers to make a Scramble among themselves who should first intitle himself to the Reprinting of a new *English Book* : and happy was he, who could get his agents in *England* to send him a copy of a supposed saleable Piece, *as soon as it was printed*, and ready to be published. This Kind of Property was never contested with them by authors *in England* ; and it was agreed among *themselves* [i.e. among the *Irish* Booksellers and Printers] to be a *sufficient* Title : tho' now-and-then a Shark was found, who preyed on *his own Kind* : as the News-papers of *Dublin* have testified. But the *present* Case will shew to what a Height of Baseness such an undisputed Licence is arrived . . . . a Law may one Day be thought necessary." THROUGHOUT the century the position was unaltered. *The Gray's Inn Journal*, commenting on Richardson's case with a show of moral abhorrence, declared that such men " should all be expelled from the Republic of Letters," but it remained true that " at present the English writers may be said, from the attempts and practices of the Irish booksellers and printers, to live in an age of liberty but not of property." Murray, the bookseller, received in 1769, from an agent whom he had sent to Dublin, the following reply : " On receipt of thine I constantly applied to Alderman Faulkener, and showed him the first Fable of Florian, but he told me that he would not give a shilling for any original copy whatever, as there is no law or even custom to secure any property in books in this Kingdom. From him I went directly to Smith, and afterwards to Bradley, etc. They all gave me the same answer."[1]   Finally in that transaction a bookseller named Ewing was found to give twenty guineas for the right to republish in Dublin, but it is clear that the property was very insecure. In fact, Ireland as a market for literature was practically closed to English writers and booksellers. They could not enter it without the danger of incurring losses, and in later years the Irish pirates made barefaced incursions into the English and Scotch markets as well. Thus Gibbon wrote of his first volume in 1776 that " the bookseller's property was twice invaded by the pirates of Dublin " ;[2] and it is said of Elliott, one of the leading Scotch booksellers of the last twenty years of the century and one of the first to give large sums for copyright in that country, that " he like other publishers in England and Scotland was grossly plundered by the Irish pirates, who printed his works and undersold him both in London and Edinburgh." The reading public of England and Scotland was the only sure support of English writers. In the early years of the century there were signs of a growing demand for books in the colonies of the West Indies and America, but by the time it had become in any degree considerable, their needs began to be almost wholly supplied by their own presses.

ANOTHER, but much less important weakness of the 1710 Act was the explicit omission from protection against importation of pirated editions of " books in Greek, Latin, or any other foreign language printed beyond the seas." Anyone who

[1] Smiles, *A Publisher and his Friends*, i. 9.   [2] *Autobiography*.

had spent years in editing a classical text was, therefore, liable to find other copies, printed possibly in Holland, being sold openly at a lower price, without any power to stop them. The only way [1] for an editor to secure the outcome of his labours was to petition Parliament for a private Bill, giving him the exclusive right for a limited period. It was an expensive procedure, costing some £80 to £100, but the bookseller Samuel Buckley thought it worth while to do so in 1734 in order to protect his rights to a costly edition of the histories of Thuanus.[2] Indeed, the disadvantage which a bookseller or an author who dealt with an ordinary bookseller incurred, was increased by the fact that the Universities were given a rebate on the tax on imported paper used for printing ancient foreign languages, and were thus enabled to print their work more cheaply on better paper. But in the case of this omission from the Act, a remedy was obtained in 1739, though not without several rebuffs, and in the end because it was merged in a wider issue.

WE shall shortly have occasion to consider fully two Bills presented in 1735 and 1737 respectively, in which the booksellers sought to gain a longer term of copyright. At present our interest in them is limited to their attitude to imported books. Their chief aim was the grant of a longer term, but they also gave considerable prominence to the question of importation, dealing not only

[1] Protection could also be gained by royal licence, where an author could command the necessary influence. Thus Theobald in 1728 was granted the sole and exclusive right of printing and publishing for fourteen years his play *The Double Falsehood*, on the ground that it was an old play the MS. copy of which he had purchased at a considerable cost. Warburton, in 1759, when the length of copyright was uncertain, was granted a similar patent for Pope's works, by then outside the terms of statute protection.
[2] Nichols, *Literary Anecdotes*, ii. 26.

with learned works which were quite unprotected, but also with the need of stronger safeguards against the flooding of the home market by all kinds of books reprinted abroad. A sheet entitled *Farther Reasons humbly offered to the consideration of the House of Commons* [1] was very much concerned at "the Liberty taken of late Years by Foreigners to Print our best Books abroad, and import them into this Kingdom," and both this and another pamphlet demonstrated that great loss was resulting to the revenue through such a state of affairs. That line of approach, the appeal to the commercial spirit rather than to any intrinsic merits based on natural rights, seemed the safest way. Much of the better paper used in England was imported from France and Holland, and it was shown that, whereas the tax on one hundredweight of paper was a guinea, the tax on the same weight of printed books was only six shillings and eightpence; the revenue was, therefore, fourteen shillings and fourpence the poorer by books being imported from abroad, instead of the same weight of paper and the books being then printed in England. The argument thence was, not that books should be taxed as much as paper, but that it should be an offence to import books at all; at least it was already an offence under the 1710 Act to import English books, but it was suggested that fresh penalties should be granted which would prove more effectually deterrent.

BOTH Bills were, however, rejected, presumably because Parliament was not favourable to the major claim for a longer copyright. The book-

[1] B.M. 816, m. 12 (51).

sellers had to begin again, and in 1738 obtained leave to bring in to the House of Commons a Bill to prohibit the importation of books reprinted abroad, and also to limit the prices of books. It was carried to the Lords by Henry Fox, got as far as its third reading, and was then rejected and dropped. But the cause was too important for the booksellers to give up, and twelve months later they brought forward another Bill, this time with the secondary purpose of abolishing and not amending the clause of the Queen Anne Act which gave power to certain authorities to limit excessive prices of books. Thus they gained their end after a struggle of four years, which had been prolonged by the mingling of their request with more controversial matters. The new Act (12 George II, cap. XXXVI) came into force on September 29th, 1739, and the penalties consisted of the forfeiture and destruction by damasking of all illegal copies, a fixed fine of £5 and another equal to double the value of every book, half of which went to the party who instituted the action, and the other half to the Crown. It proved effective, and from that time the danger of invasion of rights by importation became negligible, although in later years the Irish booksellers proved somewhat troublesome.

But it is interesting to note in all this that the author's interest is not mentioned. The old position, stated the preamble, "was to the Diminution of his Majesty's revenue, and the Discouragement of the Trade and Manufactures of this Kingdom"; on those grounds books must no longer be imported. So far was Parliament from acknowledging the author's natural right to protection in his writings, that the Act was only to last seven years, in case, no doubt, the interests of the revenue or of commerce should require some change to be made. The law was, however, successively re-enacted for periods of seven years, as long as it continued to be necessary.

(iii)

THE general re-establishment among the trade of the idea of the sanctity of copyright which was effected by the 1710 Act seems to have been so satisfactory that the outsiders in their ranks were too imbued with the spirit to snatch the first opportunity which offered of reprinting books whose rights had lapsed under the terms given. We cannot conceive that the inner circle of booksellers did not know the adverse opinions on the Common Law right given in Committee by the House of Commons, but it is possible that they managed to keep the knowledge to themselves, and that the piratically inclined may have been led to believe that the probability lay on the side of perpetual copyright still existing. In the second half of the year 1724 copies began to fall free, if the 1710 Act was the only source of protection. Addison's *Spectator*, for example, had been published after the Act came into force, and since Addison died in 1719, his papers became common property on the expiration of fourteen years from their first appearance. The last volume of Burnet's *History of the Reformation* was issued in 1712, and as the Bishop did not survive the fourteen years, that right, too, lapsed. YET there seems, for the time, to have been no action in any direction over works such as these. Booksellers were, possibly, too interested in more recent works, for the late twenties saw many publications by Pope, Swift, Gay, Young, and others, and further, the fact that Steele did not die till 1729 may have been some protection to the popular *Spectators*. But the question assumed more serious proportion after April 1731, when the period of twenty-one years " and no longer " granted in respect of old books terminated, and the works of Shakespeare, Milton, Dryden, Congreve, with many more, must have been held free for anyone to print, if a prior Common Law right did not exist or had been abridged. Even apart from those older writers there were, as the thirties advanced, a growing number of quite modern books the property of which became doubtful, those of Prior being among the most popular. We can be sure that, whatever the real opinion of men like Tonson on the actuality of their rights at law was, they would not submit to such threatened diminution of their hoped-for gains without a sturdy resistance. Acquiescence would have reduced their property to almost trivial proportions. The battle was soon joined, and in 1734 Tonson and the other proprietors of Shakespeare were keenly contesting an invasion of their time-honoured rights by Walker, who was for some years the bookseller most prominent in attacking the established order.

IN March 1735 a petition [1] of the booksellers was presented to the House of Commons, and was favourably received and delegated to a Committee, among whose members were Lord Cornbury, the

[1] B.M. 357, c. 2. (80), 1735.

friend of Pope, Lord Tyrconnel, the patron of Savage, Mr. Wortley, and Pitt. Within a week the Committee met, started their proceedings by having the Act of Queen Anne read to them, and then went on to hear the evidence of its insufficiency. The booksellers opened their case by laying stress on the great labours of authors, and the heavy expense of booksellers, as shown by the twenty years' toil of one, Mr. Aynsworth, in compiling a Latin Dictionary, and by the sum of nearly £3,000 which the booksellers were to expend in copy money (£800) and the cost of publishing; the latter, it was said, could expect no profits at all on the first edition. From this they advanced to the question of risks; a paper was handed in containing the names of twenty-nine different authors, the prospect of whose works had been damaged by the importation and underselling of Irish and Dutch copies. To substantiate the statements of this document several authors came forward in person. One deposed to a piratical Dublin edition of sermons, sold at fourteen shillings below the authorized price; Rivington, the bookseller, to other under-cutting Irish impressions of books; others gave evidence of piratical Dutch editions; and, finally, the loss to the revenue by importation of books in place of paper was shown.

COPIES of the impressions complained of were produced before the Committee, and there is no reason to doubt that the question of importation was genuinely troublesome. From these proceedings, indeed, it would appear at first sight to be all for which the booksellers and the authors for whom they claimed to speak sought a remedy, and the evidence before the Committee seems to indicate that the imported books were chiefly sold in the provinces, and that London itself was free of them. The booksellers practically ignored the major question of perpetual copyright, although their petition followed closely on the insistence of Tonson and others that they still owned the sole property of Shakespeare's works. The only book of importance named as having been pirated, which was not well within the terms of the statute, was Shaftesbury's *Characteristics*; that had been published in 1711, and its rights had therefore lapsed in 1725; but it is alone in being thus outside the strict limits. There is no word said of any piracy of works which had been published before 1710, although it is hardly doubtful that such piracy must have occurred. The whole question, in fact, of lapsed copyright seems to have been left untouched, and a week after the petition had been presented, the Committee gave its report[1] on this evidence alone, and leave was granted to bring in a Bill.

THE text of this Bill of 1735 does not appear to have survived, for there are indications that it differed from the text of that which was put forward two years later. But some light is thrown on it by a sheet, entitled *A letter to a M.P. concerning the Bill now depending in the House of Commons*.[2] The writer of this pamphlet was no friend to the booksellers, and denounced their action for its " specious Shew of being calculated for the Furtherance of Learning, and the Securing of Property." He passed by the question of imported books, to treat fully that of a longer

[1] B.M. 357, c. 2 (73), 1735.   [2] B.M. 357, c. 2 (74).

period of protection, which seems to have been the most important part of the Bill, though it had not been mentioned in Committee. If we may believe this writer, the booksellers were trying to win support by a false representation of the facts; " many have been artfully made to believe, that the aforesaid Act passed in the 8th year of Queen *Anne* is now expired, and therefore have the more readily concurred in promoting a Bill which they look on only as the Continuance or Revival of an expiring Law." They were seeking another twenty-one years' copyright on old books, and, said the critic, if there were grounds for giving it them, there must be equal reason for granting another twenty-one when these had expired; " so that should this Bill pass, it will in Effect be establishing a perpetual Monopoly, a Thing deservedly odious in the Eye of the Law; it will be a great Cramp to Trade, a Discouragement to Learning, no Benefit to the Authors, but a general Tax on the Publick; and all this only to increase the private Gain of the Booksellers."
WHETHER all these disasters would have been the consequence of passing the Bill is more than doubtful, but there would certainly have been little benefit to the writers. The latter were made use of merely as a stalking-horse by the booksellers, who also reprinted Addison's *Tatler* paper (No. 101) against pirates to strengthen their claim. The fact was that " the Authors, for what appears, are very well satisfied with the Encouragement the Law allows them; for it is not they, but the Booksellers that make this Application." The argument that a longer copyright would be paid for more highly by a bookseller was also treated

by this critic (and with justice) contemptuously. The trade admitted by the very suggestion that it was not their custom to pay for perpetual rights, and the books would be very rare for the reversionary right to which after twenty-eight years a bookseller would be prepared to pay anything. But whatever were the exact proposals of this Bill, however much was added to the complaints preferred before the Committee, the Bill found acceptance in the House of Commons, where it was passed on May 1st, 1735, by 163 to 111. On May 6th it was carried to the Lords, whence it never returned, being shelved by the expedient of successively postponing the second reading.

MEANWHILE, what was the real opinion of the trade and the true interest of the author? It would appear that the booksellers were trying to obtain by bluff, artifice, or any other method that suggested itself, rights to which they knew they were not legally entitled, and which they openly avowed that they did not desire. Lintot's written agreement with Pope for the copyright of the *Iliad* was for fourteen years, followed by another fourteen if Pope were still alive; that is to say, Lintot was perfectly aware that all he could buy of Pope, and all Pope could sell him, was the right to publish for the term of years stated in the statute. Further, the omission of all reference to the question of perpetual copyright in their statement of their case to the Committee argues their knowledge of the futility of such action. Again, the pamphlets which they caused to be written in their support either ignore the question or explicitly disclaim any intention of seeking the perpetuity. One pamphlet[1] says clearly that "the present Application to Parliament is not proposed to establish a perpetual Right in Copies, but only to give Authors and their Assignes a longer Term." Whether this pamphlet was written while the first Bill was before Parliament in 1735 or at the second attempt in 1737 is not clear, as it is not dated, but it provides, in either case, proof of the double dealing of the trade. Such a disclaimer is convicted of insincerity when coming on behalf either of men who assert that Shakespeare is their exclusive property, or of men who are laying the foundations of what they disclaim, by seeking injunctions in Chancery.

BY June 1735 the first Bill before Parliament was dead, and in that very month an injunction was granted in Chancery by Sir. J. Jekyll to restrain Walker from selling an edition of *The Whole Duty of Man*, of which Eyre claimed the sole rights, in spite of the work having been first published as long ago as 1657. In November 1735 Motte was granted an injunction by Lord Talbot to restrain a publication of Pope's and Swift's *Miscellanies* many pieces in which had been originally published in 1701, 1702, and 1708. In January 1736 the notorious Walker was again the object of an injunction, filed this time by Walthoe, to restrain him from selling Nelson's *Festivals*, a publication of 1703. In all three cases there could be no plea of an infringement of rights secured by the 1710 Act, and the injunctions, therefore, were based on a previous right, still sound at Common Law, in the opinion of the

[1] B.M. 816, m. 12 (51).

judges. Thus the booksellers, having failed to secure an extension of their rights and apparently afraid to claim that they had perpetual rights, seemed to have found that there was prevalent a strange bias of the juridical mind in their favour, and they lost no time in setting up precedents. So strong was this legal support that in the case of Motte v. Faulkner over Swift's *Miscellanies*, we are told that Faulkner, who was a rich man, well able to support his cause, was advised not to dispute the validity of the injunction, because there could be little hope of winning the day. It must remain somewhat of a mystery why the judges in Chancery formed this view of the matter, but for the time they seem to have been quite agreed in it, and the booksellers readily adopted a view so much to their advantage, until they, too, became equally convinced of its truth.

THE interest of authors in this question of copyright does not seem to have been very great. At this time Aaron Hill was writing angry letters about the shameful neglect of talent in dramatic authorship, and advocating a private theatre which should stand in the same relation to theatrical patentees and managers as the Society for the Encouragement of Learning did to booksellers; but we do not find him complaining of the position of authors in general and suggesting that things would go better with him as a writer, if only he could have longer copyright; in that matter, neither he nor any other writer of prominence seems to have felt a grievance. Nor did writers then show the sympathy for the trade's claim which was in 1774 shown by Robertson, Hume, and Beattie; neither Pope, Thomson, nor any other gave his name in support of it, or seems to have cared much about it. In 1774 the length of copyright was still of more importance to booksellers than to authors, but in 1735 the concern of authors was far less. Unless a writer sold his copyright he had very little hope of success, and stood but small chance of combating piracy, if his book were worth pirating. The only course was to part with the copyright, and booksellers naturally paid no more for a hundred years' rights than for the statutory fourteen, since very few books live more than a few years, and many not above two or three. A longer term would only be valuable to a writer when he could appeal directly to the public and keep the copyright in his own hands. To do either was in 1735 almost impossible.

BUT in spite of the power they found they had of obtaining injunctions, the booksellers evidently continued to feel insecure and to think that fresh legislation was desirable. Of the Queen Anne Act they stated in a pamphlet [1] that " the time limited for Discovery and Prosecution being too short, and Authors being afraid of the Hazard and Expence of a tedious Law-Suit during which the whole pyrated Impression might be sold, and, which if they gained at last, they could recover only a penny a Sheet, . . . and if . . . they should be nonsuited . . . they were exposed . . . to full Costs of Suit, . . . the Remedy intended thereby proved ineffectual." Therefore in February 1737 we find that leave was again given by the House of Commons to bring in a Bill to make the 1710 Act more effectual. The members

[1] B.M. 816, m. 12 (52).

deputed to prepare and bring in the Bill included Lord Cornbury, Mr. Townshend, Mr. Pelham, and Mr. Walpole, and they were further instructed to add a clause to make it easier for the Universities to secure the repayment of the duties on such paper as they used for printing books in the Latin, Greek, Oriental, and Northern languages.

OF this Bill, which, if passed, was to come into force on June 24th, 1737, we have a copy. It began with a declaration that the Act of Queen Anne " has proved ineffectual to prevent the Publication and Sale of surreptitious Editions, and Impressions of Books ; and the mischief intended by the said Act to be prevented, hath, of late years, greatly increased, and many Works do daily continue to be printed and are openly sold to the great Detriment and oftentimes the utter Ruin " of booksellers and authors. No retrospective protection of books was proposed, but that " from and after 24th June, 1737," an author and his assigns shall have the copyright of his works " during his natural Life, and for the Term of eleven Years after his Death, in case such Author shall live Ten Years after the first Publication, . . . and, if he shall die within Ten Years after such Publication, then for the Term of 21 Years after his Death." Posthumous works were to be protected for twenty-one years. The penalties against pirates were considerably stiffened, that of forfeiture and damasking of copies remained unchanged, but the fine of one penny a sheet was raised to one of five shillings, and the whole sum was recoverable by the author, who was also to be entitled to the full costs of his suit. In addition to these penalties it was to be enacted that, as books were often printed and sold so covertly and their vending carried on and managed so craftily " that the Authors and Proprietors can seldom come to the Knowledge thereof, or be able to make due Proof," these penalties could be waived, and instead an injunction filed in Chancery for the discovery of the number and value of the piratical copies, and for an account of the profits, which were to be recovered by the owner of the copyright. There was a very detailed regulation as to registry at Stationers' Hall, and the supply of fourteen copies for the various libraries; and to distinguish a genuine book each was to have affixed to it a copy of the receipt for these fourteen copies. Security against importation was to be gained by penalties of forfeiture and fines of £5 and of double the value of every copy, half to go to whoever would sue and half to the Crown. Last among the more important clauses was the extension of the time within which an action must be brought from three months to three years.

SUCH was the Bill that was carried up to the House of Lords in April 1737, where it was read a first time and ordered to be printed. It passed a second reading, and a resolution was agreed to that it should be committed to a Committee of the whole House. It went no further; the Committee was first postponed for a week, twice postponed for a few days, and finally, on May 10th the motion to put it into Committee was objected to, and with the resolution that it should be referred to " this day month " it was indefinitely shelved, to appear no more.

IT is difficult to surmise what the nature of the

objections can have been, for although the Bill had been sought by the booksellers, its text was throughout favourable to authors to the subordination of booksellers. Possibly the extended period of copyright was held to favour the " monopoly " of the trade too much at the time, but the extension was in many cases negligible. If this Bill had become law, the rights of *The Seasons* would only have lasted two years longer, and there would have been only the same extension in the case of *Gulliver's Travels*. The only considerable extension was given to works published late in an author's life, such as *The Beggar's Opera*, where the bookseller owning the copyright would have been protected for an additional eleven years; similarly *The Castle of Indolence* would have been private property seven years longer under the proposed conditions. The prospect of this lengthened " monopoly " (for " monopoly " appears to have been a potent word, freely used by the enemies of booksellers) may have influenced the peers.

LOOKING at the matter from the standpoint of modern publishers, it may seem that these new terms were distinctly beneficial, and that it was a hardship to authors that they were rejected. Yet it is doubtful if authors would have benefited in any way. Thus Robertson, who published his *History of Scotland* in 1759, drove the best bargain he could with Millar, and was paid £600 for the copyright. It was a time when the booksellers were maintaining with considerable success the practice of perpetual copyright, so that we may assume that Millar paid in the faith that he was probably buying the right in perpetuity; and even if he had not that faith, it is reasonable to doubt if he would have paid any more if he had. Robertson, having parted with the copyright, had no further interest in its protection, even though it lapsed six years before his death. If the law had given him the copyright for a hundred years, neither he nor his descendants would have been any the richer, but only Millar, who, in twenty-eight years alone, had made a profit of £6,000. It was only towards the end of the century, when such men as Adam Smith were in a position to bargain with a bookseller for a fixed sum and a proportion of the profits, that any additional period would have been valuable.

BUT, if the peers thought that these terms were too favourable to the trade, there were other clauses distinctly aimed against the booksellers. " Forasmuch," said the Bill, " as the true Worth of Books and Writing is in many cases not found out till a considerable Time after the Publication thereof ; and Authors who are in necessity may often be tempted to sell and alienate their Right which they will hereby have to original Copies of the Books before the value thereof is known, and may thereby put it out of their Power to alter and correct their Compositions, therefore from 24th June, 1737, no Author shall have the Power to sell or alienate, except by his last Will and Testament, the Copyright for any longer than Ten Years." This clause would, if carried out, have resulted in a control of the bookseller by the author, who at the end of ten years could again make a bargain for his work, if its merits were still such as to attract the public. Certainly it was possible that authors and publishers might con-

THE COPYRIGHT STRUGGLE

nive to defeat the intentions of the clause, but it is worthy of note that a very similar scheme was suggested by Johnson as practicable in 1774.[1] Again, there was an anti-bookseller clause by which a second edition of a work sold for more than five shillings would only be protected if any additions or alterations were published separately, so that purchasers of the first edition could buy them cheaply and insert them, for at that period there seems to have been a general complaint of new editions, with considerable alterations, being made within a few months, to the great annoyance of the public. Lastly, there was some truth in the plea that the new penalties and alternative method of prosecution together with the recovery of full costs of suit would lessen the risks of an author in contesting piracy, and so would tend to make authors independent of booksellers. But, here again, the plea was more valid for futurity than the present time, and had too much of the air of being put forward as a happy afterthought of the trade, to divert the attention from the benefit to booksellers by showing the possibility of benefit to authors; it may well be that the peers considered this benefit, as far as the average writer was concerned, to be in 1737 rather theoretical than practical, since the booksellers were too completely masters of the literary market to allow any writer to approach the public successfully without their help. The unprosperous start of the Society for the Encouragement of Learning in the previous year was certainly not very promising to the idea of independence.

ON the whole, then, these anti-bookseller clauses

---

[1] *Johnsonian Miscellanies*, ed. G. B. Hill: Letter to Strahan, ii. 442.

were not likely for some years to be as efficacious as the framers of the Bill had hoped, and probably the perception of this and the disinclination to lengthen the term of copyright more to the advantage of bookseller than author were responsible for the failure of the Bill. The booksellers then ceased to petition Parliament for a Bill affecting copyright, and, as we have seen before, in 1738 asked chiefly for better security against importation of pirated works. Parliament, however, was still unfriendly, and not till 1739 was even this limited claim acceded to, four years after the evidence offered against the trouble of imported books had been heard by a Committee and its proposed remedy endorsed by the whole House of Commons.

(iv)

THE booksellers remained in uncertainty on the question of perpetual copyright despite these Parliamentary rebuffs, hoping to creep in behind the back of the legislature, fearing lest they should be too precipitate. In May 1739 another important injunction was obtained, once more against Walker, to stop the sale of *Paradise Lost*, claimed by Tonson and others. Walker presumably gave way, but Osborne, another bookseller, was in these years more audacious and would not give way. It was frequently stated in after-years, and never contradicted, that the monopolising booksellers had to buy him off with a pension " after they had threatened, prosecuted, and tried every other artifice, to intimidate him from printing Shakespear, and other works ; but all to no purpose ; he was not to be wrought upon so easily, and they were obliged to last to strike their flag."[1] Evidently they feared to lose the power of threatening by injunctions, and so always avoided pressing for a definite decision lest a full legal investigation should after all prove unfavourable to their Chancery actions. BUT the outer circle of booksellers was gradually becoming restive under the restraint of the Tonsons and Rivingtons who claimed everything for themselves, and, moreover, the booksellers of Scotland were growing in number and importance. In 1743 Millar and seventeen other London booksellers brought an action against Kincaid and twenty booksellers of Edinburgh and four of Glasgow, on the ground that they had infringed the Acts of 1710 and 1739; and so began the first case of its kind in Scotland.[2] The chief point in dispute was whether the London booksellers could claim damages in addition to the penalties under the statute and on books not registered in terms of the statute; that is, whether there did exist a Common Law right independent of that granted by Parliament. The case was long drawn out; two decisions were given in 1746, two more in 1747, and the last, in June 1748, finally defined the attitude of the Court of Session, which had at first tended to support Millar, in favour of the Scotch booksellers. It was found "that no Action lies upon the Statute, except for such Books as have been

---

[1] B.M. 518, k. 4 (13), p. 20. Cf. also B.M. 215, i. 4 (99), *Observations on the Case of the Booksellers of London and Westminster* (1774). "It is notorious, that *John Osborne*, late of *Paternoster Row*, printed an Edition of Shakespeare's Works, as a copy *that lay in common*: Upon that Occasion, the Booksellers did not venture to claim an exclusive Right by Law or Equity, but, to avoid the Question, compromised with Osborne, and bought up the Copies which he had printed, for a Pension; which, it is said, he enjoys at this Hour."

[2] Millar v. Kincaid (1743). See B.M. 816, m. 12 (54).

entered in *Stationers-Hall* in Terms of the Statute . . . and that no Action of Damages lies." The London booksellers appealed to the House of Lords, and were again non-suited in a judgment given in February 1750. Lord Chancellor Hardwicke held that the London booksellers had mixed action of an inconsistent nature and mistaken the true course of their proceeding ; and further, that the books in regard to which the action had been brought, were only owned by certain of the plaintiffs, and only pirated by certain of the defendants, so that it was inadmissible to join them all in one action. In the circumstances, he thought that "the libel being irrelevant, the best way for the plaintiffs to take was to begin again," when it would be material to consider the Common Law of Scotland, as apart from that of England. On the actual merits of the case he would offer no binding opinion. "After hearing this opinion," wrote Donaldson in a pamphlet some years later, " the London booksellers were advised, and were themselves satisfied that it was by no means to their interest to push for a decision, and accordingly for several years many editions of books to which they pretended a right, were printed without challenge in England and Scotland." As a general statement Donaldson's is accurate, but when in 1752 Walker once more took the war-path and advertised a new edition of *Paradise Lost*, with life and notes of all former editions, and Doctor Newton's notes, he was not left unprosecuted. Although nothing of this proposed edition was within the 1710 Act except Newton's notes, yet Lord Hardwicke granted Tonson an injunction against the whole; but he stipulated that the case should be brought to a trial at Common Law. Tonson, however, backed out.

DURING the thirty years following the institution of Millar *v.* Kincaid in 1743, the question of literary property, as it was called, came more and more before the public. Many pamphlets were written about it, and opinion was considerably divided. The difficulty people found in deciding the justice of the cause was well illustrated by Warburton, who in 1747 wrote *A Letter from an Author to a Member of Parliament*[1] in support of perpetual copyright, and in 1762 wrote *An Enquiry into the Nature and Origin of Literary Property*[2] in reply to his own pamphlet, demolishing his previous arguments one after another with a most un-Warburtonian mildness. Both these pamphlets (which were anonymous) are in their treatment typical of the arguments used by each side.

IN 1747 Warburton lamented that while " there was a Time, when Men in public Stations thought it the Duty of their Office to encourage Letters . . . *Letters* are now left, like *Virtue*, to be their own Reward." Authors had never been fairly used, nor dared to demand their rights, but had only ventured to supplicate a grace by means of an insinuating address, under cover of a plea for promoting the manufacture of paper at home or augmenting the revenue. It was due, he said, largely to public prejudice against enriching the booksellers, against supporting their monopoly, and against their practices in general; but, strictly speaking, they had no monopoly, for was

[1] B.M. 518, k. 4 (9).   [2] B.M. 516, c. 41.

not a monopoly the grant of a sole right of doing what all claim the right and power to do, whereas it was impossible for all to print? He next proved to his satisfaction that there was certainly a real property in books, plunging into many metaphysical subtleties concerning the nature of property, and bringing in the inevitable comparisons between the writing of books and the invention of orreries and watches, and between printing and manufacturing, by which it was demonstrated that literary property was a thing apart. Finally, he dealt with the arguments that the 1710 Act either abridged the Common Law rights or indicated that they did not exist; the limited terms, he said, were given clearly because the petitioners had desired no more, since the greatest danger of piracy is when a book is new, and afterwards the remedies at Common Law are quite sufficient; those who had concurred to represent the 1710 Act as a restrictive and not a cumulative law were led astray by "Ignorance and Knavery"; for was it not manifest that the learned judges in Chancery would not grant injunctions, if there could be any doubt?

THE more detailed enquiry of fifteen years later swept all this away. "When the Right of the Author in his Copy was first agitated, I confess that I was prejudiced in its Favour. I considered it as the noblest Inheritance which could be transmitted to Posterity." Now in 1762, however, he saw his error; and every argument took the opposite turn. How could one speak of a property dependent on the exclusive right to the perception of ideas? Even admitting the principles on which this fantastic property was founded, the consequences were inconsistent with themselves and repugnant to every other species of property. He quoted the law of Greece, the Roman Institutes, and the Common Law of Venice; he contrasted the buying of a book with the purchase of a theatre ticket; he reviewed the old argument drawn from watches and orreries, and found it wanting. If there had been a Common Law right, why was the 1710 Act sought, since a remedy at Common Law is always preferable? So did he make use of the legal studies of his early days to turn the tables on the booksellers, possibly not uninfluenced in his change of opinion by his rapid rise in the world and recent elevation to the see of Gloucester.

AT any rate, Warburton was in 1762 as decidedly opposed to booksellers as he had in 1747 been in their favour, and his later remarks anticipate those of Chatham and Lord Camden in 1774, all rather foolish in speaking of the indignity of authorship for money.[1] How sadly did Warburton, the bishop, regret the golden age of Greek authorship when " there was a mutual Exchange of Benefits between the Author and his Patron, [since] the Patron conferred Riches on the Author, which was requited with Fame and Immortality!"[2] Compared with those times the state of authorship in England was, in Warburton's estimation, inglorious. A poor author was obliged to sell his rights to the bookseller for a gross sum to relieve his present necessity, and "from that

---

[1] Letter of Lord Chatham to Lord Shelbourne, 1774: "The very thought of coining literature into ready rhino! why, it is as illiberal, as it is illegal." Lord Camden, speech in 1774: "Glory is the reward of science; and those who deserve it scorn all meaner view. I speak not of the scribblers for bread, who tease the world with their wretched productions; fourteen years is too long a period for their perishable trash."
[2] *Enquiry*, p. 18.

instant became a Slave to his Bookseller, who estimating Wit and Learning by the Bulk, imposed the severest Tasks."[1] In fact, said Warburton, from this imaginary right of literary property arose a servitude of authors to booksellers, which to a liberal mind was most intolerable, although what relation such an opinion had to the literary calling of the day, or whether it had any relation at all, Warburton probably had no clear idea, for how an author was to live in 1762 was no concern of his.

AND not only that argument but all his arguments, whether for or against, were like all the arguments brought forward in those years; the whole question of literary property was involved in a maze of abstract theories, together with a few facts of dubious interpretation, and liable to be transformed at any moment by the breath of personal prejudice. The time had come when so many suggestions had been thrown out as to what the 1710 Act might or might not mean, that no one knew where he stood, but turned from contemplation of the Act to weaving theories, was confused by problematical injunctions, and swayed by friendship or interest.

BUT Warburton's expression of a changed opinion was not allowed to pass unanswered by the booksellers, who were then involved in a lawsuit of their own making which, they hoped, would finally decide the question in their favour. An injunction had been sought in 1758 by Tonson against Collins of Salisbury in respect of an edition of *The Spectator*, reprinted in Scotland; and the right being contested, the issue was taken to

[1] *Enquiry*, p. 19.

Court for a legal decision. The defendant, however, was purely nominal, and his expenses were to be paid; it was no more than a test-case got up by the inner circle of 'the trade.' The case was heard twice in the Court of King's Bench, and it was said that the pleading on both sides was quite *bona fide*, although the probability of its being so it does not require a cynic to deny. After the decision of the House of Lords in 1750 on the Scotch appeal case, the booksellers must have been still more uncertain as to their chances in a definite trial, and it would have required more impartiality and courage voluntarily to hazard such a trial than there is any reason for supposing the members of 'the trade' to have had, especially in the light of their tactics at the time, which we shall shortly consider. Nor is the name of Collins, as defendant, the most conducive to belief in the *bona-fide* nature of this action, when we remember that in these years Collins was himself laying out considerable sums in the acquisition of shares in copyright. No decision having been reached after the second hearing, and, moreover, suspicion of collusion having arisen, the case was in 1762 adjourned to the Exchequer Chamber to be placed before all the judges.

THIS was the position when Warburton published his *Enquiry*, and it quickly drew from the booksellers *A Vindication of the Exclusive Right of Authors to their own Works*,[1] wherein the "late shrewd and ingenious writer" is told that his arguments are indefensible, and that he is simply "combatting with shadows presented by his own imagination." The reply is in substance merely

[1] B.M. 1130, d. 46, 1762.

a restatement of Warburton's earlier work, which, indeed, is often quoted as the excellent plea of a " learned author," who is not identified with the writer of the *Enquiry*. There are the same quibbles about monopoly, the same dull and useless theories on property, the same twistings of the 1710 Act. The writer asserts the great helpfulness of booksellers, that they know their business too well to be ungenerous, and that no writer need or ever can be a slave, unless he is one by nature, ruined by profligate morals and habitual indiscretion. And in that he spoke the truth, for slavery to booksellers was gone by 1762 with a writer who deserved success; but the hopeless bias is seen in the later pages. One would imagine that there was no protection at all without perpetual copyright; " if they have not an exclusive property in their works, and consequently a power of transferring such right, learning will soon be lost among us, the gloom of Gothic ignorance will darken the age, and extinguish every beam of science." To confine protection to that of the 1710 Act, it was said, would destroy literature, and the only hope of authors was that their right should " be judicially established, and preserved inviolably to the latest posterity." "May the fruits of genius never be exposed to rapine and depredation!" We may wonder how writers welcomed this tender solicitude for their welfare, and we may also wonder, in face of this hysterical outburst, how *bona fide* was the case of Tonson *v.* Collins. The Bench of Judges finally refused to give any decision, lest an undesirable precedent should be created of forcing the law by collusive actions.

WHILE this case was still before the King's Bench, the booksellers were engaged in an underhand and oppressive attempt to enforce for themselves what they considered the law ought to be. It is revealed in three letters which were published in 1764 by Donaldson,[1] of which the authenticity was never contested; and it was also stated as a fact by the Attorney-General in 1774. The first two letters were written in April 1759, by a London bookseller, Whiston, to one at Cambridge, a Mr. Merrill. The first announces that a fund is being subscribed to finance a campaign of prosecution against all booksellers who shall sell after May 1st any books which the London booksellers claim. Merrill is invited to co-operate, and to tell other booksellers who are his friends, that the proprietors will buy up any piratical copies in the possession of those who will join them. Among the books mentioned as thus sacred are the works of Shakespeare, Temple, Barrow, Milton, and Waller, and such books as *Hudibras* and *The Tatler*. A more flagrant example of illegal bullying in a trade it is difficult to imagine. The second letter confirmed the first, gave details of the Committee and of the way in which the total of £3,150 had been subscribed. Tonson, the impartial plaintiff, paying lawyers for a *bona-fide* argument, headed the list with a contribution of £500. Whiston also mentioned that anyone who refused to sign the agreement would henceforth be excluded from all trade sales. The third letter, dated November 1759, was a circular addressed to all the booksellers of England, telling them very

[1] *Some Thoughts on the State of Literary Property humbly submitted to the Consideration of the Public* (Donaldson, London, 1764). B.M. 518, k. 4 (13).

much what Whiston had told Merrill. The proceedings, it said, were based on the advice of lawyers; it was their desire to use only the most gentle methods, and if anyone were prosecuted, he must blame no one but himself. In fact, it was essentially what a pamphlet printed for Donaldson described it, " a masterpiece of low cunning, interspersed with flatteries and threats."

(v)

BUT the time for a successful and unchallenged use of such methods was gone by, and the most prominent figure in the opposition was Donaldson, an Edinburgh bookseller. It was of the year 1763 that Boswell wrote that " Mr. Alexander Donaldson had for some time opened a shop in London, and sold his cheap editions of the most popular English books in defiance of the supposed Common Law right of literary property."[1] Donaldson's efforts, moreover, were not confined to selling cheap editions; he also had recourse to propaganda altogether more forcible and to the point than the other side produced. Thus in 1764 there appeared *Some Thoughts on the State of Literary Property humbly submitted to the Consideration of the Public*, printed for Donaldson, whose address is given as near Norfolk Street, Strand.

IT is a pleasure to find something tangible after so much quibbling about the nature of property. The public wanted facts about the actual state of things, and its justice or injustice, and that is what Donaldson gave them. He protested that

[1] *Life*, i. 437.

"the booksellers of London have endeavoured of late to monopolize books of all kinds, to the hurt of all the other booksellers in England, Scotland, and Ireland in particular, and, in general, to the prejudice of all his Majesty's subjects in the three Kingdoms, as well as in the British colonies." Many of the booksellers in other parts of the United Kingdom, terrified at the thoughts of involving themselves in lawsuits with so powerful a body, had been obliged to submit to this usurped exclusive right. Progress in printing had been rapid of late outside London, particularly in Edinburgh and Glasgow, and had been a matter of umbrage and jealousy to the booksellers of London, so that they had instituted various prosecutions in Chancery and the Court of Session. Now, seeing that their threats failed, they had forced a combination and conspiracy to suppress all reprinted books no matter how long ago they had been first published. This, said Donaldson, quoting the three letters just mentioned, was sheer bluff; their circular letter was written purely *in terrorem*, with no real intention of prosecution, for "they will dread a decision as they would deadly poison." Besides, where was the grievance of an author? An inventor could get only a limited patent right for fourteen years, but authors had been singled out for Parliamentary favour by being given the possible grant of twenty-eight years. Donaldson had been assured by counsel that there was no protection outside the Act of Queen Anne, and therefore he began to sell considerably below the London booksellers, and though there had been several prosecutions against him, he was determined not to give way. In fact, after some favourable extracts from Warburton's last pamphlet, he concluded with an advertisement that his prices were from thirty to fifty per cent. below those of the rest of the trade, and that " good allowance is made to merchants who buy for exportation, and to country booksellers."

THEN in 1767 he followed it up with *Considerations on the Nature and Origin of Literary Property*,[1] which, while to some extent clogged with typical learned quotations, still had some shrewd blows and unwelcome facts. This pamphlet, indeed, has in it nearly all the truth concerning the question. The mainspring of the whole action, said the writer, was the selfishness of the London booksellers; they might say that their claim was for the good of authors, but it was noticeable that authors appeared quite indifferent, and had little or nothing to say about it; indeed, " invariably . . . the Profits of the Author are but a Mite, when compared with those of the Bookseller."[2] The Scotch booksellers maintained that limited copyright was not harmful to writers, but on the other hand very beneficial to the reading public. Moreover, were not the Scotch much more zealous for literature, since their best printing was admittedly so superior to the English? They would no longer submit to this jealous exclusion, which made them no more than retailers at a small profit. As to the honesty of the claim of perpetual copyright, it was difficult to think that the cases of Millar *v.* Kincaid and of Tonson *v.* Collins could have left the claimants honestly convinced that they were right. Several injunctions had been filed in 1763 against a

[1] Written for him by John Maclaurin, Lord Dreghorn. B.M. 518, k. 4 (16).
[2] *Considerations*, p. 2.

London bookseller, " but with no View to bring on a Decision; their sole Purpose was to incommode and distress."[1] To conclude, the result of perpetual copyright being granted would merely be to aggrandize about half a dozen London booksellers to the depression and discouragement of all others; the consciousness of security would occasion slovenliness, inelegance, and incorrectness, and enhance the price of books; whereas, if old copies became common property, there would be more printing, more employment, more trade in paper, and more revenue. Such was the very plausible case made out against perpetuity. MEANWHILE everything was tending towards a decision. The collusive action in Tonson *v.* Collins and the detailed arguments seem to have shaken the judges in Chancery out of their convictions. In 1765 injunctions in the cases of Millar *v.* Donaldson and Osborne *v.* Donaldson were dissolved by Lord Northington. Millar's action against Donaldson was in respect of Thomson's *Seasons*, Pope's *Iliad*, and Swift's *Works*, for the last of which only was the injunction continued, because with the works were incorporated a *Life and Notes* by Hawkesworth, which were within the protection of the statute. THE booksellers evidently felt that now or never the question must be put to a final test; they seemed to have lost the power of injunctions and could lose no more by an adverse legal judgment. So the decisive case of Millar *v.* Taylor over a so-called illegal and injurious reprint of Thomson's *Seasons* was instituted late in 1766. It was argued first in June 1767, for a second time in

[1] *Considerations*, p. 27.

June 1768, and the considered judgment was delivered in April 1769. Three of the judges gave their opinions in favour of perpetual copyright, while one dissented in favour of Taylor, a lack of unanimity then rare in the judgments of the Court of King's Bench.[1] It was understood that the matter would not be left there, but would be carried by Taylor to the House of Lords for a final decree; and such an expectation was expressed by the newswriters in the magazines. According to a writer in 1774, Taylor did bring a writ of error, but he " was practised upon to discontinue it." Thus were the efforts, fair and foul, of the monopolists brought to a temporary success.

BUT still Donaldson refused to give way, and went on printing and selling books which he asserted to be unprotected because they were outside the 1710 Act. Millar had died on the day following the second hearing of his case against Taylor, and in June 1769 the copyright of *The Seasons* was put up for sale by his executors and bought in various shares by Becket and fourteen others. Donaldson, who was given no opportunity of acquiring any share, being told that his presence at the sale would not be permitted, sold, according to these new owners, several thousand copies of an edition of *The Seasons* which he had printed at Edinburgh; and in 1771 Becket and his partners filed an injunction in Chancery to restrain the sale, and for an account of the profits made. Donaldson pleaded that Millar had no power to bequeath by his will any legal security in *The*

---

[1] See Sir J. Burrow, *Question of Literary Property* (1774); and *Tracts on Literary Property* (1774), B.M. 515, f. 16.

Seasons, that Becket, therefore, could not possess any rights, and that he himself was well authorized in his action by the Act of Parliament. The cause went before the Lord Chancellor in November 1772, and by Lord Apsley[1] the injunction was made perpetual (following on the precedent of Millar *v*. Taylor), with the further order that a full account of profits should be made to Becket and the others. The Scotch booksellers (for the Donaldson brothers were jointly concerned) did not follow Taylor's example, but appealed against the decree to the House of Lords.

BEFORE the decision of the House of Lords was delivered, a London bookseller named Hinton had begun an action in the Court of Session against Donaldson and Wood of Edinburgh for printing and selling Stackhouse's *History of the Bible*, a book first published in 1732.[2] The hearing took place in July 1773, and one of the counsel against perpetual copyright was Mr. James Boswell, the friend of Johnson. The London bookseller badly lost the day, and he and his fellows were made the object of many unfavourable remarks. The doctrine of the sages of St. Paul's Churchyard, said Lord Hailes, was very commodious; they enlarged or limited this Common Law right as best suited their own convenience; they abridged and abstracted right and left, and then complained that it was hard that anyone should steal from them what they had stolen from others. They even claimed anonymous works, and many pretended rights to Virgil, or Horace, or Cæsar. Even were the Court of

[1] Succeeded to the title of Lord Bathurst in 1773.
[2] See *Hinton* v. *Donaldson*, B.M. 6573, g. 11. and reports in *Scots Mag.* (1773).

Session to follow the judgment of the King's Bench, Lord Hailes said he could not grant any exclusive property in Stackhouse's *History*, a mere tedious compilation with no trace of originality. One judge doubted whether the trial in the Court of King's Bench had been so thorough as it might have been. Many were satisfied that there was no such right in the Common Law of Scotland, however much there might be in that of England, and there it appeared to be a late invention. The opinion was emphatically expressed that prices would go up and learning be oppressed if booksellers were given this unlimited power. As to the interests of authors, both Lord Kames and Lord Gardenstone were convinced that they were outside the question. The former said : "There are not many books which have so long a run as fourteen years ; and the success of books upon the first publication is so uncertain, that a bookseller will give very little more for a perpetuity than for the temporary privilege bestowed by the statute "[1]; and the latter : " It does not appear to me that this question is of such importance even to the literary trade of London booksellers as they seem to imagine ; and I am clear that authors have no concern in the question at all. The term of legal protection outlives the great bulk of books that are published. Nine hundred and ninety-nine of a thousand books have little merit but their novelty."[2] The general opinion, in fact, was that the monopoly, as most judges called the perpetuity, was " contrary to the law and ruinous to the public interest," and therefore the Court found for the defendants by

[1] B.M. 6573,g. 11, p. 20. [2] B.M. 6573, g. 11, p. 22.

twelve votes to one. The only dissentient was the eccentric Lord Monboddo, who based his opinion on the case of the few but excellent books whose merit was not known for some years, and which might result in a total loss to the bookseller, unless longer protection were given. But such cases could hardly be expected to outweigh the interests of the reading public and of the many excluded booksellers, and they were almost too rare to be taken into account. So in 1773 the London booksellers lost in Scotland what in 1769 they had won in England.

SOME six months later, in February 1774, came the complete demolition of this upstart claim which the London booksellers of 1735 had not dared to make. The judges in the House of Lords all gave their opinions *seriatim*[1] and in great detail, and when the decision was given on the seventh day, six were for Donaldson and five for Becket. Perpetual copyright, after a reign of five years, was no longer part of the Common Law of England.

AT once there was a feverish bustle on the part of the monopolists to gain some Parliamentary relief, and of the other booksellers to prevent it. On February 28th there was presented to Parliament a petition of the booksellers of London and Westminster on behalf of themselves and other holders of copyright. The petitioners, it said, " constantly apprehended that the Act [of 1710] did not interfere with any copyright that might be vested in them by Common Law." They had been confirmed in their apprehensions by the judgment in Millar *v*. Taylor in 1769, and in

---

[2] For summary see *Gentleman's Mag.* (1774), pp. 51, 99, 147.

consequence had invested many thousands of pounds in the purchase of ancient copyright not protected by statute. Theirs was a singularly hard case, and " men may be just subjects of Parliamentary tenderness, in cases where they have no legal right to redress." The House of Commons agreed, and appointed a Committee to report on the petition before which the booksellers gave evidence.

A MR. WM. JOHNSTON admitted to considering that he had rights to certain of the classics, although possibly only honorary rights ; further he had never thought the penalties of the statute worth contending for, and so did not make it a custom to enter his publications at Stationers' Hall. It was deposed that nearly £50,000 had recently been laid out in unprotected copyright bought at public auctions. On hearing this evidence the House by 51 to 25 gave permission to prepare and bring in a Bill for their relief.

BUT, in the meantime, numerous counter-petitions had been presented. We find petitions of the booksellers and printers of Edinburgh ; of sundry booksellers in London and Westminster on behalf of themselves and their brethren in the country ; of the printers and booksellers of the city and University of Glasgow ; of the Committee of the Royal Boroughs of Scotland ; of the booksellers, printers, and bookbinders of York ; and of Donaldson himself. The sundry booksellers of London and Westminster stated that only a very few of the London booksellers were affected by the decision of the House of Lords, and that many who had little or no interest in the matter had signed the petition for relief through fear, or friendship, or from other motives. The counter-petitioners also published some *Observations*,[1] which disputed that the belief in Common Law rights was ever sincere, complained of high prices and of public sales which were not public, and gave as typical examples of the class of poor ruined booksellers the late Tonson and Millar, who between then had left some £300,000.

THESE observations brought replies in the form of a *List of Books in Different Sizes and at Different Prices*,[2] to show that a good and cheap supply was always kept available for the public by the owners of copyright, and also of a *List of Payments to Authors for revising their Books or making New Editions of Old Works*,[3] to show what great expense proprietors of copy were always at to please the public, and that authors, in reality, got much more for their copyright than the first payment. Again, in a pamphlet of *Considerations*, they denied that booksellers were rich, because of the very slow return on their big investments on literary property; denied that they kept up the price of books, a course, they said, prejudicial to their own interests; and denounced the suggestion that books exclusively owned would never be improved, asserting that Donaldson's editions, at any rate, were as bad as possible, and no credit to the plea that free copy would mean better books. Further, *The Annual Register*, then James Dodsley's, spoke piteously of " near £200,000 worth of what was honestly purchased at public sale, and which was yesterday thought property, [and] is now reduced to nothing." " The booksellers of London and Westminster," it said, " many of

[1] B.M. 215, i. 4 (99).   [2] B.M. 215, i. 4 (97).   [3] B.M. 215, i, 4 (98).

whom sold estates and houses to purchase copyright, are in a manner ruined, and those who after many years' industry thought they had acquired a competency to provide for their families, now find themselves without a shilling to devise to their successors." [1]

AN extraordinary letter to *The Scots Magazine* [2] was sorry that the recent decision had " annihilated £100,000," [3] but disagreed with perpetuity. This correspondent would recommend the establishment of a board to regulate the publication of new books ! That no bookseller should be deprived of the chance of acquiring copyright, he thought that all new books, as soon as they were proposed, should be publicly announced, and any bookseller should be entitled to claim a twentieth share. Presumably no one deemed his suggestion worthy of an answer. Kenrick published a tract which claimed that, if writers were given further protection, it would be only right to extend the patents of engravers, etchers, printsellers, and inventors, for they stood in exactly the same position as writers and booksellers.

THE only author to support the booksellers (except Hurd, Beattie, Hume, and Robertson, who gave their support in letters to their personal publishers as an act of friendship) was the rabid republican and flashy historian Mrs. Macaulay, and it had been as well for her to have kept silence. Her *Modest Plea for the Property of Copyright* [4] was at once hysterical about " the eternal rule of right and the moral fitness of things," and would-be satirical. " The book-

---

[1] *Annual Register* (1774), p. 95.   [2] February 1774.
[3] The various estimates of the sum " annihilated " range from £50,000 to £600,000.
[4] B.M. T. 914 (3).

sellers," she said, " have generally smarted for what they have given for copyright, especially in their dealings with some Scotch authors, who have tasted very largely of their generosity or credulity."[1] Genius is not above the love of filthy lucre: did not Shakespeare write his " abundance of low ribaldry " for gain? Truly this legal decision " will not only be disadvantageous, but ruinous to the state of literature." Literary property is again placed " on a footing almost as bad as it stood on when this country first emerged from a state of such Gothic barbarity and ignorance, that the mighty tyrants of the land could neither spell nor scribble their names and titles." That was her strain. " Poor Mrs. Macaulay," commented Horace Walpole, " has written a very bad pamphlet. . . . It marks dejection and sickness. In truth, anybody that had principles must feel "[2]; which is a strange contrast to Horry's earlier dictum on " those most undeserving of all objects, printers and booksellers."

OF the Bill as it was presented in April 1774 we have no copy, but it seems to have proposed to give fourteen years further protection on old copyright and to make some extension of the time given in respect of new works. From the beginning the opposition was powerful. Sir John Dalrymple said that a large number of the men who had signed the petition for the Bill were proprietors of those infamous newspapers that had traduced the Sovereign and abused the members of each House of Parliament. The Attorney-

---
[1] Hamilton would have liked to have smarted many a time as he did in his dealing with the Scotsman Smollett, where he made some £10,000 profit.
[2] *Letters*, viij. 434.

General had characterized the petitioners as "a set of impudent monopolizing men who had combined to raise a fund of upwards of £3,000 in order to file Bills in Chancery against any person who should endeavour to get a livelihood as well as themselves." However, it passed the second reading and the Committee stage in the Lower House by good majorities, and went through the third reading by 40 to 22, after a sharp debate in which Charles Fox eloquently opposed it as " infamous." It was astonishing, he said, how anyone could have the assurance, supposing the Bill should pass the Commons, to carry it to the Lords. The Bill would bear no consideration, and therefore it had been hurried on through every stage in a shameful manner, its supporters never wishing to have more than forty members present, the lowest number possible for the transaction of business. His opposition,[1] however, failing, the Bill was carried to the Lords, and at its first reading on June 2nd met the reception predicted.

LORD CAMDEN said it was an affront to the House, since it insinuated in its wording that many still thought a Common Law right did exist. He had ground to say that many London booksellers were not of that opinion ; that all the country booksellers, and those of Scotland, Ireland, and America, were against it. In 1735, 1736, and 1737 there had been no plea of perpetual rights, and in all his legal experience he had found lawyers universally opposed to its existence. He held that the monopolizing booksellers were robbers who had stolen the means of livelihood

---

[1] Far from any offence being taken in literary circles at Fox's attitude, he was about this time elected a member of Sir Joshua Reynolds's Literary Club.

from others, maintaining their monopoly by iniquitous oppressions, and exercising it to the disgrace of printing. If anyone ought to be compensated, it was surely those who had been so long deprived of their rights. Lord Denbigh was equally set against it, affirming the Bill to be totally inadmissible, and that any consideration of what affronted the House was out of the question. The Lord Chancellor Bathurst " was satisfied there never did exist a Common Law right "; his judgment against Donaldson in 1772 had been no personal judgment, but a necessary consequence of the decision in Millar v. Taylor. The booksellers, too, had never, in his opinion, believed it. Therefore he held that " there were none of their allegations, nor any part of the Bill, required further enquiry." Finally, the House resolved by 21 to 11, that the second reading should be put off for two months, a course equivalent to complete rejection.

So the last hope of the booksellers died out, and, according to their gloomy prophecies, they should all have sunk quickly into bankruptcy, and vanished with literature before the onset of a new age of Gothic barbarism and darkness. The only perpetual copyright which remained was that held by the Universities and certain foundations such as Eton, whose rights were legally confirmed by Act of Parliament in 1775.

(vi)

HOW far were the interests of authors affected by all this? Were they concerned equally with the booksellers in maintaining perpetual copyright? Did they experience any loss or lowering of their status as a result of the change? To such questions we may confidently answer that neither their interests nor their position were affected in any way. It was argued that the high prices paid for Hume's and Robertson's histories were due to the confidence in perpetual copyright given by the continuance of Chancery injunctions; likewise that the £6,000 paid Hawkesworth for his *Voyages* in 1772 was a result of the King's Bench decision. But it is more reasonable to explain the two former by the growing public demand, for, if the copyright money was unprecedented, the sales had also increased to an extent before unknown; and to explain the latter by the fact that there was a very keen public interest in the recent South Sea discoveries, that Hawkesworth was a writer of considerable ability and estimation, and that to him alone had been allotted by the Admiralty the task of revising the official papers and the accompanying privilege of using the official maps, charts, and engravings. The inference drawn by counsel for the booksellers was an ingenious piece of special pleading, plausible, yet anything but convincing.

DAVIES, the bookseller (formerly an actor driven from the stage by Churchill's satire), would also have us believe that the faith in perpetual property had led to high prices. Thus in his *Life of Garrick* (1778) he discussed the posthumous publication by Mallet of Bolingbroke's works. Francklin, the printer of *The Craftsman*, hearing of this proposed edition, had in 1752 claimed as his copyright such of Bolingbroke's pieces as had been given him for publication in that journal, and two booksellers agreed to arbitrate between him and Mallet, as to the value of those pieces. They named £500, which, said Davies, "for leave to print two or three old volumes will doubtless appear exorbitant at present; but, at that time, the right of copy was esteemed a valuable perpetuity."[1] But Davies, writing more than twenty years later, was rating those papers in the light of after-events and making no allowance for that fact in his judgment on the perpetuity question. Before Bolingbroke's works were published, Millar offered £3,000 for the copyright, and Mallet, to whom the rights had been bequeathed, refused to accept it, because he felt assured, from the curiosity of the public, that he could do better. It was only when they were published that the public judgment proscribed them as worthless and declined to buy them. We cannot, therefore, agree with these verdicts, implying that the limitation of copyright led to lower prices being paid by booksellers.

THERE is more truth in the statement made in the case of Becket v. Donaldson, that "if booksellers have hitherto been dealing under the idea of a perpetual monopoly, they have not paid an adequate compensation for it, and the same phlegm will govern their future transactions." And, as has been pointed out, it is very doubtful how sincerely most booksellers believed in that claim; if they erred towards faith in filing injunctions, no doubt they erred against faith in paying authors. In addition it must be remembered that it is almost impossible to foretell of any writer that his works will be still selling after twenty-eight

[1] *Memoirs of Garrick* (1780, Dublin), ii. 37.

years; very few do sell as long as that, and booksellers, in case of doubt, would not give the benefit to the author. In fact, in the case of ninety-nine per cent. of books published, twenty-eight years are equivalent, for practical purposes, to perpetuity, for by the end of that limited period they are for ever dead. On the other hand, if the odd one per cent. were protected for ever, it would be quite impossible for any adequate remuneration to be paid. The average author was generously paid by a bookseller in the late eighteenth century, but he was only paid in proportion to the return which his publisher hoped to gather in a few years; if the book proved longer-lived, the bookseller merely rejoiced in his good fortune.

WHAT benefit, then, could perpetual copyright be to an author? It was not a business proposition for a bookseller to calculate on more than a few years' sale in buying a copyright, so that, whether perpetual copyright existed or not, payments were not likely to be affected. The grant of it would prove no benefit to an author, unless he could keep the copyright himself, and that in 1774 was not an advisable proceeding. But did authors after 1774 receive any less for their work? There is little evidence either way, but the probability decidedly is that they did not. From 1774 to 1780 there is little recorded about payment in the lives of authors, and, moreover, in these years there was a dearth of important writers, for Goldsmith, Smollett, Sterne, and Mallet were dead, Hume died in 1776, and only Johnson remained. The amount paid the latter for his *Lives of the Poets* was admittedly small (300

THE COPYRIGHT STRUGGLE

guineas), but the Doctor was a bad bargainer. We do not know how much he received for his *Tour to the Hebrides*, but it is not unreasonable to think that, if the booksellers had been insisting that they could no longer give so much for copyright, Boswell would have mentioned it.

IF the Solicitor-General's argument had been correct, that Robertson had been paid more simply because the booksellers were more sure of their perpetual monopoly, prices should certainly have fallen with the loss of the monopoly. Yet against the £500 paid by Strahan for Steuart's *Principles of Political Economy* in 1767 we can place the £500 given for the first edition of *The Wealth of Nations* in 1776; against the £150 for the copyright of *The Good-natured Man* in 1768 the £150 for Hannah More's *Percy* in 1778. Blair in 1777 received £200 for a first volume of sermons, and for the three succeeding volumes was paid £1,500. It is, therefore, safe to say that no such decline in payments took place.

IF the decision of the House of Lords had been detrimental to authors, or had seemed to authors likely to prove so, there would surely have been some stir among them; instead of which, they were mostly silent, and when they spoke, seemed chiefly concerned for the booksellers with whom they were on terms of friendship and intimacy. Thus the letters which Beattie, Hume, and others provided in their support were produced in the House of Commons at the second reading of the Relief Bill in 1774, when the main question was the grant of an extra fourteen years on old books. Even then Hume, at any rate, wrote more from friendship than conviction. " I have writ you an ostensible Letter on the Subject of literary Property," he told Strahan, " which contains my real Sentiments, as far as it goes. However, I shall tell you the truth ; I do not forsee any such bad Consequences as you mention from laying the Property open."¹ Again, writing to Strahan in April 1774 while the petition was still in progress, he recommended to the bookseller a book by Dr. Wallace, suggesting £500 as the price for copyright, which was the same as he had suggested some months earlier before the decision of the House of Lords. For, said he, " I imagine this Decision will not very much alter the Value of literary Property : for if you could, by a tacite convention among yourselves, make a Property of the Dauphin's Virgil,² without a single line in Virgil's hand, or Rusæus's or the Dauphin's, I see not why you may not keep Possession of all your Books as before."³

AUTHORS, indeed, show a conspicuous lack of interest in the matter. Walpole's voluminous correspondence dismisses it in a line or so. He tells Mason in March 1774, " I know not a word more than I told you, or you have heard, of the affair of literary property "⁴ ; and all he had told him was the bare decision and that there was a petition for relief. Johnson casually mentioned in a letter of January 1774 : " The question of Literary Property is this day before the Lords. Murphy drew up the Appellants' case, that is, the plea against the perpetual right. I have not seen it, nor heard the decision. I would not have the

---

[1] *Letters of Hume*, ed. G. B. Hill, p. 274.
[2] The Dauphine Virgil was an annotated edition, made by Rusæus for the Dauphin, the first English translation of which was published in 1686. It was thenceforth considered booksellers' property, and monopolized.
[3] *Letters*, p. 280.   [4] *Letters*, vii. 433.

right perpetual."[1] Murphy, the dramatist, was quite happy in his capacity of barrister to act as counsel against perpetual copyright, and so had Boswell been in 1773 in the case of Hinton v. Donaldson. Mrs. Macaulay said she was urged to take up her pen because she perceived " no abler advocate enter the lists " ; writers, indeed, had nothing to say, and she herself was reduced to much foolish rhetoric over " this mortal stab." In fact the silence of writers is very marked in contrast with the vigorous pamphleteering of the booksellers.

(vii)

BUT if authors did not support the plea for perpetual right, and did not feel urged to complain against their present condition, they were, nevertheless, sensible that there could be a better state of things. Their sanest aspirations are probably best expressed by a letter written by Johnson to Strahan,[2] at the time when the latter was seeking the opinions of authors in his support. There could be no doubt, said Johnson, that authors had a right to their compositions, but they also owed something to society, and must adjust their claims in accordance with the public welfare. He considered that copyright for life and thirty years after death would be a sufficient reward to the author without any loss to the public. But in order that an author should be given every encouragement to improve what he had published, he should not be allowed to alienate his rights for more than fourteen years

[2] *Life*, ii. 272.   [2] *Johnsonian Miscellanies*, ii. 442.

at first and afterwards for seven years at a time. The term of fourteen years would give ample bargaining power, and after that period, its worth being known, seven years of possession would have an assignable price. Finally, after some fifty years, the greater number of books being then forgotten and annihilated, those which had survived should become *bona communia*, " to be used by every scholar as he shall think best."

SUCH was Johnson's ideal in 1774; but he did not complain of the actual position. It was only on the first shock of Donaldson's opening a shop in the Strand in 1763 that Johnson expressed himself in favour of perpetual copyright. Even then he merely dismissed the plea of the invaders that their action was in the public interest, as a variation of Robin Hood's justification of robbing the rich to give to the poor.[1] Neither he nor Boswell spoke of their own interests being affected, and Johnson shortly came round to the opinion that the limitation of right was for the good of the public. In 1781 we hear him assuring Boswell, " Sir, I always said the booksellers were a generous set of men." There was little dissatisfaction in him, or worry about the loss of perpetual protection.

THE only people who suffered any loss were those booksellers who had recently bought lapsed copyright, and it may be doubted if they really lost much. The public was growing so rapidly that as many editions as would be published of such popular works as Thomson's *Seasons* would find a ready sale. Tonson and the others who had owned Shakespeare were still sure to find his

[1] *Life*, i. 438.

works as profitable as ever, if indeed not more so. Furthermore, the various proprietors of old copy banded together to maintain " the equitable title by usage," and for some years, when reprinting such books, the risk of the enterprise, as well as the chance of competition, was reduced by the property being placed in the hands of an apparently unlimited number of shareholders. The edition of the *English Poets* issued by the London booksellers in 1779 as a counter to the Apollo edition in a cheap, pocket form, brought out by Bell and Martin of Edinburgh, was managed on this principle. Forty booksellers were concerned in it, and Boswell says that " the Poets were selected by the several booksellers who had the honorary copyright, which is still [i.e. in 1791] preserved among them by mutual compact, notwithstanding the decision of the House of Lords."[1] But, in this question of their losing or not losing on lapsed copyright, it is difficult to have much sympathy with ' the trade '; the booksellers had too keen an eye on their profits. One feels tempted to say that men who would give Miss Burney £30 for the copyright of *Evelina* in 1778 and quickly make thousands, deserved losses.

[1] *Life*, iii, 370.

CHAPTER III

AUTHOR AND PATRON

(i) Patronage in the days of Charles II and Queen Anne. Its highest point. (ii) Decline under Walpole and George I. (iii) Pope—his rise to independence. He rejects pensions and has no use for patrons. (iv) Young, Savage, Gay, Swift, and Thomson. Their lives and the light they throw on patronage. (v) Political patronage under Walpole. (vi) Social patronage. Queen Caroline. Peterborough, Oxford, Chandos, and others. (vii) Writers themselves patrons—Pope, Warburton, Johnson. (viii) Dedications. They become scandalous. (ix) Value of the last years of patronage. Its help to Thomson, Fielding, and others. (x) Decay of patronage. Writers self-supporting. Literature passes to middle classes. (xi) Vulgar patrons: attacks by Johnson, Foote, Churchill, and Goldsmith. (xii) Revival of patronage by George III and Lord Bute. (xiii) Patronage after 1760. Sterne. Comparison of 1730 and 1770. Chatterton and Crabbe. (xiv) Conclusion: Conditions in 1780.

(i)

THE tradition of patronage in the later days of Dryden and the early days of Pope centres round Somers and Montagu, Harley and St. John. They continued that appreciation of literature which had since the Restoration been fashionable, and, what was more important, they enhanced the value of their appreciation by rendering substantial assistance to writers. The Merry Monarch and his courtiers had loved letters, but their love of wine and women had the first place. The gay luxury of Whitehall left little money for the reward of writers, however entertaining and deserving, and what money there was fell naturally to those alone who would pander to the passions and follies of the times. Good-natured Charles, fond of laughter and wit, praised Butler for his *Hudibras* and paid him with promises. A king content to reward with a kindly word loyal country squires who had lost their sons or their property in his service, could hardly be expected to trouble himself over the mere diverters of a casual hour. If the royal treasury had been overflowing, his careless bounty would gladly have made them happy; but instead it dried up, and so he took his pleasure, and gave his pleasers thanks. But still, if literature did not flourish materially, it was respected and admired; so much so in fact that the Court had its " mob of gentlemen that wrote at ease," poaching on the poor-enough preserves of the writer struggling for a living. The ability to turn out a good copy of verses was the requisite of a man of fashion. So it was only natural that, among these dilettante authors entangled for the most part too deep in the toils of beauty and debt, there should be at least one who was led by his love of letters to a practical love of men of letters. That one was the Earl of Dorset, no unworthy forerunner of Somers and Montagu. It was he who sent the boy Prior back to Westminster School from his accounting seat in the vintner's bar, and afterwards helped him in many ways.

BUT Dorset, with all the weight of Prior's eulogy, has not the reputation for patronage enjoyed by his successors. Somers, the brilliant lawyer and politician, who sprang into fame in 1688 by his defence of the seven bishops on trial for libel, was famous for his good taste and liberality. " He was at once," says Macaulay, " a munificent and a severely judicious patron of genius and learning. Locke owed opulence to Somers. By Somers Addison was drawn forth from a cell in a college. In distant countries the name of Somers was mentioned with respect and gratitude by great scholars and poets who had never seen his face."[1] Men of all shades of opinion in religion and politics were indebted to his generosity. He gave the fierce non-juror Hickes the means of pursuing his Teutonic studies. He helped Matthew Tindal, the deist; and he set on the ladder of success George Vertue, the Roman Catholic engraver.

EVEN higher than that of Somers stands out the name of Charles Montagu, Prior's collaborator in *The Town and Country Mouse*. A brilliant young man, intended for the Church until the Revolution opened prospects of greater things, he was helped at the start by Dorset, who used his influence to obtain for him a seat in Parliament. From that time his rise to the highest offices, to honours and wealth, was extraordinary, and both at the time of his political eminence and after his fall he played the part of a veritable Mæcenas of literature. In addition to his share in the parody of Dryden's *Hind and Panther* he had written a good deal of verse in a small way, and when he abandoned writing in the urgencies of office, he gave vent to his love of literature by patronage of its professors. Swift's accusation that his encouragement of men of letters was confined to "good words and good dinners" is not worthy of credence, and Pope's satiric portrait of "full-blown Bufo, puffed by every quill" in his *Epistle to Arbuthnot* is grossly unfair to his memory as a patron. The whirlwind of contemporary libels in which he lived is explained by Macaulay as being due to "the miseries of disappointed hope, of affronted pride, of jealousy cruel as the grave,"

[1] *History of England* (1858), iv. 451.

of those who were left in the cold, because even his wealth was not sufficiently inexhaustible to benefit all.

BUT, whatever the cause of the attacks upon him, his deeds of patronage make a most honourable show. He diverted Addison from the Church and a dependence on booksellers,[1] gained for him through Somers a pension of £300, and later introduced him into political life. He appointed Congreve in 1693, then only twenty-two years old, a Commissioner for licensing coaches as a reward for his first play *The Old Bachelor*, and " soon after gave him a place in the Pipe Office and another in the Customs of £600 a year."[2] For Newton he obtained in 1695 the Wardenship and four years later the Mastership of the Mint. Such acts alone would entitle him to high honour and make him undeserving of the " acrimonious contempt " bestowed on him by Pope ; but his patronage seems to have extended far and wide among the mere empty flatterers in verse as well as on the greatly gifted. Pope may indeed gibe at him as " fed with soft dedication all day long," but Tickell's statement that no dedicator went unrewarded was more than could be said of many later patrons, and contradicts the sneer of Swift that " he for poets open table kept, But ne'er considered where they slept."

HIS patronage of Addison and Newton was intimately connected with his political life, being inspired largely by the needs of his party. For that was the line patronage was to follow for the next few years, the maintenance of brilliant young

---

[1] Addison had, before gaining the notice of Montagu, been engaged by Tonson to make a translation of *Herodotus*. [2] *Lives of the Poets* (Congreve).

men for political ends. At least that motive was the dominant one, for it must be admitted that in the times of Harley and St. John appreciation and patronage of letters still overflowed the narrow bounds of party interest. In the words of Lecky, " it was the received opinion of the time that it was part of the duty of an English minister to encourage promising merit." On the one side there were still Somers and Halifax (Montagu had been created Earl of Halifax in 1700), the leaders of the Whigs; on the other Harley and St. John of the Tories, gradually becoming more and more powerful as the reign of Anne advanced. Between them their record of patronage is a credit to the early eighteenth century; in addition to Locke, Congreve, Addison, and Newton we find such men patronized as Steele, Swift, Prior, Rowe, Tickell, and Parnell. "There were great prizes," said Thackeray, " in a profession which had made Addison a minister, and Prior an ambassador, and Steele a commissioner, and Swift all but a bishop."

(ii)

THERE was, then, in the first decade of the eighteenth century a well-established custom of the patronage of authors, and it partook of a dual nature—of the patronage of literature as literature, and of literature as a political weapon. That is to say, not only political leaders were patrons, but men of wealth and rank felt it incumbent upon them, as a duty inherent in their social position, to come forward as patrons of the arts and of literature, if they wished to be considered men of taste. This, as well as the pseudo-classical style which prevailed in literature, contributed to give the Queen Anne period a reasonable claim to the distinction of being called the Augustan age of England.

THIS happy state of authorship may be said to have been at its height in the last years of the Queen. From the accession of the commonplace, sensual Hanoverian, George I, it began to decline, first on its political side, then in the sphere of social patronage. In the first place, the whole aspect of political life had changed. Queen Anne, though not a woman of any outstanding ability and without any strong political tendencies, had nevertheless not been without some considerable influence over the councils of her ministers, and in smaller matters, such as Church patronage, had been inclined to insist on her own will. That influence of the Crown died with her in 1714, and for over forty years the Government was almost free from the personal interference of the sovereign; the Court and the Ministry became henceforth separate bodies. But freedom from the influence of the Crown threatened to subject the government to control by Parliament, unless steps were taken. Those steps were the buying and cornering of pocket boroughs, and the bribery of members by lucrative offices and pensions, and those steps were quickly taken; the system of comprehensive corruption shot up in a fertile soil, and grew stronger and more deeply rooted through the following half-century. That being so, where should the successors of Harley and St. John find means to carry on the worthy tradition of supporting young writers of promise from the public funds? The means were clearly gone, and the tradition, of necessity, withered away. It was more important for a ministry to buy up the votes of recalcitrant or unprincipled members of the House of Commons than to pension another Addison, to sustain a genius that delighted the mind in the study, or boudoir, or coffee-house, or theatre, but which stumbled hopelessly in a debate, and displayed a mere competent mediocrity in the strife of party or the details of office. Several lost votes meant a ruined ministry, whereas the loss of a writer might not be felt.

POLITICAL circumstances, then, were of themselves unfavourable to the continuance of the old patronage of authors, and the new personalities in the political world were equally inimical. The Tory leaders, wavering between the Pretender and the Elector until it was too late, had fatally compromised their party; the unsuccessful rebellion of 1715 proved a death-blow; for more than a generation the Tories were politically impotent, because Toryism was identified with Jacobitism and the Whigs took care that the identification remained clear and obvious, even more obvious than was actually true. Harley was impeached, St. John banished, Prior spent some time a prisoner in the Tower, and Swift was already virtually exiled in his deanery of St. Patrick's. There was, therefore, no opposition for protection against whose efforts ministers need seriously concern themselves; bribery of the Commons was the only essential.

MEANWHILE, the rising power in the world of politics was Walpole, who in 1715 was Chancellor of the Exchequer and in 1721 the head of the ministry. From him it was useless to expect any more patronage of authors; he was above all practical, and authors were no longer of any practical use to a politician. Moreover, he had no money to spare out of the public funds. And for himself, he never read and was indifferent to literature. His attitude to men of letters was simply that of a prominent member of society, willing to add his few guineas to the subscription list of a fashionable work; he subscribed to Pope's *Iliad*, to Thomson's *Seasons*, to Dodsley's *Muse in Livery*, and so on. Otherwise his patronage was negligible, although we shall see later that he did display some. On the whole, the outstanding effect of the Hanoverian succession on authors was the disappearance of political patronage of them.

It was only natural that the same change should take place in the purely social sphere. The patronage of Somers and Montagu had been as much disinterested as political in motive, but it was from political sources that their greatest rewards came, and as politicians that the patrons were most eminent. The tradition of patronage among individual members of the aristocracy in their private lives could never be so firm and widespread. Literary patronage had been a fashion of the times, set by ministers who were intimately connected with the Court. When ministers no longer set the fashion, when the Court revolved round a German-speaking king encircled by German favourites and mistresses, when the great Tory peers were for a while in disgrace, there was no one to continue a leader of this honourable fashion. But still it did not die out so quickly as did the former class; there were many who found pleasure in the company of men of letters and delight in helping them. For years we may find many isolated examples of men who gladly set themselves up as patrons, making gifts of money or livings, helping by recommendations, and honouring as friends a worthy band of authors who would otherwise have been subjected to the drudgery of dependence on booksellers. Very often this tradition was handed on from father to son, from the first Lord Oxford to the second, from Lord Orrery to his son, from the Duke of Richmond to his son; and in addition there were such wealthy benefactors as Lords Burlington and Bathurst, the Duke of Chandos, and Bubb Dodington.

It was once said of patronage by Johnson that " in the infancy of learning, we find some great man praised for it. This diffused it among others. When it becomes general; an author leaves the great, and applies to the multitude." [1] In 1720 learning was becoming general, so that it was difficult to detect the truly learned and deserving of patronage, and, if that had been possible, it was beyond the means of wealthy individuals to diffuse their patronage among them all. There were bound to be more unpatronized than there were patronized, and, as the number of aspiring authors grew, they besieged the doors of the rich with epistles and dedications, until patronage became a scandal. The worthless scribblers loitered in the great man's hall and grumbled, or were thrust out by his servants and reviled him. Then, too, there grew up " the

[1] *Life.*

fop, whose pride affects a patron's name," who adorned his table with wits, and repaid them with his own verses. To that stage had patronage descended by 1750, but the intervening period was not without honour, and will have our attention shortly. Let us first see how those writers fared who were beginning to make their mark about the year 1726.

(iii)

THE literary world had in 1726 what is essential if the profession of letters is to enjoy the highest public esteem, a great writer, clearly recognized as the unrivalled genius of his age, prominent in society, and safely placed above the reach of that blight of reputation, poverty. It was some years since Swift had canvassed among his friends, saying that he had found the first poet of the day for whom he must have their subscriptions. In that time Pope[1] had risen triumphant over the obstacles of his religion which debarred him from holding any public office, and of his ill-health which made his life one long disease, and he was in 1726 as near the summit of his ambition as his irritable genius would ever take him. By his handsomely subscribed translation of *Homer* finished in the preceding year he had made some £5,000, and in 1725, too, he had been paid £217 by Tonson for his not oversuccessful edition of Shakespeare. Thus we see him, after a struggling public career of about fifteen years, at length securely independent, the pioneer of literature as an honourable and remunerative profession unsupported by any forced dabbling in politics.

[1] See *Works*, ed. Elwin and Courthope: *Life*, vol. v.

SETTLED in his pleasant villa at Twickenham with a modest annuity, and enjoying the friendship of the highest in society, he had reason to rejoice in his success. He stood for a new order of things, which had been impossible to Dryden and to Addison, who could have gained independence only at the cost of all their prospects. Pope, on the other hand, following literature for its own sake, preserving a strict neutrality between Whig and Tory and refusing to tune his verse to the call of any man, won his way to fame and prosperity; and once there he steadily proclaimed his freedom, his determination to " maintain a poet's dignity and ease." In the *Epistle to Arbuthnot* in 1735 he speaks of himself as—

" above a patron, though I condescend
Sometimes to call a minister my friend,"

a statement out of place as spoken of 1735, but perfectly true of his early days when he wrote the *Essay on Criticism* and *The Rape of the Lock*. He had begun as a youth with the friendship of old Wycherley, the dramatist, and of Lord Lansdowne, the politician, and they had introduced him to the circle of Swift, Harley, and Atterbury, where he gained an instantaneous and disinterested appreciation and patronage most pleasing to observe.

HALIFAX, the " Mæcenas of the nation," suggested that a pension might be secured for him in spite of his Roman Catholicism, but the project was dropped since Pope was averse to any kind of patronage. Thus we find him later reject a similar suggestion of a pension of £300 a year, made him by his friend Craggs when he was Secretary of State. Pope would not abjure his religion for any reason, and he would not condescend to the acceptance of a pension which had to be smuggled through from the secret service money of the government. Besides which, he had sufficient money to live comfortably in his careful way, and in fact took pleasure in the money he had gained by his pen, even to the talking of it. " It would be hard to find a man," said Johnson, " so well entitled to notice by his wit, that ever delighted so much in talking of his money."[1] But the sum of £5,000 for a translation, where Dryden had only got £1,200, was so bright a new star in the literary firmament as might justify its creator in some self-congratulation. He was eloquent over his independence, and we find him writing to Lord Cartaret in 1723, " I take myself to be the only Scribbler of my Time, of any degree of distinction, who never receiv'd any Places from the Establishment, any Pension from a Court, or any Presents from a Ministry. I desire to preserve this Honour untainted to my Grave."[2] So, although his political sympathies, such as they were, leaned to the Tories, he did not take advantage of his independence to abandon that neutrality which had won to his subscription list the names of Whig and Tory in the worthy rivalry of patronage. " They have scoundrels enough to write for their passions and their designs ; let us write for truth, for honour, and for posterity."[3] With such words he dissuaded Swift in 1726 from falling in with Pulteney's project of gaining the Dean for his war on Walpole.

But the unparalleled success of his *Homer*

[1] *Lives of the Poets,* iii. 204.   [2] *Works,* x. 140.   [3] *Ibid.,* vii. 87.

naturally, and perhaps justly, gave rise to some outcry against the details of its attainment. A writer in *The London Journal* of July 1726 felt called upon to say: " I have a great veneration for this admired poet; and also for his ingenious bookseller, but I hope they will not always expect to impose extravagant prices upon us for bad paper, old types and journey-work poetry." Confirmation of these charges, possibly to be taken with a grain of salt, comes in a letter of May 1726 from Fenton to Broome, both of whom were collaborators with Pope in his version of the *Odyssey*. " I find," wrote Fenton from Cambridge, " the clamour here is as great both against him and the work as it was last winter in London." [1] That is, Pope was asserting himself not only against patrons, but boldly against the public too. It was a healthy change, and a much-needed lesson for an author-grinding public to be author-ground by the only man who had the power and will to maintain the dignity of the author. They had never fairly requited authors, but now Pope was determined that they should pay for his genius at as high a price as he could wring from them. Perhaps we should condemn the attitude, but at least it was an error on the right side. It was in keeping with the stress which he laid on the honour due to literature and its professors. Authors should assert their independence, and the public must help them to do so. THE pity was, that his example of independence had no followers, but for some time stood alone as a demonstration of what lay within the power of an author to achieve. It was in vain that he

[1] Pope, *Works*, viii. 117.

himself upheld the dignity of his calling, telling his friends, when he declined a pension, that he preferred " liberty without a coach," and with the cry " O let me live my own and die so too ! "[1] shuddering at the thought of having to rely on the bounty and defer to the wishes of others. He alone could do what he had done ; the times were not ripe for lesser writers to stand on their own merits, and neither was there the spirit to make the attempt until sturdy Samuel Johnson came to complete what Pope had begun. Too many had been born into the atmosphere of patronage, too many loved ease, too many preferred pensions to freedom. Young, Gay, and Thomson were all three eager dependents on wealthy patrons, galled at times by their chains, but none the less glad of them. And, further, there was an evil spirit still unexorcised, which was the very opposite of all for which Pope stood. It was that snobbery and affectation which looked down upon authors as an inferior class, if they were authors who soiled themselves by earning a living at their calling. While Pope was proclaiming that literature was a profession worthy of any man, and that it deserved to be well paid and should be subservient to nothing, there was old Congreve, grown snobbish in his prosperous retirement, acting the elegant, idle gentleman, and affecting before his visitor Voltaire to despise his literary reputation. He wished, he said, to be visited not as an author, but as an English gentleman. THEN, again, there was Swift. The Dean had no such affectation as Congreve's, but he did not treat the literary calling as seriously as his friend

[1] *Epistle to Arbuthnot*, line 261.

Pope held that it should be treated. Pope was an apostle of the new order which was inevitably dawning, the day of that alliance between author and bookseller, which would do away with those irksome intermediaries, the patrons. To establish that alliance by making profitable bargains for copyright was an aim he had evidently close at heart. But Swift, unlike Pope, gave his copyright carelessly away and brought down upon himself his friend's reproof. It was most regrettable, Pope thought, that the rights of even fugitive essays should be given to such " mercenaries " as that Rev. Mr. Pilkington, who was always at Swift's side to snap them up ; and so he told Swift ; and later we note that he involved himself in a quarrel with Bowyer the printer, when the latter was bringing out an edition of his and Swift's *Miscellanies*, where these rights of Pilkington's came in question.

Nor was it any better, in Pope's opinion, that the equally " mercenary " booksellers should get the copyright for nothing, and his dislike of this led him to negotiate with Motte, the bookseller, for the purchase of *Gulliver's Travels* in 1726. It was the only book, with the exception of Temple's *Works*, for which Swift got a farthing. Motte agreed to give £200, " if the success would allow it," and Swift acknowledged in a letter to Chetwode that it was solely due to Pope's prudent management. Pope, in fact, was the protagonist of the literary calling, and, when we consider him thus sinking himself in a cause common to all his fellow-writers, we find a pleasing contrast and compensation to the petty spite and malice born of the selfishness of his exaggerated sensibility. In his view the literary labourer was worthy of his hire, and the public and the booksellers must all be made to recognize it. Meanwhile he held, and rightly, that every grain of mortar was needed to cement and consolidate the alliance of bookseller and author. That way only would the prospects of authorship be improved, and patrons dispensed with.

BUT Pope the satirist could not always do without the help and protection of those more powerful than he, as Pope the poet pure and simple had been able to do. The author of the *Dunciad* might well stand in need of some substantial shelter against the crowds of miserable wretches to whom his attack was almost a decree of unemployment, ignominy, and starvation, since booksellers hesitated further to employ one whose name had been thus publicly proscribed. There was likely to be great danger of prosecutions for libel, and Pope felt the wisdom of diminishing his risks. He, therefore, prevailed upon his friends Lords Bathurst, Burlington, and Oxford to undertake the distribution of the second edition of 1729, which contained the key to the allusions, stripping aside the tolerable disguise so far allowed to the poor victims. The peers were to act as his nominal publishers, as though possessed of the copyright, and it was hoped that by this means even the most daring adversaries would be overawed. The plan presumably succeeded, and the danger being considered past, the rest of the impression was made over to the booksellers to be dispersed in the usual way. What had doubtlessly increased the security was that higher patronage still had been gained, or at least implied, for the King and Queen had openly received a copy at the hands of Sir Robert Walpole. It says much for the position Pope had won, that such support was his.

IT was in connexion with the *Dunciad* that Thackeray gave expression to an opinion upon Pope's relation to the profession of authorship, amazing in its onesidedness and exaggeration. Far from allowing Pope to have contributed even in the smallest degree to the bettering of his calling, he accuses him of fouling it in mire, and lays upon him the burden of being responsible for much of the unavoidable stress and uncertainty through which men of letters were compelled to struggle while the old system of patronage was dying, and the new system of mutual alliance between author and bookseller was still subject to the fits and starts of its childhood. " It was Pope," he fears, "who contributed more than any man who ever lived to depreciate the literary calling. It was not an unprosperous one before that time. . . . The condition of authorship began to fall from the days of the *Dunciad* : and I believe in my heart that much of the obloquy which has since pursued our calling was occasioned by Pope's libels and wicked wit."[1] Such a judgment could only come of brooding too deeply and too exclusively on Pope's repulsive and sombre landscape and on the distressing story of spendthrift Goldsmith. Thackeray, too shocked in his somewhat sentimental heart to make use of the customary protective blinkers of his affected cynicism, had not only fallen a victim like Macaulay to that Grub Street myth which

[1] *English Humorists* (1853), pp. 215–16.

grossly magnified conditions admittedly wretched, but he would have us believe that Pope was the cause of those conditions and of their continuance. AGAINST this we may place what has already been considered, the complete change in politics consequent on the change of the reigning dynasty, the gradual decay of extensive personal patronage on the part of the wealthy, and the rapid growth of an army of scribblers out of all proportion to the growth in size of the reading public. The earlier " not unprosperous " state of things was gone before the *Dunciad* appeared, and its continuance was in no way due to Pope. It would be as reasonable to argue that an attack on quack doctors would sink in " obloquy " the whole medical profession.

As for this " obloquy " that was said henceforth to attach to the literary calling, it is worthy of note that his elevation to the throne of Dullness did not overwhelm in distress and contempt Theobald, the Shakespearean critic. The latter had in 1726 ventured to point out with all respect the failings of Pope's *Shakespeare*, and met in return the outraged spleen of the poet who was, at the best, no appreciator of critical scholarship, even in a Bentley. But " piddling Tibbald " survived the ordeal with almost undamaged prospects. Pope's *Shakespeare* was only once reprinted; of Theobald's there were many editions, some 12,680 copies in all being sold, and Theobald's profits were £652 10s. against Pope's £217 10s. Literature continued so respected that the Prince of Wales in 1737 sought to attain popularity by taking authors into his patronage; Thomson was associated with eminent peers on the committee of the Society for the Encouragement of Learning; Chesterfield recognized the honour he might derive from patronizing the *Dictionary*. Obloquy did not pursue the literary calling as a result of the *Dunciad*; indeed, it would have been interesting to know Johnson's opinion on the " obloquy " overshadowing his profession.

THE affair of the *Dunciad* was the only cause of Pope's having to depend on the assistance of others, and we cannot call the action of the peers patronage, for it was hardly more than an act of friendship. The rest of his life was a continuous manifestation of his independence and power. Bolingbroke's exile had been allowed to terminate in 1723, and in the following years the slight acquaintance between him and Pope which had existed in the days of Queen Anne ripened into an intimate friendship. By this the poet's envenomed warfare against the Dunces was thankfully diverted, and his energies turned towards poetry of more honour to his character. The brilliant statesman, of whom Beaconsfield said that he was " the only peer of his period who was educated," had relieved his years of enforced residence abroad by philosophical studies, which were destined to determine much of Pope's later work, and indirectly to provide the means by which Warburton was set upon the road to success. He expounded his ideas to Pope, and suggested that the latter should undertake a philosophical poem setting forth some such system. The poet, who was for the time quite under the spell of his friend's powerful personality, welcomed the proposal and left the garreteers once more untroubled, except for much duller if not less spiteful attacks by himself and others in *The Grub Street Journal*, conducted under his guidance from 1731 to 1737. The result was the *Essay on Man*, which came out anonymously in four parts between February 1733 and January 1734, from the press of Gilliver, who had bought the right to print for one year at £50 a part.

POPE was extremely fond of his ethical system, and was at the same time, also at Bolingbroke's suggestion, supplementing it with moral epistles on the duties of life, and satirical chastenings of those of whom he disapproved. Such poems as the *Epistle to Bathurst on the Use of Riches*, and the companion *Characters of Men* and *Characters of Women* were conceived as illustrative counterparts to the general principles of the *Essay*. His satire marked down its victims right and left with a fearlessness which had no respect of persons, and is thereby another token of the strength and security of his social position. Standing where he did, there was scarcely any " vice too high " for him to know, and what he knew, he seemed to have little fear of publishing ; he avowed the intention of making " men not afraid of God, afraid of me," and there can be little doubt that he succeeded. It was probably more the influence of his friends Lords Bolingbroke and Marchmont that induced him to suppress the character of the Duchess of Marlborough as Atossa than consideration for the gift of £1,000 which the Duchess is said to have made him some time previously. Lord Hervey, a steady supporter of the ministry, prominent at Court and on good terms with George II, was pilloried as Sporus—

> " that thing of silk,
> Sporus, that mere white curd of Ass's milk,"

and could only reply with similar poetic invective. Perhaps he would have liked to have taken the same revenge as Rochester, the Duchess of Portsmouth, and others took on Dryden for a piece of satire which he never wrote, and have had him waylaid and beaten, but times were changed, and Pope could speak out freely without having to trim his sail to the winds of favour, or give way before the blasts of opposition.

BUT even with Pope there were, of course, limits, and he experienced a check when, after 1735, he began to show his real political bias by mingling with the supporters of the Prince of Wales, and entertaining that royal outcast and mischief-maker at his table. His partisanship went as far as the composition of two satirical dialogues entitled, from the year of their appearance, *One Thousand Seven Hundred and Thirty-eight*, full of denunciations of venality and bribery, of personal attacks on Hervey and Walpole, of sneers at the Court and reflections on the King. It went as far as even Pope could go. A much less obnoxious satire, *Manners*, a poem by Paul Whitehead, was prosecuted, and Dodsley, the printer, summoned to the bar of the House of Lords and imprisoned, chiefly with a view to intimidate Pope. It is even said that Pope was himself threatened with a prosecution, and was so incensed that he thereupon began a third dialogue, which was however suppressed as the result of a compromise.

AUTHOR AND PATRON

THE poet had evidently come to the opinion that discretion was the better part of valour; he disentangled himself once more from the strife of faction, which he had entered, unlike others, with no view to gain, and during the last five years of his life confined his satire to his old foes in the world of letters. He withdrew, likewise, from the polite world, keeping more and more to his own little circle, " now content with the friendship of a few." He could rely, he said, on Lord Cornbury, Lord Polwarth, a Mr. Murray,[1] and one or two others, and they were enough.[2]

IN fact, the world was changing, and the honours paid to literature in society were being relaxed by a new generation who left authors more alone, because they saw how they began to rely chiefly upon booksellers. If Pope had not been gradually excluded from society by growing weakness and ill-health, he would have been conscious that men of letters, in general, were not so freely given the entrée of fashionable circles as they had been in his earlier days. His last important work was the addition of a fourth book to the *Dunciad*, announcing with its splendid rhetoric the inauguration of the reign of Dullness, and, when the whole was republished in 1743, his long cherished grudge against Colley Cibber was satisfied by installing him in the place of Theobald. Soon afterwards the poet's fragile body, never healthy since his childhood and weakened by the unwise indulgence of his appetite, rapidly grew worse; for the last eighteen months he planned nothing new, became subject to delirious fits, and in May 1744 died. His will left his property and £1,000 to his friend

[1] Later Lord Mansfield, Chief Justice 1756-88. [2] *Works*, vii. 374.

Martha Blount, and £100 to his servant, the "good John" of his verse. It makes a pleasant rounding off to a life of comfortable independence, built up and maintained by his pen alone.

PATRONS, then, were of little account to Pope, even at the beginning. Introduced into society by friends, proud of the chance to help forward so promising a youth, he had won universal admiration but little money. By his *Homer* he gained the latter, aided by no more patronage than subscription to his book implied, the patronage of the small class of cultivated readers which was to become in course of time the patronage of the public. Swift said of Bolingbroke that " he began in the Queen's time to be my patron, and then condescended to be my friend." Pope's relation to such men was still more one of friendship alone, and from about 1720 his reputation opened to him nearly all the houses of the great, who felt that they were honoured by his presence, and that they at the same time conferred honour on him. Both were presumably well pleased: Burlington, Cobham, Bathurst, and others were given the honour of dedications and of poetical praise, while Pope, however much he pretended to despise wealth and rank, was as glad to have the intimacy of its possessors and to declare his friendships to the world at large. If we consider what Pope's position would have been without this friendship, we may find it difficult to draw the line between such friendship and patronage; but if, on the other hand, we compare Pope's position with that of Young and Thomson, it is clear by what a gap Pope is separated from that real patronage which entails, however slightly, dependence on the patron and compliance with his wishes. It was only the unrivalled supremacy of Pope's genius that so lifted his circumstances above those of his contemporaries; for them, patronage was still a valuable help.

(iv)

THE life of the poet Young is the best example of the continuance of political patronage. Five years older than Pope, he was slower in his advance, and first spent some years in the pursuit of academical learning. However, by 1712 he had won an outer seat on the benches of Addison's little senate more by the wise use of friends, by persistence, and by the promise of genius than by anything he had so far achieved. The Augustan age of patronage, though on the wane, still appeared prosperous and hopeful, and Young's eye was always on the main chance; he was of no mind to let slip opportunities by being backward, and he did not fail to prosper, albeit inconsolably below the mark of his soaring expectations. He left no avenue to fame untried. Beginning with the grossest flattery of men of wealth and station, he gained the patronage of the Duke of Wharton; proceeding to flatter and also to help Sir Robert Walpole, he received a pension; with *Busiris* (1719) and *The Revenge* (1721) he had some success on the stage; finally, entering the Church, he obtained a rectory, married a daughter of the Earl of Lichfield, and spent the rest of his days bewailing the shabby treatment of those in power, which denied him preferment.

PERHAPS, after all, he overdid things, and flattered

too freely, and showed himself too sensitive to the winds of opportunism. He began his literary career in 1713 with an *Epistle to the Marquis of Lansdowne*, and the flattery which hailed that peer and politician as an Augustus, a second Shakespeare, " born to make the Muse immortal," a philosopher whom perusal of the Grecian sages " only taught With more respect to value his own thought," must have taken the edge off that peer's appetite long before he finished the five hundred lines, if he ever did. Apparently, nothing came of this, and in view of the changes of 1714 it was distinctly unfortunate. The *Epistle* had been frankly Tory, interspersed with lavish praise of Bolingbroke, but with a complete disregard for consistency Young turned to welcome George I in a poem brimming with Whig sentiment. Next he successfully attached himself to the none too estimable Duke of Wharton, then a minister, and in his wake began to advance. In 1719 the Duke granted him a pension of £100, because, in the wording of the grant, he considered " that the public good is advanced by the encouragement of learning and the polite arts." It was an idea, however sincere or not in Wharton, in keeping with recent tradition and honourable to patron and patronized. Actually, however, it was a mere gesture, for the poet received nothing until Walpole doubled it and secured its payment in 1726. It is almost the only piece of worthy patronage recorded of Walpole, and there can be little doubt that it was earned in some way by political service ; at any rate, it was generously rewarded by Young in a flood of panegyric on Walpole's *Installation as Knight of the Garter*, where the poet spoke rapturously of a breast "glowing with grateful fire," because—

> "The streams of royal bounty, turned by thee,
> Refresh the dry domains of poesy."

MEANWHILE, the connexion with Wharton had been ended by the latter's not unadvised departure to the Continent, there to direct scandalous attacks on the Government, and intrigue with the Pretender. It was probably a good thing for Young that he thus lost this patron before he became too deeply entangled with him, or had to break the connexion himself; but Wharton did not leave him without another *beau geste*, and one more profitable to Young if we may believe the anecdote given by Spence. "A little after Dr. Young," says Spence, "had published his *Universal Passion*, the Duke of Wharton made him a present of two thousand pounds for it. When a friend of the Duke's, who was surprised at the largeness of the present, cried out on hearing it: 'What! two thousand pounds for a poem?' the Duke smiled, and said: 'It was the best bargain he ever made in his life, for he was fairly worth four thousand.'"[1] The story, which evidently had some circulation, and the terms of the pension earlier, at least show that there was prevalent an ideal of patronage.

WHEN Wharton was gone, Young easily found another patron, one with whom his intimacy had been increasing for a few years, Bubb Dodington, the wealthy borough-monger. "Charmed with his burgundy and wit," Young was a frequent inmate of the politician's fine country seat at

[1] Spence, *Anecdotes* (1858), p. 193.

Eastbury, celebrated in many a poem. But still he baited his hook for possible patrons; he plied George II with Odes, sought to insinuate himself into Pope's good graces by supporting him in his war against the Dunces, and seemed at one time likely to drift towards the Opposition, because Walpole showed no signs of doing more for him. In the end he settled down in 1730 in the rectory of Alwyn in Hertfordshire to which he had been appointed by All Souls' with the intention of awaiting that patronage which he considered should lead him to a deanery at least, and which seemed to be promised from his appointment in 1727 as a chaplain to the King. That preferment never came; in the early years Queen Caroline beneficently guided church patronage without recognizing his claims, and after her death neither Walpole nor his successors gave him any attention; all he got more was the post of Clerk of the Closet to the Dowager Princess of Wales in 1761, when he was seventy-eight.

BUT, on the whole, he had little to complain of: he was patronized by Wharton, Walpole, and Dodington; he formed the only striking exception to Walpole's practice of not patronizing authors; and he had an assured and comfortable income. Then, his *Night Thoughts* in 1742 brought him over £600 from the booksellers for copyright, so that he had none of the claim to patronage that many had, and which is most pressing, the want of the means to live. The greatest reflection thrown on the condition of patronage by Young's life is the seeming necessity of gross flattery, indicated by its abundance on Young's part. We find him lamenting that—

"All other trades demand, verse-makers beg;
A dedication is a wooden leg," [1]
and probably authors had to exert themselves in that way to obtain notice, although Young's flattery seems rather excessive, and later he did his best to withdraw his dedications. Meanwhile he had prospered by them, and soothed his conscience by mingling in the same poems with his flattery equally strong denunciations of flatterers. Had he begun earlier, his flattery and political adaptability would probably have carried him further, but the change had commenced before his career was properly started.

IN many ways the life of Savage resembled that of Young. Some fourteen years younger, he was forced at an earlier age than the latter to seek a living, because he was the son not of a Dean of Salisbury, but of parents doubtful in character or origin. That Savage was the adulterous son of the Countess of Macclesfield by Earl Rivers was an accepted fact with his friend Johnson, was apparently admitted by certain of the lady's relatives, and was never effectively contradicted, but has never been satisfactorily substantiated. If it was true, his mother's actions presented an amazing instance of maternal cruelty and persecution, and it seems pleasanter, where corroboration is untrustworthy, to believe that Savage was born of humble parents, and that, having found out some of the Countess's history (she had by then become Mrs. Brett), he chose to assail her with claims that he was her son. It was a possible way of frightening her into patronizing him, as Young and others tried to force the gates

[1] *The Universal Passion*, iv. 191-2.

of patronage by flattery. In any case, he had been brought up in poor circumstances, and in 1717, still in his late 'teens, having aroused the bitter enmity of Mrs. Brett by his claims and painful probings into her past, " he was obliged to seek some other means of support ; and having no profession, became by necessity an author."
FIRST, he entered the lists of controversial writing with *The Convocation*, a weak poem attacking the Bishop of Bangor ; that failing to gain him notice, he wrote for the stage with little success beyond gaining the friendship and occasional help of Steele, and Mrs. Oldfield, the actress. In 1723 he secured the acting at Drury Lane of his tragedy, *Sir Thomas Overbury*, which brought him a very welcome £100. Meantime, the claims to the recognition of his birth had convinced Aaron Hill, an author of some note and comfortable means, and a friend of Lord Peterborough and a wide circle. At last his claims began to bear some fruit, and in 1724 Hill published the story in *The Plain Dealer*. It gained him a considerable degree of public sympathy, so that in 1726 he was enabled to publish by subscription a volume of *Miscellaneous Poems and Translations by several hands* which brought him another welcome sum. Then, just as he seemed in a fair way to succeed, he became involved in a drunken brawl, killed a man, and was sentenced to death.
BUT people of importance had now come to hear of him, patrons came forward, and Lord Tyrconnel, Mrs. Brett's nephew, the Countess of Hertford, a prominent patroness of literary men, and finally Queen Caroline interested themselves in his behalf, and secured his reprieve and release

in March 1728. Tyrconnel settled on him a pension of £200 a year, and for a few years he enjoyed the sunshine of social favour. His life so far reflects the prospects around 1720 of social patronage; his merits extorted some success on the stage; but there were no patrons to lend him help until his misfortunes clamoured in their ears. As a result he was driven to work for Curll, the bookseller, in every variety of shady and disagreeable hack-work; then, more by his claims on their sympathy than by his merits as a writer, he attained the shelter of patronage, and found himself a dependent, in what Johnson called his golden age. Tyrconnel's motives being less those of literary patronage than of stifling the scandal in his family, we can hardly be surprised that he expected Savage to use his pen in his service, for there were very few avowed literary patrons who did not expect as much. Thus, out of deference to Tyrconnel, Savage composed a very eulogistic *Epistle to Walpole* in 1732, which told the minister that his—

> " spreading worth in various bounty fell,
> Made genius flourish and made art excel."

Walpole displayed a fitting appreciation by making the poet a present of £20. In the interval Savage had been trying to get for himself the Laureateship rendered vacant in 1730 by the death of Eusden, but that post, being considered the reward of political service, went to Cibber, whose claims in that way were much superior.[1] Savage, however, had a recompense from Queen Caroline,

[1] Cibber's claim was based on his political play, *The Non-Juror*, which had been of service to the Government by its popular Whiggism at the time of the Jacobite rising of 1715.

who, till her death in 1737, paid him £50 a year in return for an annual birthday poem, no very hard condition.

BUT the golden age was tottering; in 1734 he quarrelled with Tyrconnel, broke off the connexion, abused him as the "Honourable Brute and Booby," and turned expectantly to Walpole, who in view of his support of Lord Chancellor Talbot in a dispute with the Bishop of London promised him a place worth £200 a year. But he was his own enemy, and his outspoken avowals of attachment to Bolingbroke were probably the cause of Walpole's failure to fulfil the expectations, for Walpole was not the man to help a poet who would not help himself, and whose gratitude was, at best, likely to be very dubious. So Savage, in a fit of spleen and disappointment, wrote *A Poet's Dependance on a Statesman*, a poem which appeared in *The Gentleman's Magazine* of April 1736. Its sentiments were lofty:

" Be posts dispos'd at will !—I have, for these,
    No gold to plead, no impudence to teize . . .
  I have no pow'r, election votes to gain ;
    No will to hackney out polemic strain ; . . .
  Where lives the *statesman*, so in *honour* clear,
    To give where he has nothing to hope, nor fear ? "[1]

Such was the strain, and it was largely true. Yet why should a statesman, however liberal, give pensions to a man like Savage, as ready to be an enemy as a friend, who at once showed his aversion to political time-serving by trying to gain the patronage of the Prince of Wales, the centre of the opposition ? Patronage had served him well

[1] 1736, p. 225.

enough, and would doubtlessly have continued to do so, had he continued to deserve it. Instead, living recklessly, spending his pension from the Queen in a few riotous days, he alienated his friends by pride and petulance, and withdrawing to Bristol, died there of fever in 1743. For one who, like him, ventured on the profession of letters because he had no other resources, and who was merely a unit among countless such, hack-work for booksellers was a necessary preliminary, and dependence on a patron almost an essential condition of success; accepting the conditions and gaining patronage, he seemed likely to succeed; fate and his irregular life wrecked him.

AMIABLE, easy-going Gay, far greater than Young or Savage, was yet unable to attain the independence which Pope won. He had not in his character the fervent desire and persistence to secure it, and was born, if ever a poet of that day was, to recline in the lap of luxury, spread by patronage. In 1720 he had realised £1,000 by the handsomely subscribed edition of his poems published by Tonson and Lintot, but what with losses in South Sea stock and with idleness and good living, it was soon dissipated. In the interval he had been an honoured guest of Lord Burlington, and moreover he had one sure support of £150 a year as a Lottery Commissioner, since occasional posts of that kind remained for some twenty years open to men of letters, after Walpole had closed the majority to such incompetent and unprofitable people. Further, he was relieved from all anxiety by the imperious patronage of the eccentric Duchess of Queensberry. Pope, writing to Fortescue in 1726, could " give no account of

Gay, since he was raffled for, and won back by his Duchess, but that he has been in her vortex ever since, immoveable to appearance, yet . . . with his head turning round upon some work or other."[1] He was quite a pampered favourite of the nobility of the day; if he were not with the Queensberrys, he was with Lord Burlington, and the Earl of Lincoln supplied him with lodgings in Whitehall. He was by nature a dependent born to be a protégé, and the kindly if irksome guiding-strings of his Duchess were not far short of a necessity. In other circumstances he might have led the life of a Goldsmith.

THEN in 1727, after some delay over the illustrations, was published the first series of his *Fables* written for young Prince William at the request of the Princess of Wales. Shortly afterwards George I died, the Princess became Queen Caroline, and Gay and his friends looked for his reward. He was offered the position of gentleman-usher to the little Princess Louisa, an almost nominal office with a salary of £200, and refused in offended disappointment. He assured Swift, " I can no more be disappointed, so that I am in a blessed condition "; and the Dean in reply stormed over this insulting proposal, as they held it, " to squire a royal girl of two years old."

> " How could you, Gay, disgrace the Muses' train,
> To serve a tasteless court twelve years in vain ! "[2]

So did all his friends exclaim, and splenetic Pope not least. Yet what could they reasonably expect ? Gay's service to the ministry was negligible; in his very fables he inserted quite

[1] *Works*, ix. 110.   [2] *An Epistle to Mr. Gay* (1731).

unnecessary satire on courtiers; and he lived on the most intimate terms with powerful members of the opposition. The offer he received indicated a genuine desire to reward him, probably a greater desire than many a later minister would have evinced, who was faced by such opponents as Swift, Bolingbroke, and Pulteney.

In the next year or so he became a big thorn in the side of Court and ministry, and was used as a political stalking-horse by the enemies of the Government. The "Newgate Pastoral" proposed by Swift took shape as *The Beggar's Opera*, and its production in January 1728 at Drury Lane, with the popular Miss Fenton as Polly Peachum, was the sensation of the season. It ran in London for sixty-three nights, in Dublin for twenty, and caused Pope to withhold the *Dunciad*, lest his own success should be weakened by its unparalleled popularity. Probably without any intention on the part of Gay, the character of Captain Macheath was taken by the public for Walpole, and the identification was warmly sustained by the Opposition. Distinctly this was undesirable; but angels would have feared to tread in the path of its suppression, and Walpole was not fool enough to step in against such popular acclamation. But when *Polly*, its sequel, was ready in 1729, its performance was at once banned by the Lord Chamberlain, acting under the express instructions of the King, who was himself influenced by Walpole. The thorn might have been the merest prick, had it been left alone, but this misguided treatment resulted in an inflamed and festering wound. If *Polly* could not be acted, it could be printed. Bowyer's press supplied two large quarto editions, totalling 10,500, and at least two illegal editions appeared on the market. Walpole's opponents were determined to make the most of it, and the promotion of the sale was undertaken with all the zest of faction. The Duchess of Queensberry, for openly canvassing with characteristic impudence in the very arcana of the Court, was dismissed from her places, and retired with her husband, saucily defiant. In the words of Swift, to Arbuthnot, " the inoffensive John Gay is now become one of the obstructions to the peace of Europe, the terror of ministers. He has got several turned out of their places, and is the darling of the city."

WHEN it was all over, Gay was richer by £1,200, and, as by the thirty-sixth performance of *The Beggar's Opera* he had got from £700 to £800, politics had in two years proved very profitable to him. He did little more beyond writing a few fables, and spent his last years entirely with the Queensberrys, by whose careful husbanding he died worth £6,000 in 1732. He owed the keeping his money to his patrons, but he did not owe them the getting it. The wide popularity of his operas and the success of his poems suggest that he, too, might have won independence, but for the failings of his character. As it is, he affords one of the best examples of patronage, for it raised him from the humble status of a mercer's apprentice, gave him a life of ease and plenty, and buried him " at Westminster Abbey as if he had been a peer of the realm."

THE lives of Pope, Savage, Young and Gay illustrate the relation to patronage of authors who had already in 1726 made their mark. Swift we can overlook, for he was now for some years retired to Dublin, secure in his deanery, from which he refused to stir, content for the most part with an intermittent long-range bombardment by essay and poem of the Court, and Walpole and Grub Street. The Queen Anne days of political patronage had taken him there, would doubtlessly have taken him higher if the Queen had not been so self-willed in the matter of Church appointments, and the fate of Toryism had left him stranded there, bitterly mounting guard over " the accepted hell beneath." Pope stood high enough to patronize others, but with Swift it was not so ; his genius had made him feared rather than loved, and literature was in him respected at a distance. " My popularity," he told Pope in 1736, " is wholly confined to the common people. . . . I have not the love, or hardly the civility, of any one man in power or station ; and I can boast, that I neither visit nor am acquainted with any lord, temporal or spiritual, in the whole Kingdom ; nor am able to do the least good office to the most deserving man, except what I can dispose of in my own cathedral upon a vacancy."[1] Therefore, since the life of Swift is more or less unrelated in any way to the course of literary patronage, let us consider that of James Thomson.

BORN in 1700, Thomson[2] had stayed on at Edinburgh University till 1724, trifling with the idea of entering the ministry, and chiefly occupied in writing miscellaneous poems, which by no means improved his ecclesiastical prospects. Then, although he did not admit to himself that

[1] Pope, *Works*, vii. 340.   [2] See Leon Morel, *J. Thomson, Sa Vie et ses œuvres.*

he was going to abandon divinity altogether, he at length determined to try his fortune as a writer in London, which he reached in February 1725. His mother was connected with the Homes of Bassendean, an influential family, and he had a distant kinswoman of some influence, Lady Grisel Baillie of Jerviswood, so that his descent on London was not a rash project. He knew that there was little hope of success unless he had some helpful patronage at the outset, and that he had reasonable hopes of securing through his connexions. He quickly gained access to the houses of the rich, was introduced to people of literary and social eminence by Duncan Forbes,[1] was appointed tutor in the family of Lady Grisel's son-in-law, Lord Binning, at East Barnet, and resumed a friendship with his college acquaintance David Mallet, who had preceded him, and was then tutor to the sons of the Duke of Montrose.

BUT there seemed at the beginning, in spite of these favouring circumstances, some hesitation, some failure to appreciate his merit, and to foresee the honour that would come of patronizing him. *Winter* was finished, but there was singularly little enthusiasm over the manuscript. Millan, at the inducement of Mallet, agreed to advance £3 on it to relieve particularly pressing financial straits, and probably gave more for it later; but for some time he had cause to regret even this £3. The public passed by this new departure in verse; someone was needed to give the word that blank-verse nature descriptions deserved to

---

[1] Duncan Forbes followed his father's example in patronizing men of letters. He became in 1737 President of the Court of Session and was said to be the Mæcenas of every man of genius in science or belles-lettres.

be read or praised, and this necessary part was played by a Rev. Mr. Whatley, afterwards Prebendary of York, " a man of some taste in letters . . . [who] went from Coffee-house to Coffeehouse, calling upon all men of taste to exert themselves in rescuing one of the greatest geniuses that ever appeared from obscurity. In a short time the impression was bought up."[1] Sir Spencer Compton, to whom the poem had been dedicated, sent Thomson a present of twenty guineas, after Aaron Hill had assured him that it was the only proper thing to do; and Thomson, in thanking Hill, was " very ready to own that the present was larger than his performance deserved." Certainly at this time of day it seems a thing to have been thankful for, that a poet could extort so welcome a gift from a person whom he had never before personally approached.

ONCE Thomson's claims to patronage were thus established, the potential patrons began to come forward. He was taken up by those great ladies the Countess of Hertford and the eldest daughter of Sir Hans Sloane, was recommended to Charles Talbot, became a frequenter of Pope's circle, and found a pleasant country house at Eastbury, the seat of Dodington, who had sent his services through the poet Young, expressing his desire to see him. Society was, perhaps, too slack in seeking out subjects for its patronage, but it was not backward in helping a good writer on the path to fame when he had achieved a footing on the first rung of the ladder; nor was Thomson backward in celebrating in poem and dedication those who were or might be prominent in so doing.

[1] Cibber's *Lives*, v. 196.

In 1727 appeared *Summer* with a dedication to Dodington, who had been suggested for that honour by the poet's late master and friend, Lord Binning, for whom the dedication had been first intended, because Dodington, as Johnson said, " had more power to advance the reputation and fortune of a poet."[1] The same year he published a *Poem sacred to the Memory of Sir Isaac Newton*, prefaced by a richly baited hook for Sir Robert Walpole, whose failure to bite he soon after repaid in *Britannia* with an equally thorough denunciation. In 1728 *Spring*, dedicatd to Lady Hertford, brought him fifty guineas from the bookseller Millar, who had replaced Millan as his publisher; and in 1730 *The Seasons* appeared in a subscription edition at a guinea a copy, of which the list ran to 454 names, and included those of Pope, Bolingbroke, Walpole, Arbuthnot, Somerville, Spence, and Young, peers, politicians and poets joining in his support. By the time the copyright of the whole was finally in Millar's hands, the poet is said to have reaped £1,000, a most satisfactory result at a time when subscriptions were beginning to go out of fashion, as a result of their abuse by rascally authors who gathered in the cash but published no book.

MEANWHILE, avid of success, he determined to seek it in the most lucrative quarters. The tradition of the theatre audience was older, more engrained, and more generous than that of the reading public. Failure on the stage might be more complete, but success there contrasted very favourably with success in other walks, and where the bookseller paid in tens, Drury Lane or

[1] *Lives*: Thomson, iii. 287.

Covent Garden paid in hundreds. The playwright was sure of £100 for his copyright on publication, and, in addition, he drew the receipts of the author's third nights, three of which could be relied on with a play of any merit. It is no matter for wonder, therefore, that more or less a complete lack of dramatic talent did not keep back the crowds of would-be dramatists from the managers' doors. How a particular play might appeal to the public was often uncertain; friends had not been over-confident about *The Beggar's Opera* before its performance, and in 1773 it needed a kind of force to wring from Colman a dejected and fearful acceptance of *She Stoops to Conquer*. But, in the eyes of an author, the tedious siege of a manager, the risk of a hurricane of catcalls and the utter downfall of his labours, weighed lightly in the balance against the possibility of popularity and a heap of gold. Influential patrons, too, might considerably affect success even on the stage by bringing their troops of friends, and a mediocre play with a powerful backing might in favourable circumstances have a good run.

THOMSON had a good backing, and he was following a hard-wearing custom, when in 1730 he laid aside for the first time his poetic genius and worked instead his mediocre dramatic talent; the pecuniary argument had been even more forcible in the time of Dryden, it was not even worn out as late as 1780. *Sophonisba* had a degree of success in spite of itself. It " raised such expectation that every rehearsal was dignified with a splendid audience, collected to anticipate the delight that was preparing for the public; it was observed, however, that nobody was much affected, and that the company rose as from a moral lecture."[1] But Thomson's name and Mrs. Oldfield's acting filled the footmen's seats with men of fashion, so great was the first crush; the play ran some ten nights, went through four editions in a year, supplied the wits with a butt, and died. The author's share of the profits cannot have been inconsiderable, and for the copyright he had eighty guineas. He felt justified in resting on his laurels, and late in 1730 left England for the Continent on a grand tour as tutor to Talbot's son.

His achievement in the four years 1726 to 1730 suggests that the profession of letters had quite attractive rewards to offer a man of high ability, yet very moderate social position (and the success of such a man is a very fair criterion of the prospects of a profession). It shows, too, that patrons if possessed of less initiative, were far from extinct, neither unhelpful, nor unconscious of the traditions of Somers and Halifax, nor unmindful that nobility had its obligations as well to literature as elsewhere; and it indicates that a reading and book-buying public had grown up which, though still small, was rapidly increasing and gave a fairly wide circulation to those whom it favoured. But Thomson in 1730, in spite of his success, was not independent, as he longed to be. His holiday on the Continent as travelling tutor to the Solicitor-General's son was very pleasant, but there was always the feeling that he was not his own master, which haunted him even while " storing his imagination with ideas of all-beautiful, all-great, and all-perfect Nature," and

[1] Johnson, *Lives*, iii. 288.

imbibing from a view of the tyranny of foreign governments very lofty convictions of the glorious qualities of Liberty. When living with Dodington at Eastbury in 1729, he had complained of being " far from that divine freedom, that independent life which the Muses love." It should not long be thus, he proclaimed. But, in fact, he never attained such independence as was Pope's, partly, no doubt, because being a " bard more fat than bard beseems," he was too indolent and fond of self-indulgence to follow the path necessary for its attainments, and partly, perhaps, because his genius was not of sufficient universality to support him without resort to patronage. At any rate, during this tour he was preoccupied with the idea of doing that which should secure him independence. Yet not so much ambitious of the glorious summit of Parnassus as of " some little dear retirement in the vale below that gives the right relish." [1] But he found that he could write nothing, the Muse having, it would seem, remained in the woods of Eastbury, reluctant to cross the Channel.

BACK in England in December 1731, he stayed with his " pupil," waiting till Talbot should become Lord Chancellor, when some sinecure was bound to be his reward. It came in 1733 in the form of a Secretaryship of Briefs in the Court of Chancery, of which the duties were negligible and the income £300, and for the time the poet was content. He was able to help his family in Scotland, to pretend he was independent, to patronize others, including his own early patron Aaron Hill, whose *Zara* he recommended to

[1] Letter to Dodington, October 24th, 1731.

Dodington, and he lived on terms of intimacy with Pope. Meantime he had been working on his lengthy poem, *Liberty*, and in 1735 the first part was published by Millar, who printed 3,000 ordinary and 250 special copies to meet the demand which the success of *The Seasons* led him to expect. But however much the public were beginning to clamour for the liberty which Walpole never endangered, they were not prepared to buy such tedious blank verse as this. Of the second and third parts only 2,000 and 250 were printed, and of the fourth and fifth only 1,250. Thomson, seeing the loss which was incurred by Millar, spoke of bearing it himself, and probably did so, although Aaron Hill wrote that such an action would stand out to the lasting shame of ungrateful England. Yet why the public should be disgraced by not buying pompous bombast, or patrons by not encouraging its further production, it is difficult to say. So did Thomson's hopes of a real independence like Pope's crumble away, and in disgust and chagrin the poet sought to heal his wounded feelings in the air of his native country. What was still more unfortunate, the circumstances which had " blossomed pretty well of late " were now threatened by " the blight of an idle inquiry into the fees and offices of the courts of justice "[1]; the salary of his office was reduced to £100, and when it lapsed in 1737 on Talbot's death, he did not care to ask for its renewal.

THOMSON's first recommendation to the Prince of Wales was probably made by Dodington, who had earlier been the Prince's secretary, but

---

[1] L. Morel. *James Thomson*, p. 106.

beyond the dedication to the Prince of *Liberty* there was little result ; nor did the dedication, as we have seen, much benefit the poem. Meanwhile, through the autumn of 1736 Thomson, turning again to the stage, had " spurred and whipped " his Muse into producing the tragedy of *Agamemnon*, which was accepted at Drury Lane in January 1737, but postponed till April of the next year. In the interval he had published a second volume of works, and had been honoured by being chosen a member of the directing committee of the newly founded Society for the Encouragement of Learning. But Talbot had died early in 1737, and Thomson's affairs were passing into " a more poetical posture than formerly." Lord Lyttelton, however, a man of some literary taste and merit, had in August 1737 become secretary to the Prince, and to him it occurred that patronage of men of letters would contribute to make popular his master, now finally banished from the Court after the discreditable episode of the Princess's childbirth. Thomson, therefore, received the very welcome pension of £100, which continued until, on offence being taken by the Prince with Lyttelton in May 1748, he with West and Mallet, also nominated by Lyttelton, " were all routed in one day."

THE firstfruit of this pension was an *Ode on the Birth of the Princess Augusta*, and, in addition, his plays were not improved by the liberal insertion of political bias. *Agamemnon*, when it at length appeared, was honoured by a rare visit of Pope to the theatre, and, after a varied reception, lived for ten nights, giving the author three benefit nights by which he realized a fair sum. Its success was, however, chiefly due to the allusions to the " ten loosely-governed years " under Walpole, to the frequent absences of the King in Hanover, and to " bounty's pleasing chains " which involved Englishmen in slavery. The printed edition, which was dedicated to the Princess of Wales, was very successful, a second edition of 1,500 being called for four days after the issue of 3,000 of the first. The next play, *Edward and Eleanora*, was even fuller of attacks on the King and Walpole, but a Licensing Act had, in the meantime, legalized the censorship of the Lord Chamberlain, and it was prohibited, after rehearsals had begun and the date of the performance been fixed. Edward, the deliverer of his country from corruption, was too obviously the Prince of Wales, who was assured that " on thee alone our weeping country turns her distressful eye." The lines

" Has not the royal heir a juster claim
  To share his father's inmost heart and counsels,
Than aliens to his interest, those who make
  A property, a market of his honour ? "

are typical of the spirit of the play, and, though quite consistent in their historical setting, they had too topical an illustration at hand to be sanctioned by those in power. Thomson had, therefore, to be content with the profits on the sale of an impression of 4,500 copies, a number which speaks of a moderate public for such efforts, although they were doubtlessly much the more acceptable for the flavour of faction, whose existence was made no secret of in the dedication. And again in 1740 his pension was responsible for the writing of *Alfred*, a masque performed in the gardens of the Prince's house, and so evading the Licensing Act, which would have found in it equal matter for prohibition.

THIS completed his political service, which must have been irksome, even though his personal political convictions were in harmony with those he expressed. It is a matter for regret that he had thus to employ time which might have given us more poetry of the quality of the *Castle of Indolence*. But it was a time when an assured income was a thing he could not afford to pass by; his dubious prospects, in fact, absolutely turned against him the mother of the Amanda with whom he had fallen in love and whom he only wanted her mother's consent to marry. "What! would you marry Thomson? He will make ballads, and you will sing them." So did the mother sum up the poet's hopes to her daughter. The Prince's patronage, however, did not call any more for politics; Walpole's long reign was at last over, and in a year or so Lyttelton was Chancellor of the Exchequer in the Pelham Government.

THOMSON was more and more in Lyttelton's company. Together they worked at the revision of *The Seasons*, of which the new edition appeared in 1744; and in December of that year Lyttelton named him Surveyor-General of the Leeward Isles, to fill one of those offices which might still be given to authors or others at a loose end, who could draw the salary and execute the duties by deputy.[1] Thomson, however, only retained the

---

[1] Thomson's deputy was Paterson, whose play of *Arminius* is said to have been prohibited by the censor because it was in the same handwriting as Thomson's *Edward and Eleanora*, for which Paterson had been the amanuensis. In 1746 Paterson succeeded to the full salary. The incident is typical of Thomson's kindly patronage of his fellow-writers.

office for little longer than a year, being presumably rendered more independent by the profits of his new editions of *The Seasons* in 1744 and 1746 and of his successful play, *Tancred and Sigismunda*, patronized by the vigorous exertions of Lyttelton and his late fellow-patriot Pitt. So in 1748 his career ended in circumstances " more settled and of late considerably improved," and Lyttelton rounded off his consistent patronage by securing the posthumous production of Thomson's *Coriolanus*, which had been delayed by quarrels over the division of the acting parts, and which, when finally performed, resulted in a good sum for the poet's family.

WHAT light, then, do the lives of Pope, Savage, Young, Gay, and Thomson throw on the state of patronage in the third and fourth decades of the century, and on its effect upon literature? First of all, it appears that there was a widespread recognition among the upper classes of the dignity of literature, and that they considered that men of letters were worthy of admittance into the best society. Gay's poem of 1720, written in celebration of the completion of Pope's *Iliad*, is a great testimony to the fact that there was no social barrier over which an author could not step. The names of peers and peeresses, of essayists, poets, and dramatists, are mingled in the list of those represented as paying homage to the great translator. Wit was still a powerful passport to its possessor, though he were poor. The patrons generally thought in their hearts that they were the superiors of their protégés, but they did not show it as their decadent descendants did, but gave considerable help, and acted as friends who merely expected due deference. The honour of looking after Gay was so keenly sought that, in Pope's expressive phrase, he was " raffled for." The Duke of Wharton openly declared, it matters not how sincerely, the opinion that patronage was worthy and honourable in a government or a rich man. It only had to be pointed out to Sir Spencer Compton that a man in his position was expected to reward a poet who honoured him with a dedication, and he did so. Perhaps there was not so much of that spontaneous patronage which was shown by Dorset in his assistance to the boy Prior. The patrons of these later years did not seek out, but waited to be given the cue ; then they stepped forward, and those who did not play the leading rôle were not less useful together, with their guineas for subscription copies of a work.

THAT this patronage was very necessary is shown by all but Pope setting out to seek it, and, in spite of their success, never being able to free themselves from the necessity. Savage rashly broke away and was ruined ; Gay grumbled but kept to it ; Young was never tired of seeking it ; Thomson had to make it his jumping-off board, hoped to leave it behind, but could not, and was very thankful for his pension from the Prince. Nor was a patron really difficult to obtain by a writer of any merit ; among lesser men who found patrons were Mallet, Christopher Pitt, and Ambrose Philips. It is reasonable to believe that Johnson himself could have found a patron had it not been for his inflexible pride, and so might have been spared that long period of drudgery under booksellers, relief from which was the great boon of patronage. The existence of patrons was the only safeguard of good literature, enabling a man to write what he would, not what he must because the booksellers wanted it. But patronage had its evil, too, for it also entailed at times the writing of what patrons wanted. Yet where the dependence on a bookseller's wishes was absolute, that on a patron's was conditional. A patron might demand a political bias, but a wide scope was still left for the writer's own self-expression. Thus Young was writing *The Universal Passion* while he enjoyed a pension from Walpole. Thomson's *Liberty* was the fruit of his own aspirations while maintaining himself on his office from Lord Talbot, and Savage was little troubled by the call for trifling birthday odes in return for his £50. A writer for a bookseller was unceasingly at the beck and call of his employer to produce lives, dictionaries, histories, or pamphlets, but the demands of a patron were more occasional and better paid.

THE most depressing side of the relation to political patronage of Savage, Young, Gay, and Thomson is their readiness to sell their pens without any hesitation, swaying greedily from side to side. Thomson was the steadiest, and his later principles were actually those of his patron; but in his early days he first plied Walpole with flattery, and when it failed, turned abruptly against him. Gay and Savage seemed to think that they could side with the Tories and his Whig opponents, and yet receive money from Walpole. Young dodged from party to party as interest directed. Judging from the complete absence of such tactics on the part of Pope, we may doubt whether so much subserviency was needed; if it were, it was the greatest blot on the patrons of 1730, but further consideration would suggest that it was not. The general position in Queen Anne's day was summed up by Goldsmith thus : " Writers were sufficiently esteemed by the great, and not rewarded enough by the booksellers to set them above dependence." It was still so in this later period.

(v)

POLITICAL patronage has been earlier dismissed, because it was rendered comparatively negligible by the changed conditions of politics coincident with the rise of Walpole, but it is worthy of more consideration. The causes of Walpole's unrivalled supremacy have been explained ; and the disintegration of political patronage was inevitable from the passage of time and the nature of Walpole's character. The minister had in the beginning practically no opposition of any power, and by 1726 he had bought so many newspapers and their writers under his control that he could well afford to disregard attacks, and for some time employed few writers in his defence, and rarely oppressed his libellers with prosecutions. His chief organ was *The Daily Gazetteer*, which was as well supplied with the general news which he desired published as *The London Gazette* was with the official announcements. " Into this, as a common sink," said a note to the *Dunciad*, " was received all the trash which had been before dispersed in several journals, and circulated at the public expense of the nation. The authors were the same obscure men; though sometimes relieved by occasional essays from statesmen, courtiers, bishops, deans, and doctors. The meanest sort were rewarded with money; others with places or benefices, from an hundred to a thousand a year."[1]

THOMAS GORDON, more honourably known as a translator of Sallust and Tacitus, gives a typical example of Walpole's attitude to political writers. He had first distinguished himself as a supporter of Hoadly, so obtaining the help of a Whig politician Trenchard, with whom he wrote in 1720 a weekly paper, *The Independent Whig*. That having too strong an air of "patriotism," Walpole thought it worth while to silence him, and so took him into his pay with the office of First Commissioner of Wine Licences, which he held till his death in 1750. Then there was the notorious Orator Henley, who "had £200 a year given him for the secret service of a weekly paper of unintelligible nonsense called *The Hyp Doctor*," as a note of Pope's tells us, for these were the kind of people whom he pilloried in the *Dunciad* and its notes. Concanen was another "hired scribbler in *The Daily Courant*," a friend of Warburton and Theobald in the late twenties, who for his seasonable Billingsgate, specially in support of Sir William Yonge and the Duke of Newcastle, was rewarded in 1732 with the post of Attorney-General of Jamaica.

BETWEEN the years 1731 and 1741 nearly £50,000 was spent by Walpole on writers and printers out of the secret service money, and Arnall, the chief of his hired penmen, is said to have received in four years some £11,000 for his own services

[1] *Works*, iv. 153, note 5.

and to pay his subordinates. This profuse expenditure shows that Walpole had found that more writers were necessary, for his long-continued, absolute rule had begun to create opposition. Many had hoped that the death of George I meant the downfall of his minister, but the latter's astute handling of the matter of the new Queen's income kept him in the saddle, and the sight of his re-establishment incited his opponents to more vigorous efforts. Further, he had himself swollen their ranks by his overbearing character, which thrust out from his Cabinet, at its inception unusually strong, such men as Pulteney, Chesterfield, and Townshend, who would not submit tamely to his yoke, but asserted their position as equals. One result had been the appearance in December 1726 of *The Craftsman*, an able journal directed by Pulteney and Bolingbroke through their tool Nicholas Amhurst, a capable political writer. Walpole never read any papers, neither his own nor those of his opponents, but he was aware that more propaganda was needed on his side, and he secured it from third-rate men, quite incapable of the task of combating their adversaries, whose strength Walpole never appreciated. He hired, said Coxe, " several known disseminators of infidelity," and " many warm remonstrances were frequently made by the minister's friends against such low mercenaries, but usually disregarded."[1] He had, asserted Swift, " none but beasts and blockheads for his penmen." That was a grossly biassed judgment, but certainly he

[1]. Coxe, *Memoirs of Sir R. Walpole*, i. 761. Coxe also says (p. 759): "Nor can it be denied, that this neglect of men of letters, was highly disadvantageous to his administration, and exposed him to great obloquy."

employed none who are an honour to literature except Young, who probably gave him some help, if we judge either from Walpole's character or the lines of Swift that—

> "Young must torture his invention
> To flatter knaves or lose his pension."

His acts of pure patronage, without any service being required, were few, but they include Congreve's Commissionership and Gay's. Also, his treatment of the men he did employ was liberal. A certain Phillips, " dubb'd Historian by express command,"[1] had a pension of £200 a year; Guthrie was pensioned; the Mitchell known for his steady dependence as " Sir Robert Walpole's poet " was doubtlessly not unrewarded; Entinck, also a bookseller's hack and school-book compiler, had £200 a year; and Arnall was finally rewarded with a pension of £400. Even Swift admitted that " he pays his workmen on the nail." And in that he makes a pleasant contrast with Pulteney and Bolingbroke, who, when they had gained their end in 1742, and seen Walpole gone for ever, neglected their associate Amhurst and let his broken heart and starved body pass unheeded to a grave paid for by a bookseller.

WALPOLE, then, was not directly of any great account as a patron of literary men. His patronage was confined to feeble, mercenary writers, to buying subscription copies of fashionable works, and to occasional donations to a well-recommended dedicator. But, indirectly, he brought into being a sphere of political patronage of some importance. With every day of his

---

[1] i.e. Historiographer-Royal.

continuance in office the opposition grew, the crowd out of office plotted to get in, the country suffered from delusions that its liberty was being undermined, and the clamour against oppression increased in violence. " It is but refusing to gratify an unreasonable or an insolent demand, and up starts a patriot "; so did the minister express his own sense of prevailing politics. At first, the opposition consisted of powerful individual politicians like Pulteney and Bolingbroke, agreeing only in their desire to overthrow Walpole, but the complete break (in the true Hanoverian spirit) between the King and the Prince of Wales gave a rallying-point to the malcontents in 1737.

IT was a happy day for several men of letters. The Prince was himself no lover of literature, but his secretary, George Lyttelton, was, and to him it occurred that patronage of the arts might assist his master to some of that popularity which he desired, but which he neither possessed nor deserved. Probably the rôle of patron was not without some success, and, at least, it makes one redeeming feature in no very princely character, though the honour should really be given to Lyttelton, " still true to virtue, and as warm as true," for it was the latter, together with Bubb Dodington,[1] who was responsible for the distribution of the Prince's favour.

THOMSON was the worthiest recipient of a pension, but Mallet, Glover, Brooke, and Ralph were among the others who benefited from the appearance of him whom Smollett called " a munificent patron of the arts, an unwearied friend of merit." Mallet was in 1742 appointed Under-Secretary

---

[1] For Dodington, see L. C. Sanders, *Patron and Place-hunter*.

at £200 a year; Glover, it is said, was once sent by the Prince a complete set of classics elegantly bound, and at another time £500; and undoubtedly there were many small presents given to authors from time to time. Paul Whitehead was a paid hanger-on of the Prince's faction who was prosecuted in 1739 together with Dodsley, the opposition bookseller, for his satirical poem *Manners*, and who was made use of to compile advertisements and pamphlets. Brooke's and Thomson's plays, by being adapted to the quarrels of the day, owed much of their success to the Prince's circle. It was a formidable opposition on all sides, as Burke testified when he said: " Sir Robert Walpole was forced into the war in 1739 by the people, who were inflamed to this measure by the most leading politicians, by the first orators, and the greatest poets of the times. For that war Pope sang his dying notes. For that war Johnson, in more energetic strains, employed the voice of his early genius. For that war Glover distinguished himself in the way in which his merit was the most natural and happy." But the patronage was neither very creditable nor very secure. It was only Lyttelton who pretended that literature deserved to be honoured for its own sake, and he could not deny that his patron must be repaid with political service. When he was dismissed because of his master's displeasure, his protégés were also deprived of their places. THE pleasantest incident is that recorded by Cave in regard to Johnson and his *Rambler*: " When the author was to be kept private (which was the first scheme) two gentlemen, belonging to the Prince's Court, came to me to inquire his name in order to do him service . . . soon after Mr. Dodington sent a letter."[1] Johnson of course did not accept, but there is an indication in the proposal of really honourable patronage, which might have been helpful to authors whose writings, though excellent, were not of a kind to be very popular. It was, however, a rare proposal, counter-balanced by the too frequent occurrence of writers like James Ralph, whose careers illustrate the evil of political patronage. This man was at one time put to edit *The Remembrancer*, a party organ, for which the money was found by Dodington and others. It was sufficiently bad for a writer of his talent to sell himself to any party, but he was " ready to be hired to any cause —and actually put himself up to auction between the Bedfords and the Pelhams, and after several biddings was bought by the Pelhams." That was the evil of reliance on political patrons by men of weak principle.

THE fall of Walpole in 1742 broke up the existing opposition. The Whigs who had rebelled against the Premier's personal dictatorship had gained all they desired, and were mostly willing to join the succeeding Whig Government headed by Pelham, Newcastle, and Pitt. The Prince's opposition, having been mainly against his father, survived the change of minister, yet with diminished strength, and what was better, a cessation of the demand for political service from Thomson. The Tories were still out of the running, with their prospects in no way improved by the second Jacobite rising of 1745. Political patronage, therefore, dwindled once more. Almost the only

[1] Nichols, *Literary Anecdotes*, v. 39.

literary man to receive a government pension was the persistent Guthrie, who was one of the first to claim the title of " an author by profession."[1] He was a good but undistinguished writer, who wrote innumerable histories for the booksellers to which he never troubled to put his name, who had written the Parliamentary debates in *The Gentleman's Magazine* before Johnson, and had been in Walpole's service. From the Pelham Government he obtained in 1745 a pension of £200.

His is the only name that stands out. Ralph, in his *Case of Authors by Profession or Trade*, published in 1756, when discussing the several kinds of writing open to an author who had to earn his bread, stated : " I do not make Ministerial Service a Province ; because Service of that kind is at present rarely called for. . . . And when they do condescend to employ the Pen, they either take the first that comes to hand out of the public Offices, or else have Recourse to the Colleges : in which latter Case, the Church furnishes the Reward ; and in the former the State."[2] That was the position of affairs from the fall of Walpole until the death of George II in 1760 led to the reawakening of the fiercest political strife of the century. Reviewing the existing state of polite learning on the eve of that new impulse, Goldsmith lamented that " since the days of a certain Prime Minister of inglorious memory, the learned have been kept pretty much at a distance." He, however, would have been one of the last to accept such patronage on the only terms at which it could in those days have been purchased.

[1] I. D'Israeli, *Calamities of Authors*, i. 5.   [2] *Case*, p. 20.

(vi)

MEANWHILE, social patronage in the sense of patronage by a wealthy and influential man out of his own pocket, not out of the State Treasury, had been steadily declining. We have seen from the lives of Young, Gay, Savage, and Thomson that it was by no means passed away or unnecessary in 1726, and a more detailed examination shows it to have been still widespread and beneficial for some years after. At Court the tradition of patronage had always been weak, and in 1736 Pope complained that poetry was simply discouraged there. George I had been succeeded by George II, and " still Dunce the second reigned like Dunce the first." " Among his many kingly virtues George II could not enumerate the patronage of science and the love of Virtú. Poetry, painting, sculpture, and all the imitative arts were neither understood nor encouraged by him. When Hogarth presented him with his admirable picture of the March on Finchley, he thought the painter well rewarded with a guinea." Beyond commanding performances at the theatres, he showed little interest in the artistic world, and even on the stage he could not appreciate Garrick. " In truth," said Horace Walpole, " I believe King George would have preferred a guinea to a composition as perfect as *Alexander's Feast*."[1] The king's remark to Lord Hervey is expressive : " You ought not to write verses ; 'tis beneath your rank ; leave such work to little Mr. Pope, it is his trade." His attitude, however, was of little moment ; the royal family were then

[1] *Memoirs of the Reign of King George II*, iii. 304.

in something of a social backwater; moreover, the activities of Queen Caroline for some years made compensation.

QUEEN CAROLINE, from the accession of her husband to the throne in 1727 till her death in 1737, was the most popular member of the royal family, the support of Walpole, hated by the Tories, and loved by many men of letters. Her leanings were predominantly philosophical and theological, and a sign of her taste was her correspondence with Leibnitz. From the time she became Queen she generously assisted the Arian Whiston with a pension of £50 a year, and the old man did not flatter her by saying that her people " justly esteemed her, as a Lady of great abilities, a Patron of Learned Men and a kind Friend to the Poor."[1] She interested herself in Dr. Courayer, a French Catholic who had written in defence of English ordinations and had been compelled, in consequence, to seek refuge in England; he had already been granted a pension of £100, but the Queen doubled it. Over Church patronage she exercised a great and useful influence, notably in the lives of Butler, Berkeley, Sherlock, Hoadly, and Secker; " she endeavoured to draw the saintly Wilson from his obscure diocese in the Isle of Man to a more prominent and lucrative position, but he declined." There was some talk of her having Warburton as a director of her theological studies, which would probably have borne fruit had she not died shortly after.

AMONG more purely literary men whom she patronized were Savage and Stephen Duck. The former first came to her notice through the Coun-

[1] Nichols, *Literary Anecdotes*, i. 304, note.

tess of Hertford, when he was lying in prison under sentence of death, and it was through her efforts that the reprieve was granted. Then in 1732 she made him her Laureate, with a salary of £50 a year, for which he was to compose birthday odes, no very arduous task. Stephen Duck was a local celebrity whose verses in a Wiltshire village had finally come to the Queen's hearing, and she sent a manuscript copy of them to Pope for his opinion. That being favourable (Pope judging by character instead of poetry), Duck became the favourite poet of the Court, had £30 a year, and was in 1735 appointed Keeper of the Queen's Library at Richmond.

THUS she assisted many deserving cases from her private means, and kept alive a worthy tradition in a Court otherwise little known for its recognition of letters. That her patronage was not very powerful was shown by her inability to obtain more for Gay than the offer of the post of gentleman-usher; it was rather in a small and unostentatious way that her good work was done. Neither was she able to set a fashion, for Handel's music made no headway for years, in spite of the support of King and Queen. A story is told of Chesterfield leaving the poorly-filled theatre in which one of Handel's oratorios was being sung before the King, and giving as his reason that he did not wish to intrude on the privacy of his sovereign. In fact the taste of the Court was not of any influence on that of society in the reign of George II, and the absence of literary patronage there gave little if any impetus to its decline in the outer social world. The Queen merely held out prospects for a space to such authors as were in holy

orders; at her death, says Lecky, " Church patronage, like all other patronage, degenerated into a mere matter of party or personal interest."
THERE was in the years centring round 1730 as yet none of that intangible barrier between the great and men of letters which existed later. If a writer of 1770 was admitted into the highest society, he was conscious that he was in rather than of that society; but in 1730, and even more so earlier, there was an intimate familiarity of intercourse. While Gay, Pope, Swift, and Arbuthnot on the one hand, and Burlington, Oxford, Peterborough, Chandos, and the Queensberrys on the other, were still actively prominent in society, the mingling of literature and society was sure to continue. In such conditions patronage was seen at its best, disinterested, generous, and accompanied by sincere friendship. One of the oldest of these patrons was the gifted and eccentric Earl of Peterborough, a survivor of the wars and policies of the reigns of William III and Queen Anne. He had a genuine respect for men of letters, was glad to seek their acquaintance, and was at home in the company of them all, from Pope at the top down to such lesser lights as the notorious novelist Mrs. Manley. Dryden spoke of him gratefully, and his relation with Pope is pleasantly indicated in a letter of the latter to Aaron Hill in 1731, where he says: " I this day have writ to Lord Peterborough a letter with your poem. The familiarity in which we have lived some years makes it not unusual, either in him or me, to tell each other anything that pleases us."[1] Hill, indeed, had been known

[1] *Works*, x. 23.

to Peterborough some twenty years earlier through the composition of his *Camillius* as a vindication of Peterborough's conduct in Spain. That nobleman was so pleased with it, that he sought out the author, and appointed him his secretary. Similarly he had befriended Berkeley in 1713, taking him to Italy as his chaplain upon Swift's recommendation. After his severance from public life he was far from rich, but continued to do such kindnesses as were in his power.

THE Duke of Chandos was another great patron, of whom Gay said that " his daily pleasure is in doing good," and Pope that " gracious Chandos is beloved at sight." His palatial home, ridiculed inexcusably by Pope, had led his patronage to architects, and the splendid chapel was placed at the service of Handel, while literature profited constantly at his hands by such benefactions as his contribution of £200 towards the publication of Hudson's *Josephus*. Pope's friend, the second Lord Oxford, " preferred to surround himself with the more distinguished poets and men of letters of the day," since " habitual indolence rather than incapacity prevented him from taking a prominent place in public affairs." He made considerable additions to his father's library, gave men like Joseph Ames and Samuel Palmer free access to it for their antiquarian research, helped Oldys in compiling his *Life of Raleigh*, promising him £200 a year as his secretary, was a great benefactor to Vertue the engraver and Zachary Grey the editor of *Hudibras*, and was a manager of the Society for the Encouragement of Learning. Maittaire, too, the critical scholar, was helped by his patronage, and rescued from notoriety by the deletion of his name from the *Dunciad*, in whose manuscript Oxford had found it. Lord Cartaret, as Lord-Lieutenant of Ireland, is known to have given occasional, unimportant pieces of preferment to Swift's friends, and had in England the reputation of being a generous patron. The fourth Lord Orrery, who died in 1731, is immortalized for his scientific leanings by the naming after him of the orrery, an astronomical instrument, and his memory as a literary patron lives by his magnificent gift to Theobald of an Egyptian pebble snuff-box minted on gold, with a £100 note enclosed, as a present in acknowledgment of the dedication to him of an alteration of *Richard II* in 1720. His son, probably impelled by paternal disparagement of his tastes, implied by his father's leaving his library to Christ Church, kept up the tradition, was an intimate friend of Pope and Swift, and, says Johnson, whom he later attempted to patronize, " would have been a liberal patron if he had been rich."

AGAIN, there was Boulter, Archbishop of Armagh, who had won his promotion by able service to the Government in 1718, when he and Ambrose Philips had written a paper called *The Freethinker*, and who did not neglect Philips, but appointed him in 1726 secretary to the Lord Chancellor and in 1733 Registrar of the Prerogative Court, to the disgust of Pope, who had not forgiven the poet's rival *Pastorals* of 1709. Nor should we forget the Earl of Granville, who was so impressed by the sad case of Cleland, summoned before the Privy Council for his indecent work written to get bread, that " he nobly rescued him from the like temptation by getting him a pension of £100 a year." The Earl of Pembroke, too, exemplified the continuance of patronage in its best form, when he, " with his usual generosity," employed Psalmanaazaar to finish Palmer's *History of Printing*, defraying all expenses, and gave the edition to Palmer's widow " not without some farther tokens of his generosity." Such scattered names are evidence how patronage continued to flourish among private individuals, mostly out of their personal means, during Pope's generation.

(vii)

THIS period, also, gave rise to a very notable departure in patronage. For the first time there was a man of letters, himself a powerful patron. Pope, mingling with his aristocratic friends, could and did bring to their notice deserving cases, and that writers appreciated the fact was shown by the court they paid him. He was possessed of a very moderate income, so that his assistance had generally to be in the way of influence, although Johnson tells us that he managed by his frugal living to put aside £100 a year for charitable purposes. The ill-fated Savage, who had supplied him with first-hand material for the *Dunciad*, was one of the more important writers whom he occasionally aided. The reckless nature of the man would hardly allow of anyone doing much for him, but Pope seems to have been steadily his friend, to have earnestly attempted to affect a reconciliation with his former patron Lord Tyrconnel, and in the last resort to have contributed twenty guineas towards a yearly subscription for him. For Fenton, his collaborator in *Homer*, he secured the post of tutor to the son of Sir William Trumbal, whose widow later provided for that minor poet for life by making him the auditor of her accounts. Duck he established in the Queen's favour, and had " the condescension and humility frequently to call on at Richmond." Harte, author of an *Essay on Reason*, he supported for the professorship of Poetry at Oxford; and he canvassed for subscriptions to enable the old father of the Wesleys to publish a commentary on *Job* in 1730. Such were instances of the kindly helping hand which he was always ready to hold out where he was satisfied of desert and untroubled by envy. His influence in the dramatic world was shown by his persuasion of Rich, the manager of Drury Lane, to produce Dodsley's *Toy Shop* in 1734, and is indicated in a note to Mallet in 1729 about the latter's *Eurydice*, of which he says: " I have but yesterday been able to have the Lord Chamberlain spoken to by Lord Burlington. Your play is delivered into my Lady Burlington's hands to give to the Duke."[1] Dodsley, too, had gained his interest by his *Muse in Livery* published in 1732, when its author was still a footman to the Hon. Mrs. Lowther, and by her and other great ladies encouraged to exercise his undoubted talent; then Pope lent him £100, which enabled him to set up in 1735 that bookseller's shop in Pall Mall for which he is chiefly remembered to-day. The greatest author on whose behalf he exercised his influence was Samuel Johnson, for whom he and his friend Lord Gower tried to obtain an M.A. degree of

[1] *Works*, x. 81.

Dublin in 1738, although Pope knew no more of him than his *London*.

BUT the writer for whom his influence did most was Warburton, whose life affords an interesting link between the literary monarchies of Pope and Johnson. It was Warburton who rescued Pope from the clamant theologians who were on the track of those unfortunate non-Christian doctrines implied in the *Essay on Man*, into which Pope had been drawn by the Puckish Bolingbroke without perceiving whither he was tending. De Crousaz, in particular, had assailed the poet, and the latter was intensely grateful to the unsought aid of Warburton in extricating him. Warburton " thought M. de Crousaz maliciously mistaken, and considered it of service to Religion, to show our Libertines that his noble genius was not of their party." As a result Warburton became an intimate friend of Pope, and therefore known to such of Pope's circle as Ralph Allen, Murray, and Chesterfield. This introduction was the making of his career. He married Allen's favourite niece, was brought into prominence as a preacher by Murray, when Solicitor-General, and finally became Dean of Bristol and Bishop of Gloucester on the nomination of Pitt, who was probably guided in his choice by the representations of Allen, who was politically powerful in the neighbourhood of Bath.

THEN we find Warburton himself carrying on this line of patronage by his support of Hurd, who seems to have won his notice in the usual way by lavish flattery. Hurd first praised Warburton as a critic, next judiciously dedicated a text of *Horace* to him, completed his conquest by literary assistance in disputes with Jortin and Hume, and was at length rewarded with the Bishopric of Lichfield in 1774. Such was the progress of a writer whose literary merits, contained almost wholly in the *Letters on Chivalry and Romance*, would of themselves never have carried him far. Consistent flattery and useful service he found the only avenues to advancement.

BUT to return to Pope the patron of Warburton, we see exemplified in his patronage the half-way stage between the patronage of individuals and that of the public. Dryden did not have the power to help others as Pope did, and Johnson and Goldsmith had neither the power nor the need. Pope's powerful friendships enabled him to gain the necessary influence to advance writers, but to Johnson those friendships were not open with the same intimacy, and the many poor hacks whom he assisted owed what help he gave them to his private means while they were trying to make a successful appeal to the public. The influence of Pope was useful with men of wealth and position, that of Johnson with the booksellers, to induce them to buy a manuscript or employ a writer.

(viii)

THERE had long been a minor form of patronage, which, also, had been disinterested at the beginning, but which by 1730 had sunk very low indeed. It was that of payment in return for dedications,[1] a practice which had flourished in the seventeenth century as a forerunner of publication

---
[1] See H. B. Wheatley, *The Dedication of Books to Patron and Friend*.

by subscription. A writer in those days canvassed with his dedications, as he or his booksellers did later for subscriptions, no less than fifty dedications being sometimes necessary to cover the expenses of publishing. Gradually there had evolved a rate of exchange for these prefatory laudations, and in the time of Queen Anne it was usual to give an author from five to ten guineas for the dedication of a play; under George I this donation increased to twenty guineas; and during the reign of George II it went the way of all patronage, the least to be mourned. Although there was an average rate, the largess naturally varied according to the estimation in which the writer was held, and some poor wretches are said to have undergone for a paltry sum the humiliation of having to put their names to pieces of flattery penned by the patron himself. Thomson received twenty guineas for the dedication of *Winter* to Sir Spencer Compton in 1724; Savage in 1724 had a gift of ten guineas from a certain H. Tryst, Esq., of Hereford, for the dedication of *Sir Thomas Overbury*; Theobald was given a benefit night at Drury Lane for the dedication to Rich, the manager, of his pamphlet *Shakespeare Restored*. Royal dedications, too, were worthily recompensed, as we see by the £300 which George I gave Eachard in respect of his *History of England*, and the hundred guineas presented to Hickes for the dedication of his *Thesaurus* by George II while Prince of Wales.

THERE were always good exceptions to the profanation of this custom, and they continued for a long time. Of such was the dedication by Borlase of his *Antiquities of Cornwall* in 1754 to Sir

John Aubyn, who in return bore the cost of that expensive publication. But the exceptions were swamped by the multitude of scribblers who dedicated without restraint, a tribe fostered by the unwise generosity of the Halifaxes who would let no dedication go unrewarded. While Swift and Pope were leading the way back to disinterested and honourable dedications, these others were degrading the practice until it nauseated. It was not necessary for those men to know the person to whom they dedicated a work, and it was not an infrequent occurrence for the meaner kind of writer to hawk about his dedications for the highest bidder, and only compile a trashy volume when he had secured a sufficiently profitable dedicatee. Thomas Gordon (d. 1750) was satirizing, but hardly exaggerating what often happened, when he wrote : " I have known an author praise an Earl, for twenty pages together, though he knew nothing of him, but that he had money to spare. He made him wise, just, and religious for no reason in the world, but in hopes to find him charitable ; and gave him a most bountiful heart, because he himself had an empty stomach."[1]

As the middle of the century approached, the vogue of dedications for money passed away, one of the latest prominent examples being that of Hoadly's *Suspicious Husband* to George II, who acknowledged it with the gift of £100. The attitude in 1736 was summed up by Fielding thus : "Asking leave to dedicate is asking whether you will pay for your dedication, and in that sense, I believe, is understood by both

[1] Anonymous, *Dedication to a Great Man concerning Dedications.*

authors and patrons."[1] Fielding also gave the view of dedication, that "a patron is a kind of god-father to a book—and if he give a present also, what doth he more than a god-father?" If it could have been purely so, dedications for money might have stayed a while to tide over the slow growth of the public to support writers, but, as Wheatley justly says, "in course of time the evil of bought dedications worked its own cure, for the practice sank so low in public estimation that it went out of fashion, and may be said to have almost gone out of existence."[2] Fielding in 1736 dedicated the *Historical Register* (in which the above quotations occur) to the public, thus showing signs of the change. Foote in 1753 ridiculed dedications to the great by inscribing his *Englishman in Paris* to Vaillant, the bookseller, because he held himself obliged to him "for the correctness of the press and the beauty of the type, and the goodness of the paper." Goldsmith dedicated *The Traveller* to his brother in 1764; and while Johnson wrote many dedications for others, "the loftiness of his mind prevented him from ever dedicating in his own person." So another of the stains of servility faded out of the texture of the literary profession. As late as 1817 Peacock felt justified in satirizing "virtue-spyers" who survived, but at any rate there was no open and avowed rate of exchange by which flattery could be turned into cash. By 1780 dedications had become merely a graceful and expected introduction to a work. "The known

---

[1] Cf. Fielding's *Pasquin*: "Fustian: 'A dedication is generally a bill drawn for value therein contained; which value is a set of nauseous fulsome compliments which my soul abhors. . . .' Sneerwell: 'Yes, faith, a dedication without flattery will be worth the seeing.'"
[2] Wheatley, *Dedication of Books*, p. 47.

style of dedication is flattery," said Johnson ; " it professes to flatter."

(ix)

THE last lingering years of patronage gave welcome protection to many writers, and left free for better work the talents of authors who might have otherwise been condemned to the drudgery of transient hack-work, starving in a cellar, pining in a spunging-house, or driven in misery " to flourish o'er a cup of gin." It would have been a grievous age for literature if social patronage had declined with the suddenness and completeness of its political counterpart. Although Thomson regretted his dependence, he would have been helpless without it ; the failure of his *Liberty* showed how insecure was his hold on the favour of the small public, and the loss of his government pension made him very grateful to Lyttelton for opening the purse of the Prince's bounty. It is always unprofitable to consider what might have been, but it helps us to value the existence of patronage if we consider what might have been the lot of Thomson and Mallet without their pensions from the Opposition, and how much poorer their contribution to lasting literature. It is pleasant to reflect how much the munificence of a man like Benson meant to such minor writers as Christopher Pitt and Dobson, of whom the latter at one time received £1,000 for translating *Paradise Lost* into Latin verse for that Milton-worshipper, his patron. The difficulties of many small authors must have been alleviated in those days by great folk like the Duke of Dorset, whom Johnson was able to call

" a universal patron," and there was probably more than one Cleland relieved by the kindness of a patron from the wretched necessity of writing indecent novels. Between 1720 and 1750 these scattered patrons seemed to continue, like lowborn Allen, " to do good by stealth."

ALLEN, too, was among those who helped Fielding to keep his head above the kennels of Grub Street, before, as novelist and magistrate, he was comparatively secure. But while he plied the public twice or thrice a year with his generally profligate and rather second-rate plays, he was only sustained by the " princely benefactions " of the Duke of Bedford, which he gratefully acknowledged in the preface of *Tom Jones*. Nichols, probably with some exaggeration, tells us that the " pecuniary disappointments from the drama which Mr. Fielding met, were nobly alleviated by the patronage of the late Duke of Richmond, the Duke of Bedford, the Duke of Argyll, the Duke of Roxburgh and Lord Lyttelton."[1] Allen, we know, once sent him a present of £200 as a tribute to his genius, even before he had made his acquaintance. And it is difficult to conceive Fielding's position in those days without such patronage, for even so, working at dramatic writing, then the most profitable sphere for an author, he was in constant distress, gladly accepting loans from his bookseller, Millar, and with his best clothes as often as not in pawn. Before he turned to the novel, he could not command a large enough public to support him, and the only alternative to the acceptance of patronage was a life like Johnson's. It was not a

[1] *Literary Anecdotes*, iii. 365.

pleasant alternative, and dependence on the great seems certainly preferable. As Johnson said, "You may be prudently attached to great men, and yet independent." Fielding was independent, inasmuch as his life had no trace of subserviency, and his acknowledgment of Bedford's gifts and his praise of Dodington as "Mæcenas, thou in no Augustan age," do not speak in the language of the paid flatterer, for his half-brother also bore witness years later to the Duke's "princely generosity,"[1] and Dodington was an excellent patron whose memory has been too much depreciated because of his politics and ostentation.

PATRONAGE was, in fact, a serviceable shelter of which the weaker brethren might take advantage without being ashamed. Not everyone who possessed a talent for authorship could create a public like Pope's, or endure the hardships braved by Johnson, whose strength could battle through and keep his genius unimpaired. These others were, therefore, justified in enlisting under the banners of patronage as tutors or otherwise, and many in those days found their first support as tutors in the families of the great. Mallet began his literary career as tutor to the sons of the Duke of Montrose, and Thomson as tutor to the son of Lord Binning, and afterwards to the son of Lord Talbot. Such a position removed from patronage any of the savour of charity, introduced an author to people of importance, and gave him ample leisure to cultivate his literary talent. Among the smaller men who found this the path to success was William Whitehead, successively

[1] Probably in reference to the Duke's gift of a house in Bow Street to Fielding when he was magistrate.

tutor to the sons of Lord Jersey and Lord Harcourt, throughout his life more or less dependent on his social superiors, but yet without any of those degrading accompaniments consequent on the political patronage of a Lord Sandwich, for which an author must—

" indulge his patron's hate and spleen,
And stab the fame of those he ne'er had seen."

Whitehead pleasantly travelling with and guiding the studies of these young men, and meantime gently working his own mild Muse, reached the " two genteel patent places usually united " of Secretary and Registrar of the Order of the Bath, and in 1757 succeeded Cibber as Laureate.[1]

SUCH were the advantages, such the condition of patronage at its best in the second quarter of the century. It was not till 1730 that the public began to expand, stimulated to a demand and liking for literature by the new magazines, and the demand was slow in having an effect on the position of the writer. The time was not come of which it could be said that writers were able to turn from patrons to the public; they might only turn from patrons to booksellers, from men whose support often was helpful and disinterested to men whose support could only be oppressive and uncertain, varying with the fluctuations in the market of literary commerce. Patronage enabled Thomson to produce *The Castle of Indolence*, while want of it left Johnson writing Parliamentary debates, and odd scraps of popular learning on Roman newspapers and similar topics. Johnson, it is true, so far overcame the pressure of hack-work

[1] See E. K. Broadus, *The Laureateship*.

as to compose *London* and *The Vanity of Human Wishes*, but Thomson was also enabled in comfortable leisure to complete his laborious, careful, and excellent revision of *The Seasons*. Again it is profitless to consider what might have been Thomson's literary output in Johnson's position, and whether it would have maintained the same excellence; we can only look at what patronage did do for him, and admit that it was almost wholly good.

FURTHER, patronage meant not only maintenance without the full severity of the struggle, in Grub Street, but also the possibility of helpful influence in bringing a writer forward to the notice of such public as there was. A man like Joseph Spence, the friend of a wide aristocratic and literary circle, with a genuine love of literature and active desire to bring forward deserving but neglected writers, could do much in those days by canvassing in their behalf among his acquaintance. They are little figures, viewed against a Halifax or a Bedford, but not the less patrons in their small way, because they exercised their influence, not their money, to help writers who had no claim on them but merit. Such another was the philanthropic and untiring General Oglethorpe, in whom Boswell praises the " kind and effectual support which he gave to Johnson's *London*, though unacquainted with its author." Patrons had considerable influence, also, on the acceptance or rejection of manuscript by theatrical managers, and on the vagaries in the use of the Lord Chamberlain's licensing functions. Pope, we have seen, intervened for Dodsley's *Toy Shop* and Mallet's *Eurydice*; and the value of this influence is indicated significantly by Boswell's dictum on *Irene*, that "Fleetwood would not accept it, probably because it was not patronized by some man of high rank." Theatrical managers were throughout the century markedly cautious, and patrons alone could sometimes persuade them.

(x)

FROM about 1750 patronage and individual patrons began to be assailed from all sides, and the tradition, once so universal and so highly esteemed, dwindled because of a change in the conditions of the literary calling, and in face of the volume of abuse and contempt drawn upon it by the preponderance of the decadent and unworthy patrons of the day ceased to be any longer openly cherished. And coincident with these forces was a lowering of the appreciation of authorship among the upper classes. Wits were no longer found mingling intimately with the aristocracy, because wit was no longer considered an equivalent of wealth. There was a renaissance of the spirit that authorship was a mean pursuit if followed for money, and although the new race of gentlemen authors generally took money from the booksellers for what they wrote, they would not have it thought that they treated literature seriously, or had profit at all in view. "You know," wrote Horace Walpole, "how I shun authors, and would never have been one myself, if it obliged me to keep such bad company. They are always in earnest, and think their profession serious, and dwell upon trifles, and reverence learning. I laugh at all those things, and write only to laugh at them, and divert myself."[1]

THAT was the attitude in the highest society of the middle of the century, in the days of that second "mob of gentlemen that wrote at ease," Walpole, Chesterfield, Pulteney, and Lovibond, who proclaimed their writings to be "the most hasty trifles in the world." Such men could not fail to appreciate literature themselves, but even their judgment seems to have been strangely warped. "What a library of poetry, taste, good sense, veracity, and vivacity!" exclaimed Horace Walpole, "ungrateful Shebbear! indolent Smollett! trifling Johnson! piddling Goldsmith! how little have they contributed to the glory of a period in which all arts, all sciences are encouraged and rewarded."[2] Nor was Horry alone in his estimate. Possibly those who had known the giant Pope were prejudiced against his successors, diminishing the greatness of the present by dwelling on the splendour of the past; but if they decried the new literature out of love of the old, the tendency of society as a whole seems to have been to neglect literature indiscriminately, being too much occupied in politics or industry. Hume was always exalting Parisian society over the "barbarians who inhabit the banks of the Thames,"[3] asserting that "letters are held there in no honour." Burke, too, wrote to a friend in Ireland about 1750: "I don't think there is as much respect paid to a man of letters this side the water as you imagine. I don't find that Genius, 'the rathe primrose, which forsaken dies,' is patronized by any of the nobility."[4]

[1] *Letters*, viii. 268. [2] *Letters*, viii. 184. [3] Burton's *Hume*, p. 196.
[4] Forster's *Goldsmith*, i. 89.

It was to an outer public that the love of letters was beginning to spread, and the class which had before supported literature was no longer distinguished for its literary taste. Emblematic of the orientation of literature and the rise of an *esprit de corps* among authors and artists was the foundation of the Literary Club. If we compare that assembly of writers, painters, and politicians with its prototype the Kit-Cat Club at its height in the early years of the century, we see in what direction literature was tending. It was disentangling itself from peers and dependence, passing towards the middle class and independence.

MEANWHILE the growth of the public began to create a demand for writers, in place of booksellers having to try to create a public for the writers who flocked round them. The effect was most considerable on the best authors, who could henceforth reasonably rely on supporting themselves by their pens alone. Hume reaped £3,400 for his *History*, Smollett £2,000 for his, Johnson lived till 1762 on his earnings, and Churchill was by his poems "raised to an affluent lot." Apart from any other considerations, this was a state of things sufficient in itself to put an end to patronage. The earlier attitude had been, that it was the duty of ministers and rich men to patronize authors, because great literature was a national credit, a glory to be admired and cherished, and because authors could not devote themselves to their calling and give of their best, unless they were placed in favourable circumstances. Towards 1760 there had come to be little point in such an argument. Rather might people of the upper class declare that writers could very well support themselves, if they would. Why should they have any more claim to patronage than barristers, since the prospects of the literary calling were now quite as good? Doubtless there were many who said that patronage only encouraged a naturally idle class to remain idle. If authors would only work at authorship, the superior man of wealth would declare, they could live very tolerably indeed, and when authors, quite as ready to cast off such patrons as the patrons were to cast off them, did start to earn a living by their pens, the late patronizing class turned round and banned authorship as " low," till the condemnation went in widening circles through the sea of genteel snobbery. Horace Walpole expressed his surprise in 1761 that so sensible a man as young Mr. Burke should not have " worn off his authorism yet—and thinks there is nothing so charming as writers, and to be one—he will know better one of these days."[1] In fact as their patronage ceased to be necessary, those who composed the world of society began to exclude authors from their circle, if they were not one of themselves. It was as Walpole told Hume : " we think them sufficiently paid if their books sell, and of course leave them to their colleges and obscurity, by which means we are not troubled with their vanity and impertinence. . . . I, who am an author, must own this conduct very sensible ; for in truth we are a most useless tribe."[2] So the old order yielded place to new, and plebeian authors were for the future kept at a distance. Patronage was dead ; " writers of the first talent," said Burke in 1750,

[1] *Letters*, v. 86. [2] *Letters*, vii. 70.

"are left to the capricious patronage of the public." Eminent authors were still honoured by the great, but it was the honour graciously given by superiors, not that which sought to lose itself in equality. Thus Johnson, we are told, on his tour in Scotland in 1773 received courteous attention from the Duke of Northumberland, the Duke and Duchess of Argyll, and the Duke and Duchess of Devonshire, but it was not the attention which Pope might have received from the Duke of Chandos or Lord Oxford; there was always the indefinable air of restraint inseparable from "courteous attention." Nor would Johnson, or Goldsmith, or their best contemporaries have desired it otherwise; there was nothing to be gained by such mingling with aristocracy, and the great betterment of conditions in the secondary strata of society was creating a congenial sphere for the man of letters, beyond whose bounds he had no need to step.

(xi)

IN addition, the tradition of patronage had been disintegrating fast from abuses native to the whole custom. There were not only despicable patrons, but contemptible writers. Between them their unblushing shame, their meanness and servility, their combination to prostitute the fair name of literature, overwhelmed them in ridicule and condemnation. From all sides came the chorus of denunciation, from Johnson and Goldsmith, Foote and Churchill. Patronage had become a foolish fashion among vulgar, illiberal, and ostentatious people, the fops " whose pride affects a patron's name," and who were pleased to adorn their tables with wits, hanging on in base flattery and expectation of some reward, while the patron himself held " he overpays in condescension," and turned them off when their flattery became tiresome.

SOME deserving writers still paid their court to such men, and crowds of undeserving scribblers besieged the great with poems and dedications, creating the discreditable scenes portrayed in *Roderick Random*. It was no wonder that such a scribbler had soon to say, " I never see a nobleman's door half-opened, that some surly porter or footman does not stand full in the breach,"[1] and " that the nobility were never known to subscribe worse than at present." Such was the abuse of patronage by writers, and it was equalled by that of the patrons. Johnson, in the fifties, told how " there are some whom long depression under supercilious patrons has humbled and crushed," and how " a man infatuated with the promises of greatness, wastes his hours and days in attendance and solicitation " ; he was reminded, he said, of the story of Aurantius, who kept a witty author at his table eight years, and when he saw the writer was in extremity, offered him a small office and hinted the expectation that he should marry a young woman with whom he had been acquainted.[2]

SUCH creatures were held up to scorn by Foote in the character of Sir Thomas Lofty, of whom his flatterers said that he was " the modern Midas, or rather, (as fifty dedications will tell you), the Pollio, the Atticus, the patron of genius, the protector of arts, the paragon of poets, decider

[1] Goldsmith, *The Proceedings of the Club of Authors*. [2] *The Rambler*, No. 163.

of merit, Chief Justice of taste, and sworn appraiser to Apollo and the tuneful Nine"; in the eyes of others, "a rank impostor, the Bufo of an illiberal, mercenary tribe; he has neither genius to create, judgement to distinguish, nor generosity to reward; his wealth has gained him flattery from the indigent, and the haughty insolence of his pretence admiration from the ignorant." So Johnson defined the patron of 1756 as " commonly a wretch who supports with insolence, and is paid with flattery." Churchill, in his *Independence*, contrasted them with the old patrons who " never bilked the poet of his pay"; about the new there was neither money nor honour,

> " They patronize for fashion sake—no more—
> And keep a *bard*, just as they keep a *whore*; . . .
> They promise little, and they give not much,"

and they take heed to keep the bard at arm's length. In his *Author* he again satirized the mean-spirited, servile writers who fawned, like Paul Whitehead, in dependence on the great, and thought they were honoured by the notice of " a mere, mere lord." Johnson, too, in revising his *Vanity of Human Wishes*, changed the ills which assail the scholar's life, by the substitution of " patron " for " garret," as being in those later days more apt.

So was the last age of patrons buried in obloquy, the worthless dishonourers of patronage were ridiculed out of their pretences and ignoble dependents driven to other resources, while the honourable few who continued to help authors did so privately, reverting to the basis of helpful friendship. " We have done with patronage," said Johnson in 1773. And Foote in his *Author* of 1757 had been equally emphatic. " Where," cried one character, " are the Oxfords, the Halifaxes,—the great protectors and patrons of the liberal arts ? " And " Patron ! " replied another : " the word has lost its use. A guinea subscription at the request of a lady, whose chambermaid is acquainted with the author, may now and then be picked up—Protector! Why, I dare believe there's more money laid out upon Islington turnpike, in a month, than upon all the learned men in Great Britain in seven years."[1]

ALONG with these changes in the general conditions of the literary calling there had grown up new leaders of literature, in particular Johnson, who zealously carried out in practice the principle of independence, which had been first realized in the life of Pope, but too early then for the average writer to follow. While Pope was still at the height of his power, Johnson had come to London with a hopeful admiration of Cave's *Gentleman's Magazine*, and a determination to make his own way by wholehearted work in the everyday departments of literature. In 1738 he nearly gave up the struggle and sought to be a schoolmaster or a lawyer, but he won through and could thankfully say at the end, " No man who ever lived by literature, has lived more independently than I have done."[2] He took heed never to be " near enough to great men to court them," and was, if anything, too much inclined to take offence at any signs of would-be patronage on their part, as was pre-eminently shown in his

[1] Act I, scene i.   [2] *Life*, i. 443.

repudiation of Chesterfield. Preferring to live in "poverty, and the pride of literature," rather than approach any for help which he could not earn by his labours, he extorted respect, and achieved notice by his own merit. "No man," said Boswell, "had a higher notion of the dignity of literature than Johnson, or was more determined in maintaining the respect which he justly considered was due to it." In all this he typified the new spirit at its best, and Churchill, asserting "we may be independent if we will," and Goldsmith, working for Griffiths and Newbery, joined him in their turn.

GOLDSMITH, in fact, was as averse to any manifestations of patronage as Johnson. He had at one time become acquainted with the Earl of Northumberland, and for the amusement of the Countess the ballad of *Edwin and Angelina* had been first printed privately. Shortly after, the Earl, having been appointed Lord-Lieutenant of Ireland, offered to do something for the poet through the powerful interest which the Lord-Lieutenant then had in the disposal of posts on the Irish establishment. Goldsmith, however, declined the offer for himself, suggesting that it would be more helpful to his brother, and telling his friends, "I have no dependence on promises of great men." "Thus," said the pompous and unsympathetic Sir John Hawkins, "did this idiot in the affairs of the world trifle with his fortunes, and put back the hand that was held out to assist him! Other offers of a like kind he either rejected or failed to improve, contenting himself with the patronage of one nobleman, whose mansion offered him the delights of a splendid table, and a retreat for a few days from the metropolis."[1] That nobleman was Lord Clare, and his patronage was of that kind which Johnson and Goldsmith did not reject, for he was hardly a patron, but a friend. His favours were not those of which Goldsmith complained, that "every favour a man receives, in some measure sinks him below his dignity."

BUT of other patronage Johnson or Goldsmith would have none, and sought to spread their ideals of independence by their writings as well as their lives. We have seen Johnson's condemnation of patrons: now let the following sentences from Goldsmith's *Anecdotes of Poets* speak of the state of the literary calling which was being realized in 1760, and of the new ideal; they are typical of the crusade of preaching undertaken by the best writers to declare and maintain the dignity of their profession: "At present, the few poets of England no longer depend on the great for subsistence; they have now no other patrons but the public, and the public, collectively considered, is a good and a generous master. . . . A man of letters at present, whose works are valuable, is perfectly sensible of their value. Every polite member of the community, by buying what he writes, contributes to reward him. The ridicule, therefore, of living in a garret, might have been wit in the last age, but continues such no longer, because no longer true. A writer of real merit now may easily be rich, if his heart be set only on fortune; and for those who have no merit, it is but fit that such should remain in merited obscurity. He may now refuse an invitation to

[1] Forster, *Life of Goldsmith*, i. 380.

dinner, without fearing to incur his patron's displeasure, or to starve by remaining at home. He may now venture to appear in company with just such clothes as other men generally wear, and talk even to princes with all the conscious superiority of wisdom. Though he cannot boast a fortune here, yet he can bravely assert the dignity of independence."

(xii)

BUT in 1760, while patronage was thus at its last gasp, it suddenly had a brief and not unhonourable revival, irradiating from the young King and Lord Bute. In the hands of those two it was generally good, but there had started a year or so earlier a less honourable resumption of political patronage, which mingled with the good and was sometimes confused with it. On the purely political side we note the names of Mallet, Guthrie, Shebbeare, Murphy, and Home. Mallet, " ever ready for a dirty job," was in 1757 " employed to turn the publick vengeance upon Byng, and wrote a letter of accusation under the character of a *Plain Man*. The paper was with great industry circulated and dispersed ; and he, for his seasonable intervention, had a considerable pension bestowed upon him, which he enjoyed till his death."[1] That little incident had been in the time of Newcastle's ministry, and he continued in Bute's ministry (1761-3) to use his pen in political service. Bute, however, required nothing so vile, but was content with the help afforded by Mallet's tragedy of *Elvira*, for which the writer was rewarded in 1763 with the office

[1] *Lives of the Poets*: Mallet.

of Keeper of the Book Entries for ships in the Port of London at £300 a year. Guthrie, who had wrung a pension of £200 from Pelham in 1745, was still sufficiently powerful and unscrupulous to extort its renewal by Bute in 1762, promising to deserve his " Lordship's future patronage and protection, with greater zeal if possible than ever."[1] Shebbeare ceased to libel the Government, probably served Bute, and was granted a pension by Grenville in 1764, that he might " be enabled to pursue that laudable inclination which he has of manifesting his zeal for the service of his Majesty and his Government." Murphy was employed to edit *The Auditor* in opposition to Wilkes's *North Briton*, and was paid with the office of Commissioner of Bankrupts. Home had come to Bute's notice by his persecuted tragedy, *Douglas*, in 1757, was appointed his private secretary, flattered him incessantly, and was spoken of in 1759 as " now entirely at the command of Lord Bute, whose nod made him break every engagement." Bute provided for him with a sinecure, primarily because he wished to secure his services to answer and confound the political pamphlets of opponents, but also because he respected his literary talent, and showed it by strongly backing his second play, *Agis*, to which he " dragged " the Prince of Wales. SUCH was the brief return of political patronage at the beginning of a period of the bitterest party strife. Politics plunged into yet deeper corruption ; the various Whig " gangs," the Bedfords, Grenvilles, and Conways, were shamelessly struggling for office, and buying their way to

---

[1] I. D'Israeli, *Miscellanies of Literature* (1840), p. 52.

power, until " the Paymaster's Office became a regular mart where Parliamentary votes were bought and sold as unblushingly as humble folk bought and sold groceries across a counter." It was no atmosphere for good writers, nor were they wanted nor thought of. " Faction only fills the town with pamphlets and greater subjects are forgotten in the noise of discord." Moreover, in eight years of Lord North's ministry, George III was himself virtually his own minister, controlling the whole body of political patronage, and using it to create a party of his own, who gained the title of " King's friends."

LATER instances of patronized writers are few. Kelly had a pension from North for his articles in *The Public Ledger* ; Macpherson was employed to combat Junius under the signatures of Musæus and Scævola, and was specially made use of about 1776 to support the Government's American policy ; " the Ossianite," said Walpole, " had a pension of £600 a year from the Court to supervise the newspapers, and he inserted what lies he pleased, and prevented whatever he disapproved of being printed." There were also the venomous and servile mercenaries like Parson Scott, who were hired by the Sandwiches to bespatter their adversaries, but of them it is needless to take account. Nor is any general tendency betrayed by the pension which North's secretary, Brummel, obtained for his literary friend Richard Tickell in 1781 for writing a play in support of the ministry. These belated examples of patronage were very occasional exceptions to the average prospects of a writer, and for the most part were happy products of personal friendship. The only great author who received help for political reasons was Gibbon, who had supplied Lord Weymouth with a Memoir Justicatif for use as a State document in reply to a French manifesto. So he was made a Lord Commissioner of Trades and Plantations at some £700 a year, until the rhetoric of Burke and the vote of the Commons destroyed that "perpetual virtual adjournment and unbroken sitting vacation," of which he said, "I enjoyed many days and weeks of repose, without being called away from my library to the office." There were not many such places in those days, and they became fewer and fewer, "strangely reduced by our modern reformers," as Gibbon told Robertson after his own reduction.

BUT though George III gathered into his own hands the reins of patronage in order to further his intention to "be a King," he was not so completely absorbed in politics as to be undesirous or incapable of patronizing writers, and of doing so disinterestedly. Boswell, in a eulogy on the King's education, taste, and beneficence, declared that "his accession to the throne of these Kingdoms, opened a new and brighter prospect to men of literary merit."[1] Much was undoubtedly due to the influence of Lord Bute, who had been the young Prince's guide and confidant in the years preceding his accession, and who succeeded Pitt as chief minister shortly after it.

MOST notable among the recipients of this new patronage was Johnson, and his acceptance of it was the most complete confirmation of its honourable character. The Doctor's enemies might make their taunting comparisons of the He-bear and

---

[1] *Life*, i. 372.

the She-bear, but there was no excuse for doubting that it " was granted solely as the reward of his literary merit, without any stipulation whatever, or even tacit understanding that he should write for the administration "[1]; in fact he had received it for over seven years before he wrote his political pamphlets, which, when they did come, were perfectly consonant with his own opinions. The grant reflects honour on Lord Loughborough for suggesting it, on Lord Bute for pressing it forward, and on the King for his ready acceptance. Johnson's expression was : " I must have recourse to the French. I am *pénétré* with his Majesty's goodness."[2]

NOT less pleasant was the attention paid by George III to Robertson and Hume. The former came immediately to his notice by his *History of Scotland*, and was appointed a Chaplain in Ordinary. Lord Cathcart was deputed to tell Robertson that, if he would come to London and undertake a *History of England*, he should have an establishment and every means of study. The historian intimated that he preferred to live in Scotland and did not wish to encroach on Hume's work, so that this proposal dropped; but Robertson received another mark of royal favour by the gift in 1764 of the office of Historiographer-Royal for Scotland at £200 a year, especially revived in his favour. Hume, after his last tenure of office in 1768 as Under-Secretary for Scotland, had his pension doubled at the desire of the King, who was so far interested as to express a wish to see the history continued; but Hume did not see his way to do so.

[1] *Life*, i. 373.   [2] *Ibid.*, i. 375.

GEORGE III was, in fact, by no means so wanting in taste as it has been too customary to infer from his remark on Shakespeare's " stuff." His kindly and courteous audience with Johnson, of which the Doctor spoke with such pleasure, showed that he esteemed men of letters more highly than did his grandfather, George II, and his appreciation of the arts, though not the most enlightened, inspired his patronage of the Royal Academy at its foundation in 1768, giving it a strong impetus on the way to success. It is probable that the pension of £100 given to the historian Henry in 1781 on Lord Mansfield's recommendation was granted as a result of the King's approval, and that Blair's pension of £200 settled the year before was similarly due to him. There is no doubt of his interest in Beattie, the poet of *The Minstrel*, on whom he conferred a grant of £200 a year in 1773 in recognition of his *Essay on Truth*, which was then considered a most able refutation of the materialistic doctrines of Hume and others. At a pleasant interview, forming no unworthy second to that with Johnson, the King is said to have chatted with Beattie for some time on the state of moral philosophy, telling him that " he could hardly believe that any thinking man could really be an atheist, unless he could bring himself to believe that he made himself."[1] From which instances it is clear that, however mediocre his intellect was, and however deplorably he " aired himself in the character which Bolingbroke had invented of the ' Patriot King,' " George III respected men of letters, and did very good service to some who were fortunate

---

[1] A. Dyce, *Memoir of Beattie* (Aldine Edition), p. xlv.

enough to gain his notice, without casting on the patronized any shadow of dependence. Wedderburne said in defence of Johnson's pension, that it was " the resolve of the ministry no longer to restrict the bounty of the Crown by political considerations, provided there was ' distinction in the literary world, and the prospect of approaching distress.' "[1] That statement is confirmed by these examples, and the only name whose omission we lament is that of Goldsmith. Truly his eminence and distress, albeit of his own making, should have reached the royal ear.

BUTE was hated even more than most unpopular ministers in his own day, because he was a Scotchman and a favourite, and his merits have always been obscured by that obloquy. Yet he was well-intentioned, less corrupt in his government than others, and, far from clinging to office, was willing to " retire on bread and water and think it luxury " compared with what he suffered. As a patron of literature he was rivalled by none but the King,[2] using his brief reign to the benefit of several authors. Politically, we have seen, he found use for Mallet and Murphy and Home ; he did Sir Steuart Denham, the Jacobite political economist, a service by securing him a formal pardon ; his passionate interest in botany, his favourite hobby in the Isle of Bute, led him to patronize " Sir " John Hill's *Vegetable System*, and to get that encyclopædist writer the post of royal gardener at Kensington, worth £2,000 a year. Horace Walpole characteristically tells how Richard Bentley carried his play *The Wishes* to Dodington in 1761

---

[1] Forster's *Goldsmith*, ii. 387.
[2] Anderson, in his *Life of Smollett*, said of Bute that he " had, in many instances, been found a generous patron of men of inferior importance and ability " (p. 88).

"with a recommendatory copy of verses, containing more incense to the King, and Lord Bute, than the Magi brought in their portmanteaus to Jerusalem. The idols were propitious. . . . A bank-note of 200*l*. was sent from the *Treasury*, to the author, and the play was ordered to be performed by the summer company."[1] Finally, his patronage of Macpherson is noteworthy. He invited the Scotchman, then doing hackwork for the Edinburgh booksellers, to London in 1762, and bore the expenses of the publication of *Fingal* and *Temora*, by which poems Macpherson thus made about £1,200. Then he used his influence to appoint him secretary to the Governor of West Florida, with the attendant offices of Surveyor-General and President of the Council in that colony. It made Macpherson's fortune, so that when he returned to England in 1766 he kept the salary, and was employed by Lord North.

(xiii)

BY such patronage Bute stands out from his contemporaries. There were only one or two others with some claims to be called patrons, and it is noticeable that they were lawyers or politicians. Social patronage by the upper classes was after 1760, generally speaking, dead. In that year there was an outburst of fashionable applause over *Tristram Shandy*, but it was just a passing tribute to one whose originality happened surpassingly to take their fancy. Warburton hailed Sterne as the "English Rabelais," Lord Rockingham took him in his suite to Windsor, Lord Fauconberg gave him a curacy, Lord Ossory

[1] *Letters*, v. 69.

commanded his portrait by Reynolds, and Lord Bathurst in his old age paid him the courteous deference he had shown Pope. It was a blaze from the ashes of patronage, and soon died. While it lasted, the chorus of abuse in the press testified to the new attitude of writers. Even Goldsmith denounced the " bawdy blockhead," and told him that when he " thus breaks in on the community, he sets his whole fraternity in a roar nor can he escape, even though he fly to the nobility for shelter."

WRITERS who accepted patronage in those days were liable to the attacks of their fellows, even were it as honourably given as Johnson's. An author had to be particularly cautious if he accepted political patronage and still sought the favour of the public. Of such a man Churchill asked in 1763, " What's his reward ? " and replied, " Why, his own fame undone ";[1] and of that a good example was the damnation of Kelly's *Word to the Wise*, because the public had heard that Kelly was in the pay of the Government.

BUT there was little patronage, either political or social, by acceptance of which a writer could run these risks. Lords Loughborough and Mansfield were friendly to writers and served them if they could, and more prominently Lords Shelburne and Thurlow took pleasure in the company of men of letters. Shelburne's house was the centre of the most cultivated and liberal society of the day, where diversity and freedom of thought flourished. Price, the fiery republican polemist, was welcome there, and, according to Boswell, " Johnson was at

[1] *Independence*: Chalmers' *Eng. Poets*, xiv. 373.

a certain period of his life a good deal with the Earl of Shelburne."[1] But the man who owed most to Shelburne was Priestley, whom he pensioned as a literary companion and helped in his scientific researches. As for Thurlow, he too surrounded himself with men of letters and helped some unimportant writers, while he deserves to be remembered for his offer to advance Johnson £500 for his proposed excursion to Italy for the benefit of his health in 1784.

YET what are such few patrons compared with the many and generous patrons of 1730? They only emphasize the fact that patronage had passed away. The aristocracy no longer expected to be looked to as patrons, and were not prepared to act as such. When Macpherson was making £1,200 by two poems, Mickle £1,000 by his translation of the *Lusiad*, Boswell £100 by the copyright of his *Corsica*, Henry £3,300 by his *History*, and Goldsmith £500 by his *History of England*, it could fairly be asked why writers should need patronage. Arthur Young, the political economist, is said to have earned £1,167 by his pen in the year 1770, and other good writers were also making satisfactory incomes. Patrons might well perceive that they were not wanted, and leave writers to themselves. It was true what Goldsmith had said in 1761, that " men who can prudently be content to catch the public, are certain of living without dependence."

So Chatterton's lack of patronage and Crabbe's early difficulties are perfectly explicable. Horace Walpole had no reason to think that Chatterton could not make his way to a living by authorship

[1] *Life*, iv. 191.

without his help, and was, in addition, not prepossessed in his favour by what Gray and Mason had declared to be an attempt to impose on him. The youth, by offering Dodsley for a guinea what he was pleased to call "the oldest dramatic piece extant," doubtless excited that bookseller's suspicion, and he was at the same time stifling any chance patronage by satirizing even those who had before helped him. At his death he had eleven guineas owing from booksellers, which shows that he had every prospect of earning a living and might soon have established himself, if nineteen-twentieths of his composition had not been pride, which took offence even at the offer of a meal from his landlady. Chatterton would not seek patrons, and Crabbe's experience shows that seeking them was not also finding. His intention was not to write for booksellers, but to gain a patron by whose aid he might produce his best. With that design he wrote to Lords North, Shelburne, and Thurlow with a result typical of 1780. North and Shelburne did not reply, and Thurlow sent a cold refusal. Nor was he any more successful in appeals to Lord Rochford, and his position was serious when he implored the assistance of Burke, at length to be heard sympathetically. He was taken to Beaconsfield, his success was established by *The Library*, which was hastened forward by Burke's warm advocacy, and his patron secured him the place of chaplain to the Duke of Rutland, who told him to consider Belvoir Castle his home, until he was better provided for. Thus he had gained the most generous patronage, but from Burke, and there was only one man like that. Thurlow apologized afterwards, and made Crabbe a present of £100; but he had been tested and had failed, and in his person the patronage of 1780 had been found wanting.

(xiv)

PATRONAGE had in 1726 been a necessity; in 1780 one might call it a luxury. A writer might still expect some difficulty at the start, but if he deserved success, he was assured of it in the long run. There was no reason why he should not earn his living independently, as well as those who belonged to other professions; for though only the most favoured could hope for wealth, competence was within the reach of a hard-working writer, content to satisfy the literary appetite of the day. In fact, to be in advance of one's day, an unheeded prophet, a Wordsworth defying the canons of criticism, was the only excuse for failure, and the most justifiable claim to patronage. Yet it must always be the very case where patronage is most unlikely, since the herald of a "fresh perfection" is too often deemed a crank or an impostor, and would demand as patron one of a perception equally above the contemporary mind. For such men the path of literature is seldom made smooth, and their period of probation must be long, where that of the average good writer is short.

To good writers the advantage of patronage was relatively slight, and its absence little felt. It gave Crabbe a quicker appeal to the public, without much intermediate miscellaneous writing, and it gave men like Blair, Tickell, and Beattie the security of an assured modicum which should save them the necessity of writing poor stuff for money, and provide a support against illness. But the public had by 1780 become large enough to make even those risks negligible. The demand for good general literature could absorb all that writers were able to produce, and even if authors did find it necessary to mingle with their best more popular and ephemeral work, there was no harm done. Such lesser literature had its task of feeding the mind and raising the taste of the reading public, and rather than distracting the energies from more arduous composition it afforded an equable relief. If literature was little enriched by Coleridge's political articles, the articles did not deprive it of better things, and in any case it was better that writers should serve the public than depend on patrons. Literature was in a healthy condition, and the free connexion between author and public was the best possible one. " While a man is in equilibrio," said Johnson, " he throws truth among the multitude, and lets them take it as they please : in patronage, he must say what pleases his patron, and it is an equal chance whether that be truth or falsehood " ; nor need he flatter the public, for " the world always lets a man tell what he thinks, his own way." [1]

LASTLY, even the most disinterested patronage had a drawback. The security it gave was liable unconsciously to relax the efforts of a writer, and so to deprive the world of literature which the necessity of earning a living might otherwise have given it. Such an effect of patronage is difficult to estimate, but we can hardly deny it to be real,

[1] Boswell, *Life*, v. 59.

when we consider how Johnson had to be fed by guineas at a time to keep him at work, since he would never write if he had a couple of guineas in his pocket. The absence of patronage in 1780 is, therefore, not to be regretted. It was enervating; it was unbecoming the dignity of the profession of letters; in politics it was open to abuse, and harmed the writer with the public; above all, it was unnecessary. Inequality in the reward of literature there will always be; it is natural and inevitable. In the words of Professor Saintsbury, " There does not appear to be among the numerous fixed laws of the universe any one which regulates the proportion of literary desert to immediate reward, and it is on the whole well that it should be so."

CHAPTER IV

THE GROWTH OF THE PUBLIC[1]

(i) From dependence to independence. (ii) Survey of patronage and its relation to authorship. (iii) Author and bookseller. Copyright up to 1774. Effect of 1744 on public and authors. Position in 1780. (iv) The reading public. Increased by periodical essay, newspapers, magazines, reviews, romances, novels, circulating libraries, education, number-books, and children's books. Women readers and writers. Improvement in morality and taste. Growth after 1750. Lackington. Popular reprints. (v) The play-going public. Prospects of dramatic authorship. Revival of Shakespeare. Position about 1770. (vi) Conclusion.

(i)

THAT section of literary history which begins with Pope, as a brilliant young man of twenty-three, dazzling the town with the precocious perfection of the *Essay on Criticism*, and ends with Johnson, as the old lion of letters, publishing the matured wisdom of the *Lives of the Poets*, was the period of a changing world in the sphere of authorship. In regard to the economics of literature, Johnson was born into one world and died in another. The only age in which the record of patronage was a record of honour was the age of Queen Anne, and, when that age passed away, Johnson was only five years old. While Johnson was growing up, patronage was in its decline, and when he came with Garrick to London, patrons worth the having were hardly to be had, and his pride forbade his seeking them. He had to swim the buffeting channel of the years from the old world to the new, from the world where the fashion of patronage had been honourable, but was so no more, to the world where the public were the patrons, and the booksellers held out the helping hand. Patronage died and the

[1] Section (iv) has appeared previously in *The Review of English Studies*, and is reprinted by permission of the Editor.

public grew, and the publishing world of to-day was born. It was just another of the changes towards our modern England that the eighteenth century, with its inventions and its industrial revolution, made in the old aristocratic order. The years between were very dark, so that even stout-hearted Johnson once looked away with longing eyes to the law and to teaching, and men did well who, like Thomson, found patrons. But as the public rapidly grew each year more numerous, the alliance between author and bookseller became firmer, surer, and wider, and the year 1780 saw authorship as a profession very fairly established. Let us, therefore, first summarize the progress, which we have earlier examined in detail, and then see more fully how it was the public grew up, until, when Johnson died, its demand was above what the booksellers supplied in quantity and authors in quality.

(ii)

PATRONAGE died because the public ousted it, but it was, moreover, undermined by internal disease and a political enemy. It was at its highest, most serviceable, and most honourable in the reign of Queen Anne, in the days of Somers and Halifax, Harley and St. John. Those men and their friends held it a duty and a privilege to help learning and foster genius from the wealth of the State or their own pockets. Ministers and noblemen were the willing protectors of men of letters, veiling patronage in friendship, so that the world of fashion and the world of letters intermingled and were one. Good writers were not so many as to exhaust the resources of patronage, nor so common as to arouse contempt. It was an age that approached the golden mean. Patronage was honourable to him who gave and him who received ; even where patronage was political, writers were more or less free to choose the side of their conviction, and their employment was not base ; Mallet was paid to condone a political murder, but Addison preserved an unspotted page.

THE political enemy of patronage was Sir Robert Walpole, the embodiment of a new system of politics whose destructive effect preceded that of the degrading disease which was to creep over patronage. The year 1714 saw the Hanoverian Succession established, which meant the lapse of Crown influence on the government and, in consequence, greater power on the part of Parliament. The members of the House of Commons used that power not to improve government, but to extort bribes, and since the blow of the Queen's death had stunned Toryism for more than a generation, bribery was a simple, unchallenged, and effective control of Whig placemen by Whig ministers. The places and pensions previously bestowed on men of letters had in future to buy votes and boroughs. Then in 1721 Walpole, who had naturally a contempt for writers as politicians and a disregard for them as artists, became first minister for twenty-one years. He harmonized with the changed conditions, and together with them reduced political patronage to a servile and ignoble existence. Patronage had been twofold, political and social, but from 1721 the political was negligible, saving the isolated attempt of

Prince Frederick in opposition. Walpole hardly felt the need of writers to support him, and, when he did, he thought the worst were good enough.

THERE remains social patronage, presenting a goodly record as late as 1730. Men of letters were breaking off from and being gradually squeezed out of fashionable circles, but Pope was still supreme there, the intimate and equal of peers. Towards newcomers patrons, though very helpful, were becoming less familiar and more condescending. There were still many patrons and good ones, of whom, to name but a few, there were Queen Caroline, the Duke of Queensberry, Lord Peterborough, and Mr. Dodington. Further, there was a ready and generous market for dedications, by which a writer who was not too sensitive could often obtain a welcome present and possibly notice that would advance him. Nor was the system of publication by subscription, which accompanied social patronage and social intimacy, yet passed out of fashion. Gay and Brooke and Thomson reaped large sums by it. Subscription lingered longer than patronage, but in 1730 both were going and, although supporting many men of letters admirably, getting rotten and near a sudden crash.

IT might have been, and probably would have been, a terrible thing if social patronage had not survived its political counterpart. It was almost essential for a man of letters to have a patron, if he were to produce his best and obtain a hearing for it. Writers in 1730 outnumbered the public, as in 1780 the public could absorb more than writers could give. The unpatronized authors had to make a living by such work as the booksellers could give them, and the booksellers, prescribing for the public, found that they wanted lives of cheats and rogues, spiced with " luscious rapes," and similar trash, and so the hack-writers had to provide that or starve. The fortunate ones who had their patrons wrote for the most part what was in them, except for some necessary flattery and occasional personal service. The writer in 1730 who prostituted his pen to the public was, as a rule, called on for worse service than a patron asked. At any rate, patronage enabled Thomson, Young, and Gay to produce work of high literary value ; while Fielding and Johnson, the former only accepting patronage after the public had failed to reward him and the latter refusing to contemplate it, were writing respectively second-rate licentious plays and ephemeral magazine articles and Parliamentary debates. Patronage from 1720 to 1740 set free a man's best powers, rescued him from a life of hardship liable to crush him, and imposed generally no grievous conditions on its recipient. It is difficult to conceive the literary world of those days without patrons. Thomson came to London in anticipation of finding a patron ; without that probability before him he might have remained in Scotland and swallowed his disinclination for the ministry.

IMAGING the public as a being, which, whenever born, had by 1700 hardly grown at all in spite of latent and gigantic potentialities, we may say that its babyhood definitely ended in 1731. In that year Mr. Edward Cave proved himself a mighty educator ; he invented the A B C capable of stimulating the baby public's mind to life, as an ordinary child may be lured to spelling by biscuit letters : *The Gentleman's Magazine* was seized with avidity. Henceforth the reading public steadily grew, and the host of patrons was as surely doomed. Patronage was already weakening from decay, but it was this growth of the public that dealt the irremediable blow ; it was this growth of the public that made possible the successful independence of Johnson.

But patronage declined for yet another reason. Like all good things it was abused and became ridiculous, at once loathsome and a common jest. Both patrons and writers contributed to its ill-fame. Foolish men, possessors of titles or wealth, took up poor writers, not from generosity, but vanity. There started a fashion of surrounding oneself with authors, and praising one's own taste and liberality, while destitute of both. A foppish patron liked to have a wit to show off at his table ; it gave the right touch, the air of patronage without the reality ; no matter that the poor wretch ate his heart in vain expectation of some reward, until his forced jesting became a bore and he was turned out. The callous patron sneered, and repeated the performance with another, since one who was a patron, or posed as one, or who had the means to be one, was always pestered intolerably with a swarm of poem-mongers from whom to choose. Mean sycophants, men driven to scribble by vice and extravagance, besieged the doors of the great and insinuated a way into their ante-chambers, begging for subscriptions, for offices, and for recommendations. Deserving writers whose talents equalled their misfortune were mingled in the unedifying throng, goaded by the fear of starvation to undergo that shameful dependence that was worse than poverty. The position of the best-intentioned patron became impossible, where good and bad were thus indistinguishable, and, massed together, no less than a common nuisance. The doors of the great were shut fast, the faces of their footmen implacable, the fiction that the patron was " tied up "[1] was the universal excuse. By 1760, even by 1750, patronage was dead as a whole; Johnson, Goldsmith, Foote, and Churchill denounced it with passionate sincerity repeatedly, preached the glory of independence, and ridiculed their bugbear beyond any possibility of resurrection. By the word " patron " was meant, in 1756, " commonly a wretch who supports with insolence, and is paid with flattery "; and of some even worse might be said.

IN 1726 Thomson looked for patrons and found them; in his early years Johnson might have found some, had he tamed his nature to seek them; after 1750 whoever thought to make his way by patronage was almost surely doomed to failure. Sterne's originality might sweep the aristocracy from their rock of aloofness, George III and Lord Bute might provide brilliant exceptions, and Burke might have the honour of patronizing Crabbe, but they only emphasize the absence of patronage. Burke's act shines the brighter because he alone helped, when others had refused. Patronage was bound to go, and its passing only excites one question: did it perish from adventitious circumstances, before the genuine need of it ceased to be pressing?

[1] i.e. his subscription-list full: see *Joseph Andrews*, book iii, chap. iii.

AUTHORSHIP IN THE DAYS OF JOHNSON

THE prospects of authorship depended on the relative speed of two movements. It was of vital importance to writers that the growth of the public should catch up, if it could not outstrip, the decay of patronage. The result was, broadly speaking, tolerable, but the decline was the swifter, and there was a gap of some few years, during which there only lingered the ghost of patronage, a delusion and an abomination, and the public was too small, too difficult to approach, and too ill-educated to supply adequate support. Johnson had resolved to have none of patronage, continued to avoid it, rejected the overtures of Dodington, and could only win some two hundred and fifty to buy his *Idler*. Akenside, with poor success as a doctor and literary gifts of too narrow an appeal to the existing public, " would perhaps have been reduced to great exigencies, but that Mr. Dyson, with an ardour of friendship that has not many examples, allowed him £300 a year." [1] It was in fact the better writers who fell to ground between patrons and public, because they would not join the scramble for places on the bridge thrown by the booksellers across the gap, and could not barter an obvious popularity (except a Fielding) to gain welcome admittance to the select footbridge, kept by the Tonsons and Millars for their most profitable passengers.

BUT the literary calling was past its worst, steadily improving. The good, fluent, popular writer was assured of paying employment by booksellers; the writer, less fluent, but as good or better, was generally discovered by the book-

[1] *Lives of the Poets*: Akenside.

sellers and given a chance of doing his best in intervals of hack-work; the good, and independent writer was paid respectable copy-money. At the worst the insufficiency of the public and the dearth of patrons resulted in a test of endurance, a hanging-on for better things, a necessity of writing histories, compilations, and miscellanies. These conditions had their centre in the decade 1740 to 1750, but are discernible both earlier and later; rough and convenient limits would appear the death of Queen Caroline and the first ministry of Pitt. In 1760 the ridicule of a writer living in a garret was no longer true; everyone was writing for money, not praise, and getting it.

(iii)

THE public was ultimately and primarily the all-important factor in the progress of literature as a profession, but the relation of author to public was not direct; the booksellers were essential intermediaries. In the preceding century they had replaced the printers as the " midwives of the Muses," and, after the Restoration, began gradually to become a considerable trade. Jacob Tonson the First gave Dryden those means of living which his Court friends forgot to. The alliance of author and bookseller to make patrons unnecessary was thus initiated and grew apace, only held back by the smallness of the public. An author exchanged his copyright for a lump sum, and throughout the century that lump sum was generally a liberal one. If he published a subscription edition, his bookseller saved him the necessity of canvassing himself, and became his agent. If he had no copyright to sell nor subscribers to hope for, he could apply to a bookseller instead of a patron, and earn a hard living by writing tales, pamphlets, and essays. While patronage lasted, most preferred a patron if they could get one; but when it was gone, they were glad of the resource.

By the booksellers we mean, as a rule, the powerful group in London who possessed all the old copyrights, bought into their hands all the new, tyrannized over their lesser brethren and usurped the title of ' the trade.' Till the middle of the century they alone counted, because the other London booksellers outside their combination were easy to keep outside and provincial booksellers were few and unorganized. The lesser men, and notably the Scotch, did themselves, the public, and the publishing trade as a whole good service by finally breaking down the fiction of the perpetual copyright, and so determining the future tendency, but the inner circle, the small strong group, had laid the foundation. It was by good sound business that the Tonsons, Millar, Strahan, and the others built up their prosperity, and with all their prudence and caution they knew how to esteem their writers and to pay them well. They were men of character, born to figure in the history of bookselling as the authors they employed were to figure in the history of literature. If we consider Cave, Newbery, and Strahan against Johnson, Goldsmith, and Hume, we see how the booksellers as well as the authors stand out above all others of their calling by ability and personality. These booksellers were very powerful, having no effective competition, and were abused as monopolists and were not unworthy of the abuse. But they did not presume too much on their powers. Good authors they treated fairly, and bad ones often better than they deserved; they tried to find work for as many writers as possible of those threatened by starvation, and if there were sweating and underpayment it was better than no work and poverty. The booksellers could not be philanthropists; but they were honestly the friends of writers, because they were " liberal-minded men," and because it paid them to be so.

'THE trade' shows up quite well in these later years of George II, when authors turned to it for a living in the murky twilight of patronage. The booksellers almost annihilated the night that might have followed, and led authors quickly on to the new day of public favour. The worst to be said of them is, that they were very human, very tenacious of their own interests. They would not, for instance, let an author print for himself and approach the public without their aid. The true source of much hardship around 1750 was in the writers themselves; in those people who thought they could write and could not, who turned to writing as a last resort, who turned author because they were failures at something else. It was their presence that damaged the prospects of good writers. But the profession of letters rapidly improved. The reading public was daily bigger, circulations multiplied, payment of authors reached sums unheard of, and the struggle to attain the recognized front rank of authorship was less severe and tolerably brief.

WHERE we must speak of the booksellers less

favourably is in the matter of the copyright dispute. Their human weaknesses are too unpleasantly evident, and their unscrupulous persistence hard to excuse. However excellent their relation to authors, their treatment of their fellow-publishers who disputed their illegal copyright was brutally and dishonourably selfish. They had asked for perpetual copyright in 1709, and the House of Commons in Committee rejected their claim and substituted a limited term. Tonson accepted the situation, and bought the copyright of Pope's *Homer* only for the term of fourteen years and such time as was granted by the Queen Anne statute. In 1735 and 1737 the booksellers petitioned for an extended term, explicitly disclaiming any idea of perpetual copyright. Meanwhile they bullied Walker for reprinting *Shakespeare*, and tried to bully Osborne, until they gave over in despair and bought him up. They obtained Chancery injunctions on the prima-facie plea of possession, but carefully avoided any real test at law, and when an injunction was granted by Lord Hardwicke on condition of the case being brought to a hearing, they backed out. They instituted a shuffling and muddled prosecution in the Court of Session, lost it, and were so far warned in an appeal to the House of Lords as to drop it, and be more cautious. Yet all the while they bullied those who would submit, and initiated a campaign of oppression in defiance of law. Not until they were refused injunctions by the judges in Chancery did they bring their claim to an honest legal trial, and they did so then because they had all to gain and nothing to lose. They won only to lose.

The Scotch booksellers stood fast; the Scotch judges sent the English booksellers home with hard words ringing in their ears and advice that the Scotch Common Law was different from English Common Law, if the slipshod judgment of the Court of King's Bench really reflected English Common Law. The House of Lords admitted by their decision that that judgment had been faulty, and so did a great service to the poorer booksellers, to the reading public, and to literature and knowledge.

It is obvious that this claim to perpetual copyright injured the many booksellers who were excluded from participation in old copies, by robbing them of their right to earn a livelihood; it is certain, though difficult to estimate, that the public were to some extent losers by the monopoly; it is doubtful how much the fiction benefited authors and how much they lost by its destruction. In any case perpetual copyright was bound to go, if, indeed, anyone had ever honestly believed in its existence. Continued legal support of the claim must have been overridden by Parliament. The monopolists stood almost alone against public and fellow-booksellers, unable even to win authors to their side with much warmth or conviction. Their greed, whose grossness was such that they were not ashamed to play dog-in-the-manger over Latin texts, had outraged common sense and common justice. The pretensions of the monopolists were humbled none too soon.

The eighteenth century was an age of co-operative publishing. Copyrights were seldom owned by a single bookseller, but shared among the small group who kept all copyrights in their own hands.

While the trade was still being built up slowly and prudently, this policy lessened risks, made expensive works easier to undertake, and produced learned and important contributions to knowledge and literature otherwise impossible. It was the best system for that early stage in the bookselling industry, but nevertheless had its weakness, absence of competition. The greater booksellers did not compete among themselves because it was not sound policy; the lesser booksellers could not compete with the greater because they were kept powerless by terrorism and show of law. The monopolists, therefore, had everything their own way, and it is unthinkable that they could be so unselfish as to serve the public as whole-heartedly in a market which was their own preserve as in one where they must face competition. The booksellers never showed themselves men of that character, nor was such unselfishness to be expected of any men.

We cannot say how much the public was worse served under the fiction of perpetual copyright than it would have been without it, but manifestly it cannot have been as well served. The booksellers published in 1774 a list of books [1] in various sizes and at different prices in order to show that there was an adequate supply kept in stock at reasonable and graduated prices. Their opponents had provoked the reply by a charge of perpetual copyright having led to costly books of poor workmanship. And though the charge was exaggerated it was not groundless. The booksellers charged as much as they could, but self-interest naturally set a limit and kept

---

[1] *List of Books in Different Sizes and at Different Prices* (1774), B.M. 215, i. 4 (97).

the prices fairly down to the needs of the public. Shakespeare's works were sold at prices ranging from six guineas to sixteen shillings; Gay's from ten shillings to two and threepence; *Paradise Lost* from fifty shillings to two shillings, and *Tom Jones* at eighteen and twelve shillings. On the other hand, the three guineas asked for Hawkesworth's edition of *Cook's Voyages* in 1773 had excited general complaint, and the growing demand for cheaper books was shown by the success of the Scotch invaders. Donaldson's shop in the Strand considerably undersold the monopolists and prospered, for the Scotchman's commercial instinct had perceived that the public was asking for books, and was only held back by the existing prices. The fact that his venture anticipated the decision of the House of Lords by some eleven years indicates that the public was growing slightly impatient with the monopolists. The public had cheap and good books, but it might have had cheaper and better. It was truly asserted that " the consequence of a free open trade, will be a competition, to print as well and as cheap as possible." And probably, too, the demand was beginning to exceed the power of the monopolists alone to cater for. Thus when the copyright of Hume's *History* was about to expire, Cooke and Parsons entertained the project of duodecimo editions to cut out the octavo edition of Cadell and Longman, the proprietors. But Cadell forestalled them with a similar edition. Both publishers, however, continued with their respective undertakings, and the sale was so great that each edition easily paid for its expenses.[1]

[1] Rees and Britton, *Reminiscences of Literary London*.

THE effect of the final demolition of the claim to old books was to set free the initiative of the trade as a whole. Bell, in partnership with Martin, " sent forth his *British Theatre* to drive out of the market the old octavo editions of Shakespeare's plays, or the cumbrous collections of the works of dramatic authors, from Dryden and Farquhar to Thomson and Colman." The new spirit was to provide the public with comfortable pocket editions of the English classics, tastefully got up and adorned with engravings by the best artists. It was only this shrewd home-thrust that stirred the old booksellers into sufficient activity to produce that edition of the English poets to which Johnson prefixed the *Lives*.

THE lesser booksellers made use of their long-withheld rights to serve the public whose needs had released them, but the old monopolizing booksellers ceased to serve the public as well as they had done. John Nichols says of Joseph Johnson, Cowper's bookseller, that " his regard for the true interests of literature rendered him an enemy to that typographical luxury which, joined to the necessary increase of expense in printing, has so much enhanced the price of new books as to be a material obstacle to the indulgence of a laudable and reasonable curiosity by the reading public."[1] Johnson consulted cheapness and the prospect of extensive circulation before appearance, but among his contemporaries of 1780 an " age of luxurious printing and high prices was beginning." The decision of 1774 gave the public cheap editions of old books, but was followed by a rise in the price of new books. The

---

[1] *Literary Anecdotes* (Joseph Johnson).

latter were restricted to a more exclusive market, publishers preferring big profits on a small sale to small profits and extensive circulation. Henceforth new publications could only be bought by the few; the many must wait for cheaper reprints.

THE effect on authors of the loss of perpetual copyright would depend largely on what had been the real opinion and practice of booksellers in paying authors between 1710 and 1774. Did they, during that period, believe themselves in all sincerity entitled to buy perpetual rights? and did they pay on a basis of perpetuity? Our earlier investigation satisfies us they did neither. " Many of the booksellers who now petition," it was said honestly in 1774, " have been so far from conceiving that they had a perpetual copyright, that they had, when the term granted by the 8th Anne was elapsed, republished their books under a Patent-Privilege for fourteen years longer "; and Watts's works, Stackhouse's *History of the Bible*, and Pope's works were given as instances. As for paying for perpetual rights, who could pay adequately, and what bookseller was likely to pay for more than an average period? Literary property was notoriously difficult to value. It was safest to assume that a book would only live a few years; for 99 per cent. of books published twenty-eight years were equivalent to perpetuity. Therefore that was the perpetuity for which booksellers paid, and it was the time allotted by law. That is to say, the decision of 1774 merely swept away a pretence, and the subsequent bargaining was on the same practical basis as it had been all along. No doubt the deplorable publicity and the final pang of disillusionment were not without some slight effect. The booksellers, a little shaken by the blow, were more cautious for a while; copy-money was probably checked in its rise; but the rapid expansion of the reading public made the check very temporary.

THAT authors did not suffer by the decision does not mean that their condition was beyond complaint. To say that perpetual copyright was harmful does not infer that the Statute of 1710 was adequate. Authors did not lose by the decision, but they still had much to gain. Especially when writers began to keep their copyrights or share the profits with the publisher, protection for only twenty-eight years was not a fair reward. Carlyle in 1839 was right in his plea for an author, that Parliament should forbid " all Thomas Teggs and other extraneous persons, entirely unconcerned in this adventure of his, to steal from him his small winnings, for sixty years at shortest." Wordsworth also had in 1838 denounced the spirit which would " to works that came from mind and spirit, grudge a short-lived fence."[1] But the demand for longer protection was quite another thing to the claim to protection for ever. The idea of perpetual copyright was intolerable, and was not supported by the best authors of 1774. It was Johnson who said that the public must have its rights respected too.[2]

REVIEWING the half-century 1726 to 1780 we see that it was the formative period both of the trade of bookselling and of the profession of authorship, for during those years they both grew from weakness to strength and passed from a condition

---
[1] *Miscellaneous Sonnets*, part iii, No. 38.
[2] " Whatever valuable work has once been created by an authour, and issued out by him, should be understood as no longer in his power, but as belonging to the publick" (*Life*, ii. 259).

of insecurity and uncertainty to one of consolidation and defined progress. The eighteenth century was an age of commercial advancement in all directions, and bookselling did not lag behind. The leading members of 'the trade' became men of importance, wealthy and influential; they were aldermen and members of Parliament, kept their coach, were generous in charity, and profuse in convivial hospitality. So had they prospered, and authors went naturally with them, since the selling of books and their writing make of the literary profession just such a unity as its two sides give to the legal. Booksellers did not only raise the price of literature (for which Johnson praised Millar), but they raised its status too. Thanks to them emancipation from patronage became possible, the gap between patrons and public support was made endurable, and the identification of literature with poverty finally broken down. In 1726 literature had been little more than a hanger-on of society and politics, and in no sense a profession; but in 1780 men of letters were independent, forming a society of their own, servants of the public like members of any other profession, and well paid for their labours. All this was achieved by their alliance with the booksellers; but the booksellers were merely the agents, enabled to play their part by the growth of the public. The reading public was at once the child and parent of authorship, brought into being by the existence of books, and then, by mere act of volition as it were, causing books to be multiplied and again multiplied. To speak of the increasing prosperity of booksellers and the improving prospects of authors is to describe effects of a great cause, the growth of the public. To be fully intelligible the cause needs further examination. Let us, therefore, consider how the reading public grew, and why.

(iv)

THE reading public of Addison's time was very small, closely limited both geographically and socially. It was confined to London, and mostly to fashionable London, since communication between the metropolis and the provinces was very imperfect, and there still lingered that division between society and city which had very sharply separated the puritanical citizens from the gay court of the merry monarch. There was no demand for literature from the " gross, uneducated, untravelled country gentleman," and the country clergyman's books were limited to the few dusty and long-untouched volumes which he had brought from college and still respected, though past reading them. There was little intellectual life outside London, and there was not much within. Indeed, what was there to stimulate the mind, to encourage reading? The mental pabulum offered to the public was for the most part either indigestible or of a flavour unenticingly rank. Wholesome light reading was in 1708 still to come; some form of light literature with a broad and healthy appeal had yet to be discovered. Steele discovered it, and Addison was at hand to perfect it. A new tide in the affairs of literature had turned, and the first slow creep was evident of a mighty sea of progress. Said Mrs. Shirley, in *Sir Charles*

Grandison, " The reading in fashion when I was young was Romances. You, my children, have in that respect fallen into happier days. The present age is greatly obliged to the authors of *The Spectator.*"[1] The romances, certainly, might well go ; far more the virulent pamphlets, abusive and scurrilous, the indecent verses, the salacious tales, and spiced biographies. They always survive for the unclean reader ; at the close of the seventeenth century it was largely a matter of read such, or read nothing.[2]

The Tatler began, but *The Spectator* was the best expression of, the periodical essay. It was a completely new departure, infinitely removed from all the gossiping and short-lived newssheets that had been the only previous periodical literature. Addison rejoices that " my paper has not in it a single word of news, a reflection on politics, nor a stroke of party " ; that he gives " no fashionable touches of infidelity, no obscene ideas, no satires upon priesthood, marriage, and the like popular topics of ridicule ; no private scandal, nor anything that may tend to the defamation of particular persons, families, or societies." " There is," says Addison, " not one of these above-mentioned subjects that would not sell a very indifferent paper, could I think of gratifying the public by such mean and base methods " ; but that he will not do, preferring to write something that " draws men's minds off from the bitterness of party, and furnishes them with subjects of discourse that may be treated without warmth or passion." He is

---

[1] *Sir Charles Grandison* (1754), vi. 204.
[2] Beljame, *Le Public et les hommes de lettres en Angleterre au 18ᵉ siècle*, chapitre iii.

ambitious to have it said of him that he " brought philosophy out of closets, schools, and colleges, to dwell in clubs and assemblies, at tea-tables, and in coffee-houses." In short, the aim of *The Spectator* was to interest the public without pandering to its weakness, to instruct in taste and morality, " to unite merriment with decency," and to popularize knowledge. The " morning lectures " were to be so brief, so varied, and so leavened with humour, that " the busy may find time, and the idle may find patience " to attend. THE venture had an immediate success. *The Tatler* ran to 271 numbers, covering a period of some twenty months, and the more frequent *Spectator* to 555 in about the same time. Of their circulation we cannot be certain, but it was undoubtedly considerable, and the doings of Sir Roger and his friends were the topic of the town. By the time *The Spectator* had reached its tenth number we find Addison writing : " My Publisher tells me, that there are already three thousand of them distributed every day ; so that if I allow twenty readers to every paper which I look upon as a modest computation, I may reckon about three-score thousand disciples in London and Westminster."[1] Johnson, reckoning from the stamp-tax figures, estimated the sale at nearly seventeen hundred ; tradition, on the other hand, tells of twenty thousand copies being sold on occasion.[2] In any case its influence overflowed the bounds of its sale, for the coffee-house copies were well-thumbed,[3] and to be the common

---

[1] *Spectator*, No. 10.
[2] Johnson, *Lives of the Poets*, ed. G. B. Hill : Addison, ii. 98.
[3] In 1729 the owners of coffee-houses asserted that by their means one issue of a paper passed through no less than 20,000 hands in a day. See *The Case between the Proprietors of Newspapers and the subscribing Coffee-men* (1729), B.M. 1093, d. 61.

THE GROWTH OF THE PUBLIC

theme of conversation is of more value than mere sale. Moreover, these periodicals were unlike the majority of that generally ephemeral race, because their popularity grew instead of decreasing. They were quickly gathered into volumes, and constantly reprinted. Not until the new spirit which they preached had permeated literature and society did their popularity wane before the recurring demand for new things.

TWENTY months may seem a short life, but they sufficed. It was the change itself that mattered, and a few months ensured it. Once there had been the awakening to fresh ideas, the discovery of the pleasure of instructive yet easy reading, the call to higher morality, to more humane feeling and gentler manners, to wider literary appreciation and deeper reflection, life could no longer be as before. We needs must love the highest when we see it, and the light of Addison was a clear beacon to his age. There was no need for a *Spectator* dragging on for years when its work was done, and it is less matter for wonder that Sir Roger was carried off by gaol-fever than his long continuance would have been. *The Guardian* succeeded *The Spectator*, and was followed by a brief revival of it; then *The Freeholder* in 1715 brought to an end Addison's periodical essays, closing on a definite party note. The new spirit was making its way, moulding the generation to come, preparing a reading public ready for the next impulse. But, meantime, the actual growth of the reading public suffered a check. It had been a great achievement for Addison to hold attention so long while keeping aloof from politics and personality. There was bound to be some reaction to the old ways. Conditions were first unsettled by the Jacobite rebellion, then came the bitter Bangorian controversy submerging divinity in politics, and on top of that the South Sea Bubble.

FOR a time the more general habit of reading was satisfied by very indifferent newspapers, whose contents were lies, scandal, libel, and gossip. Despite the stamp duty imposed in 1712 they had survived and were on the increase, indicating a steady public demand. A certain Samuel Negus has, in this connexion, left us a document of great interest, being a list of printers in London and the counties compiled as an offering to Lord Townshend, Secretary of State in 1724. Negus was an old printer, envious of interloping news-printers, and moreover he had an eye on the office of Extraordinary Messenger, wherein he "should not doubt of pleasing his Lordship." From his list and petition it would appear that printing presses were spreading everywhere, and men outside the trade were being tempted to try their hand by the public appetite for news and pamphlets. Most of the bigger provincial towns had their Press, and some had two; London had no less than seventy, many of whom, says the informer, "give great offence and disturbance to the State." Doubtless they did, but from the standpoint of the literary calling it was better that the public should grow by reading seditious matter than fail to grow for want of nourishment. The newspapers were better than nothing, and in 1724 numbered three daily, seven published three times a week (of which two were *Evening Posts*), and six weekly journals.[1] In 1729 the owners of coffee-houses complained that newspapers were too numerous for them to take in all, and suggested running a composite one of their own, forgetting that they owed their company as much to the newspapers as to their coffee. But most significant of all is the appearance in 1726 of *The Craftsman*, a forerunner of Junius in its vigorous invective. Its circulation is said to have been between ten and twelve thousand copies a week.

A FEW examples will show how in the late twenties of the century the sale of the more popular books was expanding. Foremost was *Gulliver's Travels*, of which Arbuthnot foretold its having " as great a run as John Bunyan "; of which the first impression was sold in a week, and which, Swift was told, had soon made a bookseller " almost rich enough to be an alderman." [2] The success of Gay's *Polly* was so great that two pirates thought it profitable to print illegal editions against the 10,500 issued by Bowyer.[3] Thomson's *Sophonisba* ran through four editions in a year; there were several issues of the first edition of the *Dunciad* in 1728, and a second and more elaborate edition appeared in the next year; Gay's *Fables* attained a fourth edition in 1733, and *The Beggar's Opera* in 1735; Garth's *Dispensary* a ninth in 1726, and Watts's *Divine and Moral Songs for Children* a tenth in 1729; Young's *Universal Passion* reached a third edition in 1730, and Duck, the Court poet, saw his *Poems* pass through nine editions in three years. The first collected edition of *The Spec-*

---
[1] Nichols, *Literary Anecdotes of the Eighteenth Century*, i. 288 sqq. and note.
[2] Swift, *Works* (1803), xvii, pp. 70, 81, 202.
[3] Nichols, *Literary Anecdotes*, i. 404.

tator consisted of nine thousand copies; in 1729, only seventeen years later, the ninth edition was issued.

SUCH evidence very clearly indicates the existence of a quite considerable reading public for the more important new and comparatively recent books. It is confirmed by the fact that, while the expenses of publishing had become heavier owing to a rise in the cost of materials and in the wages of printers, there had been no corresponding increase in the price of books. That remained through the first half of the eighteenth century the same as it had been in the last decade of the seventeenth. Publishers were enabled to keep down prices and yet maintain their profits by the wide extension of circulation everywhere taking place. A big sale of cheap books was the way to foster a public and establish a trade.

THE public was beginning to grow, but something else was needed to spread the taste for reading more quickly and more widely. The reader passes from the transitory to the less transitory; from periodical literature rooted in the present to literature whose appeal time has less and less power to diminish. The reading public must be brought up and will always largely continue to subsist on the everyday journey-work of letters; it needs above all something plain, substantial and wholesome, something better than the year 1730 could show. But by then Edward Cave, a journeyman printer, Commissioner of Franks in the Post Office, and writer of newsletters,[1] had saved up sufficient money to start a literary ven-

---

[1] The handwritten newsletter was still not uncommon in 1730; its continued appeal lay in its power of being more outspoken.

ture of whose success he was assured, although he had been unable to persuade any printer or bookseller to join him. He had realized that to become acquainted with the best pieces of periodical writing, such as it was, had become impossible to the average man, and foresaw that a condensation of this overflowing volume of information and opinion would, in all probability, find a ready sale. So in January 1731 there issued from St. John's Gate, Clerkenwell, the first number of *The Gentleman's Magazine*, announcing the intention " to treasure up, as in a Magazine, the most remarkable pieces " of writing and news, culled from the two hundred or so half-sheets thrown each month from the London Press. In addition there were to be a brief record of events, instructive articles, Parliamentary debates, and an outlet for the poetic muse.

IT was not the first attempt; there had been a monthly *Miscellany* from 1707 to 1709, and a *Bibliotheca Literaria* had emerged in 1722, but neither succeeded; they did not catch the public taste and possibly they were before their time. Cave's success, however, was immediate, and inspired a host of rivals. The booksellers who before had unanimously rejected his offer of a share, at once combined to produce *The London Magazine*, a formidable but not a more successful competitor. The many others lived and died in constant succession, unable to gain a permanency, but helping the good work of disseminating knowledge in a form easy and pleasant to assimilate, and accessible to those of moderate position and education. There could no longer be any excuse for ignorance of the outlines of domestic and foreign politics; geographical, historical, and literary knowledge was brought to all who could read, and the gift of a little led to the desire for more. The magazines were, in fact, a very powerful educative influence, affecting politics as well by the formation of a broad, national public opinion.

CAVE was the man not only to initiate but to advance this new form of literature; "he scarcely ever looked out of the window but with a view to its improvement." So he saw the circulation of *The Gentleman's Magazine* steadily rise until, in 1739, it was ten thousand, and a few years later fifteen thousand. Nor was its sale limited to the first issue, for its popularity was such that "before it had completed its ninth year, the fifth edition of some of its earliest numbers was printed."[1] London was not alone in its demand for knowledge, and in 1739 *The Scots Magazine* appeared. It justified itself on the "general increase of readers for some years past," and the want of something which should do away with the necessity of depending on English magazines, of which the sale in Scotland was considerable in spite of their contents being "stale before they come to hand"; and its quick and firm establishment showed that the plea was valid. Indeed on all sides there were made "attempts to suit the learning of the times to the purchase and opportunity of persons of every station." Between 1731 and 1780 no less than sixty magazines were published in London, while Scotland had ten and Ireland eleven. The provinces, too, began to have their own periodicals,

[1] Boswell, *Life of Johnson*, ed. G. B. Hill, i. 112, note 1.

the first being *The Newcastle General Magazine* from 1747 to 1760. Likewise there grew up the specialized magazine, like *The Farmer's* and those whose bias was social and homely.[1]

A LATER development was the *Review*, whose existence showed that a very considerable advance had taken place. It meant that the small section of the reading public, which it is convenient to call the literary public, had sufficiently increased to be able to support a magazine devoted to literature and science. One early attempt was the *History of the Works of the Learned*, in which Warburton assailed his enemies and defended Pope against the attacks of the theologian de Crousaz. It began in 1735, but continued only a year or two in a limited circle. Not until Griffiths started *The Monthly Review* in 1749 did this class of magazine become well established; then Smollett's *Critical Review* followed in 1756, and those two remained the leading examples for nearly half a century, imitated by a few much inferior in quality and staying power. "The judicious reader," said Smollett's Preface in 1756, "will perceive that [the writer's] aim has been to exhibit a succinct plan of every performance; to point out the most striking beauties and glaring defects; to illustrate their remarks with proper quotations, and to convey their remarks in such a manner as might best conduce to the entertainment of the public." In six months *The Critical* had reviewed some hundred and twenty British and about thirty foreign books, and given in addition short notices of painting and statuary.

[1] See G. F. Barwick, *Some Magazines of the Eighteenth Century*, Biblio. Soc. *Transactions* vol. x. (1910).

AUTHORSHIP IN THE DAYS OF JOHNSON

THE literary or more critical public was thus educated to a wider appreciation, and brought into closer relation with current literature and its writers. The advertisement afforded by criticism must have increased sales, especially to provincial readers whose ears new publications had been long in reaching. Further, the review was found, in good hands, to be very influential in raising the standard of literature and taste. No good author need fear a reviewer's abuse, although he might his neglect, for, in Bentley's words, no man was ever written down but by himself. Authors, in fact, stood chiefly to gain by the reviews; and not least because of the new field of literary work thus opened out to the aspirant in letters. Writing for the reviews was a beginning, and it was fairly well paid. Thus we find that Charles Jenkinson, later " the arch-mediocrity " Lord Liverpool, preceded his political career by writing for them in the late fifties.

THE novel, too, played a prominent part in developing the reading public. Since the Restoration the output of tales of all kinds had been steadily growing, until there existed for the reader of 1720 a very considerable library of romances. But most were too imbued with Restoration morals, or want of them, and many were merely reprints of the more popular works of the Charles II period. For example, the title, *The Maidenhood lost by Moonlight*, is expressive of the almost universal theme; and Keach's *Travels of True Godliness*, originally printed in 1683 and appearing in a ninth edition in 1726, is a typical reprint of such a moral allegory as *Pilgrim's Progress* had made popular. The most popular novelist of Queen Anne's reign was Mrs. Manley, with her *Secret Memoirs*, her *Power of Love*, and many other productions of doubtful taste. In addition, there were many translations of Scarron and Calprenède and stories like *The Jealous Lovers* from the Spanish ; *The Arabian Nights* went through six editions between 1708 and 1725 ; and on all sides were feeble and uninteresting tales of illustrious and illegal lovers.[1] THEN the novel began to improve, yet rather slowly. Mrs. Haywood succeeded Mrs. Manley, and around 1730 the novel reader had still to rely on the dullest of love-stories, whose bias was always to intrigue. The popular type was " a collection of several entertaining histories and occurrences which fell under the observation of a lady in search after happiness " ; of which there were endless variations, all alike tedious. But there had been an important advance in the work of Defoe ; he had given the novel a change of theme, and brought to it an altogether superior power of expression. Then came *Gulliver's Travels*, and after it imaginative imitations like *A Trip to the Moon*, published in 1728. For a time it would seem that the novel slackened off, dwindling away as it became more decent, reverting to translations, as if no more was to be looked for but versions of Crebillon and Marivaux. Richardson and Fielding rescued it, and gave to it that impulse which made the novel the dominant form of popular literature. So great was the demand that Millar gave Fielding £600 for *Tom Jones* and £1,000 for *Amelia*, and is said to have made more thousands than he gave hundreds.[2]

[1] See A. Esdaile, *List of English Tales and Prose Romances printed before 1740*.
[2] C. Knight, *Shadows of the Old Booksellers* (1865), p. 217.

THE rise of the great novel gave fresh life to the whole race of story-spinners. The public was ready to devour countless second- and third-rate novels, as well as a *Pamela* and a *Tom Jones*; and the latter inevitably raised the standard of the others. Indeed it is noticeable how Mrs. Haywood's *Betsy Thoughtless* and *Jenny and Jemmy Jessamy* are much stronger, more interesting, and better written than her novels published before Richardson's example had acted as an inspiration. When there was thus created something worth reading, the general reader was multiplied. "Novels," says Vamp the publisher in Foote's *Author* (1757), "are a pretty light summer reading, and do very well at Tunbridge, Bristol, and other watering-places; no bad commodity either for the West India trade."[1] The middle of the century saw Oriental tales in vogue, a favourite item in the magazine; about 1760 there became popular "a kind of fashionable family novel with which the stately mother and the boarding-school miss were instructed to fortify themselves against the immorality of Fielding and Smollett"[2]; about 1770 there was a regular supply of moral and fashionable novels like *The Fine Lady, or the Younger Sister*, in which the reader is introduced to "piety and cheerful prudence leading unexperienced youth through labyrinths of life." These latter, for which the publisher paid from ten to twenty pounds,[3] were sold at six shillings, and their number indicates a steady demand. A reader pleased by perusal of *The Thoughtless Ward*

---

[1] Foote, *The Author*, act i, sc. ii. [2] J. Forster, *Life of Goldsmith*, (1854), i. 188.
[3] John Britton and Rees, *Reminiscences of Literary London, 1779–1853*.

might be tempted to read *Sir Charles Grandison*; so the taste for reading might insensibly be acquired, until Pope and Locke, Young and Johnson, should be among the authors with whose work the averagely educated man would be acquainted.

FROM the novel to the circulating library is but a step, since fiction has been the mainstay and possibly the creator of the popular library. At least it is a striking testimony to their close connexion that the appearance of *Pamela* and the establishment of the first London circulating library coincide. Thus we find that about 1740 a dissenting minister, the Rev. Samuel Fancourt, had set up a library, for membership of which he charged a fee of a guinea a year.[1] A rival quickly appeared in the person of a Mr. Wright, who announced in 1743 that he was prepared to lend " all manner of books at sixteen shillings a year." The movement spread rapidly : in 1745 Nicholson at Cambridge was lending maps and text-books to students ; in 1750 Hutton established a library at Birmingham ; and in 1761 *The Annual Register* notes how " the reading female hires her novels from some Country Circulating Library, which consists of about a hundred volumes." [2]

" I HAVE been informed," Lackington wrote in his *Memoirs*, " that when circulating libraries were first opened, the booksellers were much alarmed, and their rapid increase, added to their fears, had led them to think that the sale of books would be much diminished by such libraries. But experience has proved that the sale of books,

---

[1] W. E. A. Axon, *London Circulating Library of 1743*: *The Library* (1900).
[2] *Annual Register* (1761), p. 207.

so far from being diminished by them, has been greatly promoted, as from those repositories many thousand families have been cheaply supplied with books, by which the taste of reading has become much more general, and thousands of books are purchased every year, by such as have first borrowed them at those libraries, and after reading, approving of them, become purchasers."[1] Lackington's observation of experience was just, and the action of the booksellers in setting up their own libraries shows that they, too, quickly appreciated the stimulus which the libraries gave to bookselling. Miss Lydia Melford in *Humphry Clinker* wrote to her friend from Bath, that " we girls are allowed to accompany them to the booksellers' shops, which are charming places of resort where we read novels, plays, pamphlets, and newspapers, for so small a subscription as a crown a quarter " ; and similarly we read in Dr. Thomas Campbell's diary of his visit to London in 1775 : " Strolled into the Chapter Coffeehouse, Ave Mary Lane, which I had heard was remarkable for a large collection of books, and a reading society. I subscribed a shilling for the right of a year's reading, and found all the new publications I sought."[2]

WE have noted earlier how, by 1724, the more important provincial towns had each its Press, from which issued a newspaper at first little more than a reprint of the London papers[3] ; we saw how the provincial magazine had come into being by the middle of the century ; and lastly,

[1] *Memoirs of J. Lackington* (1803), letter xl, p. 255.
[2] *Diary of a Visit to England in 1775*, ed. S. Raymond (1854) : March 21, 1775.
[3] At the beginning provincial papers were often beggared for want of news; one adopted the expedient of printing sections of the Bible to fill its columns

we have observed the rapidity with which the provinces adopted the lending library. All were signs of a new era whose great improvements in the means of travelling were fast breaking down the barrier between the country and the capital. *The Annual Register* of 1761 was moved to comment on this change. " The effects of this easy communication," it said, " have almost daily grown more and more visible. The several great cities, and we might add many poor country towns, seem to be inspired with an ambition of becoming little Londons of the part of the Kingdom wherein they are situated." The writer had to admit that the London influences had " cultivated the minds, and improved the behaviour of the ladies and gentlemen of the country," but he lamented that those ladies and gentlemen began, as well, to ape the " manners, amusements, fashions, vices, and follies of the metropolis." [1]

MOST important from the position of the literary calling was the enormous extension in the reading public which was the natural result. No longer were the coffee-house frequenters of fashionable London the only readers, and the illiteracy of the squirearchy was a thing of the past. Country readers in the first quarter of the century had been very naïve as well as very few. One thinks of the old gentleman who consulted his atlas for the position of Lilliput, and of Southey's Dr. Daniel Dove to whom " a book carried with it authority in its very aspect " ; and among the rural population, where reading was a very rare accomplishment, of Sir John Herschel's anecdote

---

[1] *Annual Register* (1761), pp. 205–8.

of the blacksmith reading *Pamela* to the villagers round the forge, who were so enthralled by the tale that they had the church bells rung to celebrate the heroine's marriage. But the circulating library, and the Press, and quick travel to and from London soon made one unified English reading public. The works of Defoe, in particular, seem to have been very popular; they were among the standard prize-books given in the schools. Typical of the change is Goldsmith's portrait of Livy Primrose, as being thoroughly acquainted with the dialogue in Defoe's *Religious Courtship*, with *Robinson Crusoe* and *Tom Jones*.

INSEPARABLE from the growth of the reading public is the spread of education; the one reacts on the other, for the reader is awake to the greater need of education, and education should create a desire to read. The eighteenth century began well; the Society for the Promotion of Christian Knowledge, founded in 1699, proceeded energetically to set up charity schools for the instruction in reading, writing, and the Church Catechism of boys and girls from seven to twelve years old. Queen Anne took considerable interest in them, and during her reign and that of George I they increased and flourished. Mandeville, in a typically perverse and outspoken pamphlet, decried the "enthusiastic passion for charity schools, a kind of distraction the nation hath laboured under for some time." That was in 1723; but a few years later the passion had cooled, and education fell back into the hands of the clergyman in his spare hours and of the village schoolmaster and dame, earning a pittance by teaching the three R's to some half-dozen children. Yet, even so, education remained at a fair level. Thomas Bray, a prominent missionary worker, who had been instrumental in founding the S.P.C.K., had also improved the intellectual resources of the country clergyman by his scheme for establishing parochial libraries in every deanery throughout England and Wales. By his death in 1730 there were eighty; twenty-three more were added in the next seven years, and the movement continued to make the clergy better informed and more efficient. Nor were the little dame-schools like that kept by Shenstone's schoolmistress without good influence; and if the upper classes were none too well served by the public schools, they made up for it by employing tutors. Everywhere education was to be had, sufficient to maintain the steady increase in the reading public. Indeed Johnson wrote of the year 1748 as " a time when so many schemes of education have been projected ... so many schools opened for general knowledge, and so many lectures in particular sciences attended." [1]

But one may doubt whether the Press is not a more potent educative force than the school. " All foreigners," said Johnson in *The Idler*, " remark that the knowledge of the common people of England is greater than that of any other vulgar "[2]; a statement which Voltaire corroborated in 1763. The Doctor held that " this superiority we undoubtedly owe to the rivulets of intelligence which are continually trickling among us, which everyone may catch and of which everyone partakes "; and when Voltaire said, " C'est que l'état mitoyen est plus riche et plus

---

[1] Preface to *The Preceptor*: *Works* (1825), v. 211. [2] *Idler*, No. 7.

instruit en Angleterre qu'en France," he meant virtually the same thing. " That general knowledge which now circulates in common talk was in Addison's time rarely to be found," said Johnson[1]; and its wide diffusion can hardly be credited to the schools. The honour is due to the booksellers who were so enterprising in the work of popularizing knowledge. The first edition of Chambers's *Cyclopedia* appeared in 1728, reaching a fifth edition in 1746, and the middle of the century was an age of number books, having " something of a quackish air " in the eyes of Hume, but admirably adapted to please and stimulate the general public. There was first a great run of popular histories issued in weekly numbers, of which the supreme example is Smollett's; to the disgust of Horace Walpole, " eleven thousand copies of that trash were instantly sold, while at the same time the University of Oxford ventured to print but two thousand of that inimitable work, Lord Clarendon's life "[2]; and, indeed, the sale of his sixpenny numbers reached twenty thousand a week, thanks to the efforts of the publishers, who " sent down a packet of prospectuses free (with half a crown enclosed) to every parish clerk in the Kingdom, to be distributed by him through the pews of the church." Then came Hill's popular scientific volumes; and in 1770 Walpole noted that " natural history is in fashion." Thus the booksellers educated the public and provided paying work for writers fifty years before Brougham and his circle went " education mad " and inaugurated the terrible " march of intellect."

[1] Boswell, *Life*, iv. 217.   [2] *Memoirs of the Reign of King George II*.

THE GROWTH OF THE PUBLIC

NOTEWORTHY, too, in the third quarter of the century is the abundance of good literature for children, and also the large number of women writers. Dodsley brought out in 1748 his *Preceptor*, " one of the most valuable works for the improvement of young minds that has appeared,"[1] said Boswell. Newbery both wrote and published his delightful " little penny books, radiant with gold, and rich with bad pictures and flowery and gilt binding," of which were *Giles Gingerbread* and *Goody Two Shoes*; and they were so popular that an edition of many thousands was often sold out during the Christmas holidays.

JUVENILE literature was a province to which the female writer tended, but it was by no means her only province. Nothing speaks more eloquently of the advance in social life achieved between 1720 and 1770 than the great improvement in the education of women and the rise of bluestocking coteries, poor shadows though they were of the Parisian salons. Addison had said of *The Spectator*, that " there are none to whom this paper will be more useful than to the female world,"[2] and his purpose of diverting the minds of women from the dull routine of sorting ribands, visiting the toyshop, making jellies, and sewing, bore fruit. The " green girl " and her novel became a common theme of weak satire; Lackington, at the end of the century, rejoiced that " by far the greatest part of ladies have now a taste for books "[3]; and Johnson had said in 1778, " All our ladies read now; which is a great extension."[4] Many educated women naturally turned to authorship. Mrs. Haywood had

[1] Boswell, *Life*, i. 192.   [2] *Spectator*, No. 10.
[3] *Memoirs*, p. 256.   [4] Boswell, *Life*, iii. 333.

her followers in the novel; Mrs. Macaulay was a best-seller among the popular historians; and the learned Mrs. Carter upheld her sex in the realm of scholarship. They had not to wait for a public, since they had grown up with it and were, in fact, evidence of its growth. They came at the right time, and found a good market for their writings great and small. Hannah More alone made a small fortune by her pen.

MEANWHILE, coarseness and indecency had been purged from literature as drunkenness, open immorality, and brutal manners had been from life. It was a slow process, and the effect of Addison's moral essays was evident in the next generation rather than his own. Even after Walpole's time drunkenness was no disgrace, but quite the usual result of a social evening; and in the lower classes the habit of gin-drinking was simply appalling in the middle of the century when there were said to be seventeen thousand gin-shops within the London " bills of mortality " alone. The mistresses of George I and George II were a public scandal, and the Duke of Grafton, when Premier, did not scruple to take his with him to the play. Chesterfield was ahead of his age in his disapproval of gaming and swearing. But manners and morality in the nation as a whole improved steadily in most respects; in certain spheres and certain matters there was a lingering in the old paths and even a step backwards, but the general trend was upward. " A posthumous piece of infidelity, or an amorous novel decorated with luscious copper plates," still continued to find a public as late as 1750; the scandalous memoirs of Lady Vane helped to sell *Peregrine Pickle* in

1752, and Stevenson's *Crazy Tales* appeared as late as 1762.

But such things were becoming the exception. The once inevitable double entendre vanished from the drama, where pleasanter themes and unexceptionable treatment became the rule. Fielding in the thirties continued the old strain, but he was often hissed for his pains,[1] and by his unbridled abuse of the Government brought the stage under a censorship, moral as well as political. *The Gentleman's Magazine*, after the first few years, was a model of propriety; and in the late fifties the reviews lashed relentlessly an immoral book, although their own abuse of one another was often none too decent. Then in 1757 Horace Walpole noted in his memoirs: " Indecent prints were prohibited: the Chief Justice Mansfield caused to be seized at an auction the well-known tale, called *The Woman of Pleasure*."[2] A few years later Wilkes brought upon himself infamy and legal prosecution by the privately printed *Essay on Woman*. The religious revival set on foot by Wesley[3] had much to do with hastening the progress of this change, but the change had been ensured ever since Addison's good-humoured advocacy of a more cultured and moral society. Nor is it doubtful that the growing respect for women, and their increasing numbers and importance both in the reading public and the craft of letters were powerful contributory agencies. The writers in 1770 had to be careful not to

[1] *Scots Mag* (1739): "So far is the dirty ribaldry that once could alone please, from being countenanced now, that seldom a double entendre is allowed, three of which if apparent to the spectators would be enough to damn a play of considerable merit."
[2] *Memoirs of the Reign of King George II*.
[3] Besides affecting literary taste, the religious revival contributed to the growth of the reading public by awakening intellectual interest. The Sunday-school movement, given impetus by Raikes of Gloucester in 1780, carried on the work.

offend against " the sweetness of female delicacy." Irreligion and immorality were no longer tolerated in the best literature, except for an occasional lapse. Sterne certainly captivated society, but was rebuked by Goldsmith and others for his " bawdy." Hawkesworth was widely condemned in 1773 for the looseness of description and the slights on religion, interwoven into his edition of the South Sea Voyages. By 1780 the taint of the Restoration was practically cleansed away.

The increase in the size of the reading public after the middle of the century is very evident. We find Dodsley's *World* in 1753 with a circulation of 2,500,[1] as against the 500 of *The Daily Gazetteer* some twenty years earlier. The first impression of Lord Orrery's *Letters concerning Swift* (1752) were sold out in a day, and in two years, according to Warburton, 12,000 had been disposed of.[2] The *Rambler*, while issued periodically, had a sale of only 500,[3] but by his death, Johnson had lived to see ten editions of 1,250 copies in London alone. Dodsley sold from twelve to thirteen hundred of Gray's *Odes* (1757) in a month.[4] Robertson's *History of Scotland* in 1759 met with " such unbounded applause that before the end of the month he was desired by his booksellers to prepare for a second edition,"[5] and that in spite of its clashing with Hume's volume on Mary ; before Robertson's death in 1793 it had gone through fourteen editions. The first impression of Horace Walpole's *History of Richard III* (1769), consisting of 1,200, sold so fast that another thousand were arranged for

[1] R. Straus, *Robert Dodsley*, p. 188. [2] Nichols, *Literary Anecdotes*, ii. 232, note.
[3] Murphy, *Life of Johnson*, p. 59. [4] Gray, *Letters* (1884), i. 350.
[5] D. Stewart, *Life of Robertson*, p. 169.

next day[1]; and in 1776 Gibbon was writing of his first volume: " I am at a loss how to describe the success of the work, without betraying the vanity of the writer. The first impression was exhausted in a few days; a second and third were scarcely equal to the demand." In 1768 Kelly's *False Delicacy* had been remarkable for a sale of 10,000 copies in the season,[2] while Cumberland's *West Indian* (1771) eclipsed that by a sale of 12,000,[3] and in 1778 4,000 copies of Hannah More's *Percy* were cleared in a fortnight.[4] Just before 1780 there was the extraordinary and well-sustained popularity of Blair's sermons, for which Strahan paid as much as £600 a volume,[5] and that had been preceded in 1776 by the sale of thousands of Price's pamphlet on American Independence.[6]

AND naturally the bigger sales of good literature were paralleled by a yet greater multiplication in the circulation of more popular work. In 1758 Johnson remarked that " not many years ago the nation was content with one gazette, but now we have not only in the metropolis papers for every morning and every evening, but almost every large town has its weekly historian."[7] The stamp-tax figures show that the average daily sale of papers grew in the twenty-two years, 1753–75, from 23,673 to 41,615; and despite the imposition of an extra half-penny in 1776 it had risen in 1780 to 45,422. Journalism, having finally established its claim in 1772 to report Parliamentary debates, had won through to an important and responsible position. *The Public*

[1] *Letters*, ed. Toynbee, vii. 160.
[2] Forster, *Life of Goldsmith*, ii. 119.
[3] D.N.B.
[4] Meakin, *Hannah More*, p. 113.
[5] Boswell, *Life*, iii. 98.
[6] D.N.B.
[7] *Idler*, No. 30.

Advertiser was the impartial publisher of many a great man's views in its letter-columns, and the whole conduct of newspapers was passing into the hands of better-class writers and booksellers, becoming more efficient, dignified, and restrained as the political fashions of the first decade of George III's reign died down. Then, in 1778, Johnson's *Sunday Monitor* came to lure on the reader who might be too busy during the week.[1]

BUT neither in the sale of new books, nor in the abundance of periodical literature and of books for children, nor in the prosperous number trade is the growth of the public in the third quarter of the century most evident. It was the irrepressible insistence of the provincial, and particularly the Scotch, booksellers, in attacking and finally demolishing the claim of the inner circle of ' the trade ' (as the chief booksellers were pleased to call themselves) to perpetual copyright, that showed there was a growing public, because it was the knowledge of a public demand behind them that gave birth to, and justified the attack on, the monopoly. For this conquering persistence of the Scotch booksellers can only be accounted for by the fact that the reading public was not getting all that it wanted from ' the trade.' The public was growing, and it wanted a better and cheaper supply of books. Nor was it only, nor even chiefly, Scotland, that was dissatisfied, for when we speak of the Scotch booksellers we mean those, too, who were established in England, and the greatest of those was Donaldson, an Edinburgh bookseller. It was of the year 1763 that Boswell wrote that " Mr. Alexander Donald-

---

[1] See A. Andrews, *History of British Journalism.*

THE GROWTH OF THE PUBLIC

son had for some time opened a shop in London, and sold his cheap editions of the most popular English books in defiance of the supposed Common Law right of literary property." [1]

FROM 1774 the lesser booksellers, by the lapse of copyrights, were able openly to serve the public by cheap and convenient reprints, as they had been doing furtively for some years before. The monopolists had, it is true, maintained a fair supply; there had been many good editions of Shakespeare; Dodsley had brought out his *Old Plays* because he found in 1743 that all " except Shakespeare's, Jonson's, and Beaumont and Fletcher's are becoming scarce and extravagantly dear " [2]; Percy had rescued the ballads. But all these editions were more for the upper-class, literary public. They were too expensive and too cumbersome for the humbler middle-class reader; and it was the rising importance of the middle class that was the dominant factor in the years round 1774, a factor, said Beaconsfield, which Lord Shelburne was the first great minister to comprehend. The booksellers, however, had been conscious of it for some time with their weekly numbers. Now the spirit was to provide the public with comfortable pocket editions of the English Classics, tastefully got up and adorned with engravings by the best artists. There was Bell's edition of the *Poets*, which, as we have seen, brought the counter-reply of Johnson's edition with his *Lives*. There was, shortly after, Cooke's edition of the *British Poets*, of which Leigh Hunt said, speaking of his boyhood: " How I loved those little sixpenny numbers

---
[1] Boswell, *Life*, i. 437. [2] *Proposal* in *London Evening Post*, March 24, 1743.

containing whole poets! I doted on their size; I doted on their type, on their ornaments, on their wrappers containing lists of other poets, and on engravings from Kirk. I bought them over and over again; and used to get up select sets that disappeared like buttered crumpets; for I could resist neither giving them away, nor possessing them."[1] Bell and Martin published their *British Theatre*. Hazlitt tells us how he came under the spell of Cooke's *Novelists*. And again there was Harrison's *Novelists' Magazine*, in octavo with double columns, similarly stitched in small weekly numbers for sixpence, with engraved embellishments by Stothard and others, which began in 1779, ran into twenty-three good-sized volumes, and of which at one time twelve thousand copies of each number were sold weekly.[2] So far had the supply of literature for the people advanced by the last quarter of the century.

FINALLY, we must note how the growth in the reading public is again marked by the appearance of Lackington, established as a second-hand book-seller in London, selling remainders at half-price in open defiance of the stringent unwritten laws of 'the trade.' They excluded him from sales, but the public carried him through and his first catalogue of twelve thousand books appeared in 1779. Well might he say in later years: "When I reflect what prodigious numbers in inferior or reduced situations of life have been effectually benefited, on easy terms, I could almost be vain enough to assert, that I have thereby been highly instrumental in diffusing

[1] *Autobiography*.   [2] Britton and Rees, *Reminiscences*.

that general desire for reading, now so prevalent among the inferior orders of society."[1] Lackington's motto was "small profits, bound by industry, and clasped by economy," and his small profits became a fair fortune, because, like Cave and like Donaldson, he had seen what the public wanted, and when the public was given what it wanted, it wanted more and more.

THUS, by the end of the eighteenth century, there was the sound nucleus of a comprehensive reading public in England and Scotland, which was ready in the early years of the next century to respond with the utmost eagerness to the combination of literary genius and book-selling enterprise, when Constable gave unheard-of prices, and Murray rivalled him, for the romantic enchantments of Scott and Byron. When Sir Walter Scott dined, at the height of his fame, at a gentleman's house in London, all the servant-maids in the house asked leave to stand in the passage and see him pass. The eighteenth century had sown the seed of that enthusiastic admiration of a man of letters.

(v)

SO much for the reading public and the literary public; it remains to consider the relation of author to playgoing public. If readers were capricious, playgoers were many times more so. It was almost impossible to foretell the fate of a play, and the difficulties of getting one's work before the audience were far greater than those of appealing to the reading public. Further, an author might hope to be read through in the

---
[1] *Memoirs*, p. 224.

study and not dismissed without reflection, but, on the stage, he ran the risk of being swept away by a storm of cat-calls without the pretence of a fair hearing. But writers were ready to face all these drawbacks, because, if they did achieve success, they were much more highly rewarded than their fellows content with being read. They had their play printed, and received a good sum for the copyright, and, in addition, they had the profits on every third performance. " The writer of plays has been ever supposed to pursue the quickest road to the temple of Plutus," said Osborne, the bookseller and ex-actor, in 1778; and it was very true of those who succeeded. It is pleasant to think of Kelly receiving the £150 profits of his first night of *False Delicacy*; " not having ever seen so much money of his own before, he was all astonishment; he put the money into his pocket as fast as he could, and ran home to his wife in a rapture." But those successes were few and far between.

ABOUT 1730 there were five London theatres—Drury Lane, Lincoln's Inn Fields, the Haymarket, Goodman's Fields, and Covent Garden [1] —and they seem to have been more than enough for the small theatre-going public. The drama had fallen on grievous days of decline, and, in Colley Cibber's opinion, the competition between the various companies made things worse. With decency had come dullness, and to relieve dullness there was abundance of foolery. Heidegger's masquerades held the stage until public disgust drove them into the privacy of society balls. Italian opera was the rage for years; once it was

---

[1] Opened in December 1732.

laughed out of fashion by *The Beggar's Opera*, and again by Carey's *Dragon of Wantley*, but it had a habit of reviving. Fielding groaned and fulminated [1] against Italian warblers, " wanton affected fondness for foreign music," jugglers and tumblers. Everything had to give way to pantomimes, flourishing year after year with such unabated popularity that higher prices were charged for them ; often they alone kept a theatre from bankruptcy and from the humiliation which often befell Fleetwood, of seeing the properties of Drury Lane in the hands of brokers. And again there were the companies of child-actors, called Lilliputians, for the public of 1740 loved " to see a little fellow just breech'd, take upon him the airs of his papa, leer, kiss and ogle at a little poppet who coquettes and intrigues." An audience that had sat out a regular play expected some light and showy tit-bit at the end, and a manager anxious to keep his house open had to give it them. Cibber avowed a sense of degradation in these things, and declared that it went much against his conscience to yield to the depraved taste of the public ; but actors and managers had to yield ; Rich, the manager whose genius lay in pantomimes, took care to maintain their popularity.

BUT the clownish and affected idols of the day, interfere though they did, still left the drama a very profitable sphere for the man of letters. Hogarth's cartoons, and the satire of Pope and Fielding give them a slight over-emphasis. Nor did it matter so much that the average writer was

[1] *Author's Farce* (1730) : Witmore : "When the theatres are puppet-shows and the comedians ballad singers, when fools lead the town, wou'd a man think to thrive by his wit ? If you must write, write nonsense, write operas, write entertainments." See Fielding's plays, *passim*.

a very poor dramatist. As the playwrights declined in force, the actors and actresses improved. Personality in acting developed, and the power to get across the footlights became more in evidence. A weak play was often redeemed by splendid acting; Thomson's *Sophonisba* derived most of its appeal from Mrs. Oldfield. The greatest danger to which writers were exposed was the powerful influence exercised by the pit. Faction would often damn a piece irrespective of its merits, as Cibber's *Provoked Husband* was very nearly damned in 1728 by his non-juror enemies. The band of young hooligans installed there might take offence with the management for employing French artists, or on questions of price, and the poor author had to bear the brunt; or, at times, the humour might take them to see "who can cat-call, hiss, or whistle best." But for the author who triumphed the risks were worth while. Lillo's *London Merchant* was a vast success in 1730 and honoured by all the royal family; the copyright sold in 1735 for £150, and in eight years the author's profits were £800. From about 1726 the average price paid for the copyright of a play of marked merit was £100, and such a play would have a run of at least nine nights, thus giving the author three benefit nights. Indeed, in the matter of copyrights, Watts the bookseller, who specialized in their purchase, seems to have been very generous. For two plays by James Millar, *The Humours of Oxford* (1729) and *The Mother-in-law* (1733), he gave £80 each, and lists of his payments show him giving from twenty to eighty guineas to very minor writers.

THE GROWTH OF THE PUBLIC

THERE had always been a censorship of the stage exercised by the Lord Chamberlain, but attacks on the ministry grew so outrageous about 1735, that it was felt desirable to legalize the position by statute. Fielding's *Pasquin* in 1736 increased the desire, and an ostensible cause being found in the scurillous manuscript of *The Golden Rump* the Licensing Act was passed in 1737. It gave no new powers, merely making indisputably valid those which had sufficed to suppress *Polly* in 1729. The soundness of the step was beyond doubt; whatever Chesterfield might say about organized attacks on liberty, it was not beneficial to any Government to have such faction as that of the Prince of Wales inflamed by stage presentations, which are far more effective than the printed play. And the harm done a writer by prohibition was slight; *Polly*, and Thomson's *Edward and Eleanora* sold all the better that their support was made a matter of party passion; as for Brooke's *Gustavus Vasa* in 1739, its sale cleared above £1,000.

THE stage, then, was profitable to the favoured few, but the favoured were indeed a small band. An author either made some hundreds or he made nothing, or next to nothing. His difficulties are admirably summed up in the following words of Fustian, in Fielding's *Pasquin*. "A Poet," says he, "undergoes a great deal before he comes to his third night; first with the Muses who are humorous ladies and must be attended; for if they take it into their head at any time to leave you, you will pump your brain in vain; then, Sir, with the Master of a Playhouse to get it acted, whom you generally allow a quarter of a year, before you know whether he will receive it or no, and then perhaps he tells you it won't do—or if he should receive the play, then you must attend again to get it writ into parts or rehearsed. Well, Sir, at last the Rehearsal begins; then, Sir, another scene of trouble with the actors, some of whom don't like their parts, and all are constantly plaguing you with alterations: at length after having waded through all these difficulties, his play appears upon the stage, where one man hisses out of resentment to the author, a second out of dislike to the house, a third out of dislike to the actor, a fourth out of dislike to the play and a fifth for the jest's sake, a sixth to keep the rest in company—enemies abuse him, friends give him up, the play is dam'd, and the author goes to the Devil."

TOWARDS the middle of the century the approach to the stage got worse. It was very largely the fault of the authors alone. There was so little talent among them that the public would flock to see a bottle-conjurer instead. Johnson's *Irene* in 1749 ran nine nights, which was still considered a good success, and above the £100 for copyright he got £195 for his three nights. But new plays became scarcer and scarcer. Around 1750 they were almost non-existent, and in the following years were confined [1] to tedious dramatizations of Roman and Eastern history, like *Barbarossa*, *Philelea*, and *Constantine*. Managers were afraid to try anything new, and were assailed by a storm of abuse from disappointed authors. James Ralph, in his *Case of Authors* (1759), affirmed that " even the Bookseller is a perfect *Mæcenas* com-

[1] Moore's *Gamester* (1753) was a notable exception.

par'd to the Manager "[1]; and of Garrick he wrote : " Though I am free to acknowledge he was made for the stage, I cannot be brought to think that the stage was made only for him ; or that the fate of every dramatical writer ought to be at his mercy, or that of any other manager whatsoever ; and the single consideration that there is no alternative but to fly from him, in case of any contempt or neglect, to Mr. Rich is enough to deter any man in his senses from embarking on such a hopeless voyage." Likewise Goldsmith, in the first edition of the *Enquiry* (1759), complained that " getting a play on even in three or four years is a privilege reserved only for the happy few, who have the arts of courting the manager as well as the Muse."

BUT the excessive shyness and caution of the managers must have originated with the public. The latter had grown tired of very mediocre plays, and preferred good revivals, puppet-shows, and pantomimes. The evil was that the managers hardened their hearts against good and bad alike, because they were unable to discriminate between them. Thus Home's *Douglas* appeared first at Edinburgh, owing to Garrick's refusal of it ; the enthusiastic cries there of " Where's Wully Shakespeare noo ? " and its persecution by the Presbyterians then gained it a welcome at Covent Garden. In 1773 Colman's acceptance of *She Stoops to Conquer* was most reluctant, and the very actors were convinced it would fail. No one had much confidence in those days of leading the playgoing public's opinion. They were content to provide farces and popular sentimental

[1] p. 24.

comedies. And it is noticeable how most of the new pieces were written by actors, managers, and theatrical proprietors ; by Foote, Murphy, Colman, Garrick, and Sheridan. Outside, but closely connected with that circle, were a few like the hapless Bickerstaffe, and the prolifically sentimental Cumberland, and like Kenrick and Kelly. Nor was there much in the work of any of them but Sheridan. They turned out some fairly witty dialogue, dull sentiment, dramatized novels, and translations from the French.

One redeeming feature in the stage-history of this period was the revival of Shakespeare. His best tragedies had been frequently played in Cibber's time, but the other plays were neglected. About 1740 public taste was beginning to change ; there grew up a society under the name of " Shakespeare's Ladies," devoted to the cause of bringing the bard once more into universal favour. Then Garrick came, and gave the support of his genius to the movement, so that in ten years a great change had been accomplished. Plays like *Richard II* and *Romeo and Juliet*, which had not been performed for years, had their share in the revival, and old favourites like *Hamlet* were nearly always running at one or other of the theatres. In fact on the average Garrick presented from ten to fifteen Shakespearean plays annually, nearly always, however, those in which he himself could act prominently. The chief fault lay in the bad taste of those who adapted the plays. Cibber made a typical adaptation of *King John* in 1745, re-naming it *Papal Tyranny* and inserting topical denunciation of the Pope ; indeed he said in his dedication, " I have endeavoured to

THE GROWTH OF THE PUBLIC

make it more like a play than I found it in Shakespeare." Nor was Garrick's taste much superior; he improved *The Winter's Tale*, and produced *Hamlet* " rescued from the rubbish of the fifth act." They might prune their revivals of Restoration comedy without danger, but they had better have left Shakespeare alone.[1] Finally, the new Shakespeare fashion blazed out in the Jubilee at Stratford in 1769, where Garrick was said to strut like a cockerel, and where Boswell paraded as a Corsican chief. The whole movement is one which we may claim as contributing to the education of the public.

But amid the constant revival of plays by old writers and by modern favourites like Gay and Dodsley, there were still good profits to be made. In 1768 Kelly's *False Delicacy* gave the author £700; Foote's *Devil on Two Sticks* produced from £3,000 to £4,000; Goldsmith's *Good-natured Man* £400 and £150 for the copyright. Earlier Home had made some hundreds by his *Agis*, and Murphy throughout his career as a playwright made considerable sums. The price paid for the copyright of a good play had risen from £100 in 1726 to £150 in 1770, and Kelly got as much as £200 for the copy of *Clementina*, although only the " admirable acting of Mrs. Bates kept it afloat for nine nights." That was still considered a satisfactory run, but many drew good houses much longer. Bickerstaffe's *Maid of the Mill* ran about twenty-nine times in the season of 1765, and his *Padlock* fifty-three in 1768; while Sheridan's *Duenna* had the unparalleled run of seventy-five times in 1777.

[1] Some were too much for the public. Garrick's version of *A Midsummer-Night's Dream* as a sort of opera with thirty-three songs did not survive its first night.

So the popularity and material prosperity of the stage increased. The playgoing public began to expand beyond the bounds of the select, fashionable society who had long been the chief patrons of the drama. It extended to the provinces where every year or so after the middle of the century saw a new theatre licensed. In 1780 crowded audiences and long runs were becoming usual despite the mediocrity of the plays themselves. The author was being superseded by the actor to a greater and greater extent. It was Mrs. Siddons, Kemble, Kean, who appealed to the public, and great acting made very poor words go a long way.

IN the early years of our period many a writer had deliberately turned to the drama as the most lucrative sphere for an author; towards the end of the century its attraction was less potent because the growth of the reading public had done away very largely with the difference in pecuniary prospects. The novel was soon to be more lucrative than the play. The theatre would always have its writers, but after Goldsmith and Sheridan it was neglected by the greatest and ceased to be magnetic to literary talent. Not even Smollett had been able to pass by so tempting a short cut to riches; Johnson, Goldsmith, Fielding, Horace Walpole himself, they had all written for the stage. But the great romantics, though they might write dramas, did not do so with the primary view of performance. A generation grew up finding the bookseller a better paymaster than the manager, and less exacting because his service had need of all talents. Men only racked their brains to write dramas, when dramas paid more highly than anything else. The reading public, by destroying that pre-eminence, destroyed the superior charm of drama for an author. Southey achieved independence by a life of unremitting toil in many fields of literature, but drama was not one of them, and in that he was typical of the new age. Men of letters henceforth depended for their support upon the general reader.

(vi)

BY 1780 patronage was a thing of the past, thankfully avowed to be so by *The Gentleman's Magazine*, and still the public had but begun to grow. " The reading public ! " exclaimed North to Tickler, " I well remember the days when she could spell with difficulty a simple disyllable—when she lost herself in complicated Polly, like a benighted nymph wandering through a wood."[1] So was she of 1780, merely " conning her Reading made easy," but even that had given her sufficient power to change the whole face of the profession of letters. Every year gave her more strength, and every year saw the price of successful authorship mount up. More readers and more money went hand in hand, and readers multiplied so fast that Christopher North had to deplore that " reading is placed on the list of necessaries before eating," while Tickler lamented that " a creeshy periodical, price a penny, takes precedence of a black pudding of strong bull's blood and the generous suet."
THAT is to say, the average good writer was

[1] *Noctes Ambrosianæ.*

increasingly sure of adequate support, and that fact is the only one to consider in estimating the prospects of the literary calling. Of the exceptional good writer immediate success cannot always be predicted. The public is a sound but not a perfect judge and it often wants time for its judgment. In the last resort we must agree with the dictum of Southey: " The Public and Transubstantiation I hold to be the two greatest mysteries in or out of nature." When we find inequality in the relation of reward to merit, whichever outbalances the other, we can only wonder at the mysterious public. He who appeals to her must abide her decision, for he is her servant for the things of this life.

INDEX

A

Addison, 26, 68, 72, 115, 117, 118, 120, 124, 137, 215, 232, 233, 234, 235, 250, 251, 252, 253
"Agamemnon," 157
Akenside, Mark, 31, 62, 220
"Alfred," 159
Allen, Ralph, 179, 185
"Amelia," 33, 44, 243
Ames, Joseph, 175
Amhurst, Nicholas, 165, 166
"Anecdotes," Horace Walpole's (of Painting in England), 23
Anne, Queen, 11, 34, 118, 119, 132, 149, 163, 181, 213, 214, 243, 248
"Annual Register," 101
Anstey, Christopher, 30, 33
Apsley, Lord, 97
"Arabian Nights," 243
Arbuthnot, John, 148, 152, 174, 237
Argyll, Duke of, 185, 193
Arnall, William, 164, 166
Atterbury, Bishop, 124
Aubyn, Sir John, 182
Aynsworth, Mr., 70

B

Baillie, Lady Grisel, 150
Ballax, 56
Bangor, Bishop of, 142
Barlow, Bishop, 91
Baskerville, John, 16, 22
Bates, Mrs., 267
Bathurst, Lord, 105, 122, 129, 136, 207
Beattie, James, 48, 75, 102, 109, 204, 210
Becket, bookseller, 96, 97, 99, 107
Bedford, Duke of, 169, 185, 186, 188, 200
"Beggar's Opera," 57, 79, 147, 148, 153, 237, 261
Bell, bookseller, 113, 128, 257, 258
Benson, 184
Bentley, Richard, the elder, 21, 131, 242

Bentley, Richard, the younger, 205
Berkeley, Bishop, 172, 175, 188, 200
Bickerstaffe, Isaac, 266, 267
Binning, Lord, 150, 152, 186
Birch, Dr., 58
Blair, Hugh, 32, 50, 109, 204, 205, 210, 255
Blount, Martha, 136
Bolingbroke, Lord, 32, 106, 107, 132, 133, 136, 138, 144, 147, 152, 165, 166, 167, 179, 204
Borlase, William, 181
Borrow, George, 27
Boswell, James, 31, 34, 46, 47, 48, 50, 59, 92, 97, 109, 111, 112, 113, 188, 189, 197, 202, 207, 208, 251, 256, 267
Boulter, Archbishop, 176
"Boulter's Monument," 39
Bowyer, William, 16, 22, 57, 128, 147, 237
Boyse, Samuel, 24
Bradley, Irish bookseller, 63
Bray, Thomas, 249
Brett, Mrs., 141, 142
Brooke, Henry, 58, 167, 168, 216, 263
Broome, William, 126
Brougham, Lord, 250
Brummel, 201
Buckley, Samuel, 65
Bunyan, 237
Burke, 168, 190, 192, 202, 209, 219
Burlington, Lord, 122, 129, 136, 145, 146, 174, 178
Burnet, Bishop, 26, 68
Burney, Fanny, 113
"Busiris," 137
Bute, Lord, 199, 200, 202, 203, 205, 206, 219
Butler, Samuel, 114, 172
Byng, Admiral, 199

C

Cadell, Thomas, 33, 42, 47, 227
"Cæsar," 97
Camden, Lord, 87, 104
"Camillius" 175

INDEX

Campbell, Thomas, 246
Carey, Henry, 261
Carlyle, Thomas, 230
Carnan, 47
Caroline, Queen, 140, 142, 143, 146, 172, 216, 221
Cartaret, Lord, 10, 125, 176
Carter, Mrs., 38, 252
"Case of Authors," 21, 25, 170, 264
"Castle of Indolence," 79, 159, 187
Cathcart, Lord, 203
Cave, Edward, 17, 21, 28, 31, 48, 168, 196, 217, 222, 238, 239, 240, 259
"Chambers's Cyclopedia," 250
Chandos, Duke of, 122, 174, 175, 193
Chapter, The, 19
"Characteristics," 71
"Charles I," 30
"Charles V," 34
Chatterton, 52, 208, 209
Chesterfield, Lord, 45, 62, 132, 165, 173, 179, 190, 197, 252, 263
"Chesterfield's Letters," 56
Chetwode, 128
Churchill, Charles, 29, 34, 39, 106, 191, 193, 195, 197, 207, 219
Cibber, Colley, 135, 143, 187, 260, 261, 262, 366
Circulating Libraries, 245
Clare, Lord, 198
Clarendon, Lord, 21
Clarke, Dr., 16
Cleland, John, 29, 176, 185
Clifton, pirate printer, 56
Cobham, Lord, 136
Coleridge, S. T., 211
Collins, the bookseller, 32, 88, 89, 90, 94, 95
Collins, William, 14, 36, 49
Colman, George, 153, 228, 265, 266
Common Prayer Book, 21, 22
Compton, Sir Spencer, 151, 161, 181
Concanen, Matthew, 164
Conger, The, 18, 19
Congreve, 11, 69, 117, 118, 127, 166
"Conscious Lovers," 56

Cooke, bookseller, 227, 257, 258
"Cook's Voyages," 227
Co-operative Publishing, 15–21, 225
Copyright Act of 1710, 9, 35, 54, 55, 57, 60, 64, 230
Copyright Act of 1739, 67
Copyright Bills of 1736–7, 71–82
"Coriolanus," 160
Cornbury, Lord, 69, 77, 135
Courayer, Dr., 172
Covent Garden Theatre, 260, 265
Cowper, William 47, 48, 228
Crabbe, 52, 208, 209, 210, 219
"Craftsman," 106, 165, 237
Craggs, James, 124
Crousaz, de, 179, 241
Cumberland, Richard, dramatist, 34, 255, 266
Curll, Edmund, 26, 56, 57, 143

D

Dalrymple, Sir John, 103
Davies, Thomas, 106, 107
"Decline and Fall," 19, 42
Dedications, 180–184
Defoe, 243, 248
Denbigh, Lord, 105
Denham, Sir James Steuart (see Sir James Steuart), 205
Devonshire, Duke of, 193
"Dictionary, Johnson's," 19, 20, 36, 132
Dilly, Charles, 42, 48, 50
"Directions to Churchwardens," 56
Dobson, 184
Dodington, 122, 139, 140, 151, 152, 155, 156, 167, 169, 186, 205, 216, 220
Dodsley, James, 101
Dodsley, Robert, 17, 18, 31, 33, 34, 36, 37, 38, 45, 46, 48, 49, 56, 57, 58, 121, 134, 168, 178, 188, 209, 251, 254, 257, 267
Donaldson, Alexander, 18, 84, 91, 92, 93, 95, 96, 97, 99, 100, 101, 105, 107, 111, 112, 227, 256, 259
Dorset, Earl of, 115, 116, 161
Dorset, Duke of, 184
"Douglas," 38

INDEX

"Dragon of Wantley," 261
Drury Lane Theatre, 260, 261
Dryden, 69, 114, 116, 124, 125, 134, 153, 174, 180, 221, 228
Duck, Stephen, 172, 173, 178, 237
"Duellist," 34
"Dunciad," 13, 24, 25, 46, 56, 62, 129, 130, 131, 132, 135, 147, 163, 164, 176, 177, 237
Dyson, Jeremiah, 220

E

Eachard, Laurence, 181
"Elegy," Gray's, 33
Elliott, Scotch bookseller, 64
"English Poets," 19, 113
"Englishmen in Paris," 183
"Enquiry into Present State of Polite Learning," 29, 265
Entwick, John, 166
"Epictetus," 39
"Essay on Man," 133, 179
"Eurydice," 178, 188
Eusden, Laurence, 143
"Evelina," 113
Ewing, Irish bookseller, 64
Eyre, Justice, 74

F

"Fables," Gay's, 146, 237
"False Delicacy," 260
Fancourt, Rev. Samuel, 245
Farquhar, George, 228
Fauconberg, Lord, 206
Faulkner, George, 62, 63, 75
Fenton, Miss Lavinia, 147
Fenton, Elijah, 126, 177
"Festivals," Nelson's, 74
Fielding, 14, 32, 33, 44, 45, 49, 182, 183, 185, 186, 217, 220, 243, 244, 253, 261, 263, 268
Fleming, Mrs., 47
Foote, Samuel, 183, 193, 194, 196, 219, 244, 266, 267
Forbes, Duncan, 150
Fortescue, Sir John, 57, 145
Fox, Charles, 104
Fox, Henry, 67
Francklin, Thomas, 14, 106
"Freethinker," 176

G

Gardenstone, Lord, 98

Garrick, David, 171, 213, 265, 266, 267
Garth, Samuel, 237
Gay, John, 56, 69, 127, 145, 146, 147, 148, 160, 161, 162, 166, 171, 173, 174, 175, 216, 217, 226, 237, 267
"Gentleman's Magazine," 16, 17, 144, 170, 196, 218, 239, 240, 253, 269
Gibbon, 19, 37, 41, 42, 47, 51, 64, 202, 255
Gilliver, bookseller, 56, 133
Glover, Richard, 167, 168
Goldsmith, Oliver, 24, 25, 28, 29, 30, 31, 32, 35, 36, 38, 39, 40, 45, 46, 47, 49, 52, 59, 108, 130, 146, 163, 170, 180, 183, 190, 193, 197, 198, 205, 207, 208, 219, 222, 248, 254, 265, 267, 268
Goodman's Fields Theatre, 260
"Good Natured Man," 30, 32, 109, 267
"Goody Two Shoes," 251
Gordon, Thomas, 164, 182
Gower, Earl, 28, 178
Grafton, Duke of, 252
Grainger, James, 36
Granville, Earl of, 176
Gray, Thomas, 33, 37, 209, 254
"Gray's Inn Journal," 63
"Grecian History," 30
Grey, Dr. Zachary, 42, 175
Griffiths, Ralph, 29, 197, 241
"Gulliver's Travels," 33, 79, 128, 237, 243
"Gustavus Vasa," 58
Guthrie, 166, 170, 199, 200

H

Hailes, Lord, 97, 98
Halifax, Lord (see Montagu), 118, 124, 154, 182, 188, 196, 214
Handel, 173, 175
Hanoverian Succession, 10, 119, 121, 215
Harcourt, Lord, 187
Hardwicke, Lord, 84, 224
Harley, Robert (see Oxford, Lord, 1st), 11, 114, 118, 119, 120, 125, 214

INDEX

Harrison, bookseller, 258
Harte, Walter, 178
Harvard, dramatist, 30
Hawkesworth, John, 56, 95, 106, 227, 254
Hawkins, Sir John, 197
Haymarket Theatre, 260
Hayter, Bishop, 58
Haywood, Mrs., 243, 244, 251
Heidegger, 260
Henley, orator, 164
Henry, Robert, 34, 208
Herschel, 247
Hertford, Countess of, 142, 151, 152, 173
Hervey, Lord, 133, 134, 171
Hickes, George, 116, 181
Hill, Aaron, 75, 142, 151, 155, 156, 174
Hill, Henry, 9
Hill, " Sir " John, 27, 205, 250
Hinton, Scotch bookseller, 97, 111
" Historical Register," 183
" History of Animated Nature," 30
" History of the Bible," 97, 98, 229
" History of England," Goldsmith, 45, 208
" History of England," Henry, 34
" History of England," Hume, 33, 44, 191, 227
" History of England," Smollett, 41
" History of Henry II," 34
" History of Printing," 177
" History of the Rebellion," 21
" History of the Reformation," 68
" History of Rome," 30
" History of Scotland," 33, 37, 38, 79, 203, 254
Hoadly, Benjamin, 164, 172, 182
Hogarth, 25, 171, 261
Home, John, 38, 199, 200, 205, 265, 267
"Homer," 123, 125, 136, 178, 224
" Horace," 97
" Hudibras," 91, 114, 175
Hudson, translator of Josephus, 175

Hume, David, 18, 29, 30, 33, 37, 44, 48, 75, 102, 106, 108, 109, 180, 190, 191, 192, 203, 204, 222, 227, 250, 254
Hunt, Leigh, 257
Hurd, Bishop, 102, 179
Hutton, library at Birmingham, 245

I

" Idler," 59, 220, 249
" Iliad," 73, 95, 121, 160
" Irene," 21, 38, 49, 189, 264
Irving, Washington, 27
Italian Opera, 260

J

Jekyll, Sir J., 74
Jenkinson, Charles, 242
Jersey, Lord, 187
Johnson, Joseph, 228
Johnson, Samuel, 13, 14, 16, 17, 19, 20, 21, 22, 24, 25, 26, 28, 29, 30, 31, 32, 33, 34, 35, 36, 38, 39, 40, 42, 45, 46, 49, 50, 51, 52, 59, 81, 97, 108, 109, 110, 111, 112, 122, 125, 127, 132, 143, 152, 161, 168, 169, 170, 176, 177, 178, 179, 180, 183, 184, 185, 186, 187, 188, 190, 191, 193, 194, 195, 196, 197, 198, 202, 203, 204, 205, 207, 208, 211, 212, 213, 214, 217, 218, 219, 220, 222, 228, 230, 231, 234, 245, 249, 250, 251, 254, 255, 256, 257, 264, 268
Johnston, William, 99
Jortin, 180
" Joseph Andrews," 33
" Journal of Sidney Parkinson," 56
Junius, 237
Juvenile Literature, 251

K

Karnes, Lord, 98
Keach, Benjamin, 242
Kean, Edmund, 268
Kelly, Hugh, 201, 207, 255, 260, 266, 267
Kemble, Charles, 268
Kenrick, William, 102, 266

INDEX

Kincaid, Scotch bookseller, 83, 85, 94
Kinnersley, bookseller, 56, 59
Knaplock, bookseller, 56

L

Lackington, James, 41, 43, 245, 246, 251, 258, 259
Lansdowne, Lord, 124
Leibnitz, 172
"Liberty," 48, 156, 157, 162, 184
Lichfield, Earl of, 137
"Life of Garrick," 106
"Life of Savage," 39
Lillo, George, 262
Lincoln, Earl of, 146
Lincoln's Inn Fields Theatre, 260
Lindsay, John, 42
Lintot, Bernard, 46, 73, 145
Liverpool, Lord, 242
"Lives of the Poets," 19, 32, 33, 34, 108, 213, 228, 257
Lloyd, Robert, 29
Locke, John, 115, 118, 215
"London," 29, 49
"London Journal," 126
"London Magazine," 17, 239
Longman, Thomas, 227
Loughborough, Lord, 203, 207
Lovibond, Edward, 190
Lowther, Mrs., 178
Lyttelton, George, Lord, 34, 45, 157, 159, 160, 167, 168, 184, 185

M

Macaulay, Lord, 24, 115, 116, 130
Macaulay, Mrs., 102, 103, 111, 252
Macclesfield, Countess of, 141
Macpherson, James, 201, 206, 208
Madden, 39
Maittaire Michael, 175
Malone, 33, 34
Mallet, David, 32, 106, 107, 108, 150, 157, 161, 167, 178, 184, 186, 188, 199, 205, 215
Mandeville, Bernard, 248
"Manilius," 21

Manley, Mrs., 174, 243
Mansfield, Lord, 204, 207, 253
Marchmont, Lord, 133
Marlborough, Duchess of, 133
Martin, bookseller, 113, 228, 258
Mason, John, 42
Mason, William, 110, 209
Melford, Lydia, 246
"Memories of a Woman of Pleasure," 29
Merrill, Cambridge bookseller, 91, 92
Mickle, William, 208
Millan, bookseller, 150, 152
Millar, Andrew, 31, 32, 33, 42, 44, 45, 48, 49, 51, 79, 80, 83, 85, 94, 95, 96, 97, 99, 101, 105, 107, 152, 156, 185, 220, 222, 231, 243
Millar, James, dramatist, 262
Milton, 69, 91
"Miscellanies," Swift's, 74, 75
Mitchell, Joseph, 166
Monboddo, Lord, 99
Montagu, Charles (see Halifax, Lord), 114, 115, 116, 121
Montagu, Lady Mary, 14
Montrose, Duke of, 150, 186
Moore, Edward, 14
More, Hannah, 34, 109, 252, 255
Motte, Benjamin, 74, 75, 128
Murphy, Arthur, 110, 111, 199, 200, 205, 266, 267
Murray, John I., 33, 63, 135, 179, 259
"Muse in Livery," 121

N

Negus, Samuel, 236
Nelson, Robert, 74
"New Bath Guide," 30, 33
Newbery, John, 27, 32, 40, 45, 47, 197, 222, 251
Newcastle, Duke of, 164, 169, 199
Newton, Dr., 84
Newton, Isaac, 117, 118
Nichols, John, 19, 22, 32, 41, 42, 48, 185, 228
Nicholson, 245
"Night Thoughts," 34, 140

INDEX

Norne, bookseller, 30
North, Lord, 201, 206, 209
North, Roger, 25
Northington, Lord, 95
Northumberland, Duke of, 193, 197

O

"Odes," Gray's, 37, 254
"Odyssey," 126
Oglethorpe, James, 188
Oldfield, Mrs., 142, 154, 262
"Old Plays," 18
Oldys, Willliam, 175
Orrery, Lord, Charles, 122, 176
Orrery, Lord, John, 45, 254
Osborne, 33, 82, 95, 224, 260
Ossory, Lord, 206
Oxford, Lord, First, 122, 174, 196
Oxford, Lord, Second, 129, 175, 176, 193,

P

Palmer, Samuel, 175, 177
"Pamela," 244, 245, 248
Pantomimes, 261
"Paradise Lost," 82, 84, 184, 227
Parnell, Thomas, 118
Parsons, bookseller, 227
"Pasquin," 261
Pelham, Henry, 77, 159, 169, 170, 200
Pembroke, Earl of, 177
Penny Books, 251
"Percy," 34, 109, 255
Percy, Bishop, 34
"Peregrine Pickle," 45
Peterborough, Earl of, 142, 174, 175, 216
Philips, Ambrose, 161, 176
Philips, historiographer-royal, 166
"Pilgrim's Progress," 242
Pilkington, Rev., 128
Pitt, Christopher, 161, 184
Pitt, William, Earl of Chatham, 70, 87, 160, 169, 179, 202, 221
"Pleasures of Imagination," 31, 62
"Polly," 56, 57, 147, 237, 263
Polworth, Lord, 135

Pope, 12, 24, 25, 28, 31, 46, 57, 61, 69, 70, 73, 74, 75, 95, 114, 116, 117, 121, 123, 124, 125, 126, 127, 128, 129, 130, 131, 132, 133, 134, 135, 136, 137, 140, 145, 146, 147, 148, 149, 151, 152, 155, 156, 157, 160, 161, 162, 164, 168, 171, 173, 174, 175, 176, 178, 179, 180, 182, 186, 188, 190, 193, 196, 207, 213, 216, 224, 229, 241, 245, 261
Portsmouth, Duchess of, 134
Prayer Book, Common, 21, 22
Price, Richard, 207, 255
Prideaux, John, 56
Priestley, Joseph, 208
"Principles of Political Economy," 34, 109
Prior, Matthew, 69, 115, 116, 118, 120, 161
Psalmanaazaar, George, 177
Pulteney, William, Earl of Bath, 125, 147, 165, 166, 167, 190
"Public Ledger," 40
"Public Register," 17

Q

Queensberry, Duchess of, 145, 146, 148, 174
Queensberry, Duke of, 146, 148, 174, 216

R

Ralph, James, 21, 25, 167, 169, 170, 264
"Rambler," 168
"Rasselas," 30, 56, 59
"Recollections of an Old Bookseller," 26
"Reliques," Percy's, 34
"Revenge," 137
Reynolds, Sir Joshua, 51, 207
Rich, John, 178, 181, 261, 265
Richardson, Samuel, 49, 59, 62, 63, 243, 244
Richmond, Duke of, 20, 122, 185
Rivers, Earl, 141
Rivington, Charles, 70, 83
Robertson, William, 33, 34, 37, 38, 48, 59, 75, 79, 80, 102, 106, 109, 202, 203, 254

INDEX

Robinson, George, 41, 42
"Robinson Crusoe," 248
Rochester, Earl of, 134
Rochford, Lord, 209
Rockingham, Lord, 206
Rolt, Richard, 62
"Rosciad," 39
Rowe, Nicholas, 118
Roxburgh, Duke of, 185
Rutland, Duke of, 209

S

St. John (see Bolingbroke, Lord), 114, 118, 119, 120, 160, 214
Sandwich, Lord, 40, 187, 201
Savage, Richard, 14, 24, 26, 70, 141, 143, 144, 145, 148, 161, 162, 171, 172, 177, 181
"Scot's Magazine," 102
Scott, "Parson," 201
Scott, Sir Walter, 259
"Seasons," 18, 79, 95, 96, 97, 112, 121, 152, 156, 159, 160, 188
Secker, Archbishop, 172
"Shadows of Old Booksellers," 51
Shaftesbury, 71
"Shakespeare," 49, 131, 224
Shakespeare, 16, 69, 71, 74, 82, 91, 103, 112, 123, 204, 226, 228, 257, 266, 267
Shebbeare, John, 14, 190, 199, 200
Shelburne, Lord, 207, 208, 209, 257
Sheridan, Richard Brinsley, 266, 267, 268
Sherlock, Thomas, 172
"She Stoops to Conquer," 153, 265
Siddons, Mrs., 268
"Sir Charles Grandison," 62
Smith, Adam, 34, 50, 80
Smollett, 18, 24, 33, 35, 40, 41, 45, 108, 167, 190, 191, 241, 244, 250, 268
Society for Encouragement of Learning, 20, 21, 49, 81, 132, 157, 175
Somers, Lord, 54, 114, 115, 116, 117, 118, 121, 154, 214

Somerville, William, 152
"Sophonisba," 153, 237, 262
Southey, 247, 269, 270
South Sea Bubble, 236
S.P.C.K., 248, 249
"Spectator," 68, 88, 233, 234, 235, 237, 251
Spence, Joseph, 139, 152, 188
Stalkhouse, Thomas, 97, 98, 229
Stamp Tax, 255
Stationers' Company and Hall, 8, 9, 53, 78, 84, 99
Steele, 56, 69, 118, 142, 232
Steevens, George, 49, 50
Sterne, Lawrence, 38, 108, 206, 219, 254
Steuart, Sir James (afterwards Denham), see Denham, 34, 109
Stevenson, John Hall, 253
Stothard, Thomas, 258
Strahan, William, 32, 34, 42, 47, 48, 50, 56, 109, 110, 111, 222, 255
Straus, Ralph, 58
"Suspicious Husband," 182
Swift, 13, 28, 33, 61, 69, 74, 75, 95, 116, 117, 118, 120, 123, 124, 125, 127, 128, 136, 146, 147, 148, 149, 165, 166, 174, 175, 176, 182, 237

T

Talbot, Charles, 151
Talbot, Lord, 74, 144, 154, 155, 156, 157, 162, 166, 186
"Tatler," 9, 72, 91, 233, 234
Taylor, bookseller, 95, 96, 97, 99, 105
Temple, 91, 128
Thackeray, 24, 118, 130
Theobald, Lewis, 131, 135, 164, 176, 181
Thomson, James, 18, 20, 45, 48, 75, 95, 112, 121, 127, 131, 136, 149, 151, 153, 154, 156, 157, 158, 159, 160, 161, 162, 167, 168, 169, 171, 181, 184, 186, 187, 188, 214, 216, 217, 219, 228, 237, 262, 263
Thomson, J., printer, 57

INDEX

Thurlow, Lord, 207, 208, 209
Tickell, Richard, 201, 210
Tickell, Thomas, 117, 118
Tillotson, Archbishop, 58
Tindal, Matthew, 116
"Tom Jones," 32, 33, 185, 227, 243, 244, 248
Tonson, Jacob (1656 – 1736), 56, 69, 123, 145, 221, 224
Tonson, Jacob (d. 1767), 49, 50, 71, 82, 83, 84, 85, 88, 90, 91, 94, 95, 101, 112, 220, 222
"Tour to the Hebrides," 109
Town and Country Mouse," 116
Townsend, Charles, Viscount, 165, 236
Townshend, Mr., 77
"Toy-shop," 57
"Traveller," 30, 183
"Treatise on Human Understanding," 30
Trenchard, John, 164
"Tristam Shandy," 38, 206
Tryst, H., 181

U

"Universal Chronicle," 59
"Universal Museum," 17
"Universal Passion," 162
University Presses, 21, 22, 65, 77, 105, 250

V

Vaillant, bookseller, 183
Vamp, 244
Vane, Lady, 45
Vertue, George, 116, 175
"Vicar of Wakefield," 30, 32
"Vindication of Church of England," 42
"Virgil," 97
Voltaire, 127, 249
"Voyages, South Sea," 106

W

Walker, Jeffrey, 57, 69, 74, 82, 84, 224
Wallace, Dr., 110
Waller, Edmund, 91

Walpole, Horace, 16, 22, 23, 28, 43, 103, 110, 171, 189, 190, 192, 201, 205, 208, 250, 253, 254, 268
Walpole, Sir Robert, 11, 12, 77, 120, 125, 130, 134, 137, 138, 140, 143, 144, 145, 147, 148, 149, 152, 156, 158, 159, 162, 163, 164, 165, 166, 167, 168, 169, 170, 172, 215, 216, 252
Walthoe, bookseller, 74
Warburton, William, 35, 36, 38, 85, 87, 88, 89, 90, 94, 132, 164, 172, 179, 180, 206, 241, 254
Watson, bookseller, 56
Watts, Isaac, 229, 237
Watts, bookseller, 262
"Wealth of Nations," 34, 42, 109
Wedderbourne, 205
Wesley, John, 253
Wesley, Samuel, 178
West, Gilbert, 26
West, William, 157
"West Indian," 34
Weymouth, Lord, 202
Wharton, Duke of, 137, 138, 139, 140, 161
Whatley, Rev. Mr., 151
Wheatley, H. B., 183
Whiston, John, 91, 92
Whiston, William, 172
Whitehead, Paul, 29, 134, 168, 195
Whitehead, William, 186, 187
"Whole Duty of Man," 74
Wilkes, John, 29, 200, 253
Wilson, Bishop, 172
Wise, Rev. Francis, 42
Wood, bookseller, 97
Wortley, Member of Parliament, 70
Wright, his circulating library, 245
Wycherley, William, 124

Yonge, Sir William, 164
Young, Arthur, 17, 208
Young, Edward, 34, 69, 127, 136, 137, 138, 139, 140, 141, 145, 148, 151, 152, 160, 161, 162, 166, 171, 217, 237, 245

For Product Safety Concerns and Information please contact our EU representative GPSR@taylorandfrancis.com
Taylor & Francis Verlag GmbH, Kaufingerstraße 24, 80331 München, Germany

www.ingramcontent.com/pod-product-compliance
Lightning Source LLC
Chambersburg PA
CBHW070556300426
44113CB00010B/1270